25-7

Fair Fights and Foul

OTHER BOOKS BY THURMAN ARNOLD

The Symbols of Government

Cases on Trials, Judgments and Appeals

The Folklore of Capitalism

The Bottlenecks of Business

Democracy and Free Enterprise

Fair Fights and Foul

A DISSENTING LAWYER'S LIFE

Thurman Arnold

HARCOURT, BRACE & WORLD, INC., NEW YORK

Dedicated to my partners
Abe Fortas and Paul Porter

Preface

Autobiographical writing happens to be difficult for me. It is too much like dressing yourself in striped pants, putting on a high silk hat, and watching yourself go by. But go by I have, and this book is an attempt to record and understand that passage. It is not greatly personal—not only because the impulse to the autobiographical is low in me, but also because the impulse to review the causes, cases, and patches of history I have known is high. Ideas have their history as much as men, and this book, in some measure, is an attempt to bring up to date the ideas expressed in my book *The Folklore of Capitalism*. I tried this out in the Judge Nelson Timothy Stephens lectures, which I gave at the University of Kansas in 1962. The result then was rather abstract. I found later that if I mixed some autobiography in the revision of those lectures the result picked up in pace and life what it lost in pomp and dignity. But the purpose of this book remains what it was in my lectures. It is a serious attempt to describe the legal, economic, and religious ideas—and to me these words all mean the same thing—that were accepted as a matter of faith in my early days in the West from 1895 to 1910, in my time at Princeton and Harvard from 1910 to the First World War, in that fabulous period of the 1920's, in the changes that took place during the Great Depression, and in the desperate conflicts that arose out of our attempts to adjust our ideas to the great and continuing industrial revolution of the twentieth century. I have seen the certainties of simple religious faith that gave me and others comfort prior to the First World War give way to the gross materialism of the early period between the two wars, to be in turn replaced by the despair and frustration of the Great Depression and, in the years following the Second World War, by the feeling that we were living in economic sin and that there was no health in us. This last conflict is happily on the way to being resolved, I believe, and the United States is on the verge of coming to terms with life as it must be lived in the twentieth century.

Acknowledgments

I acknowledge my great indebtedness to Leon H. Keyserling, former Chief Economic Adviser to President Truman, for the economic ideas in this book and to Bray Hammond, whose book *Banks and Politics in America* is the best analysis yet printed of our monetary mythology. I also wish to thank Sir Raymond Hinchcliffe, Judge of the English Queen's Bench Division, and the Honorable Carl D. Aarvold, Recorder of London (Chief Judge of the Criminal Courts of Old Bailey), for their generous assistance in correcting my observations on the English judicial system, and my partners Abe Krash and Robert Herzstein, for their critical reading of the manuscript. I want to express my particular appreciation to my secretary, Marguerite O'Brien, for her invaluable assistance in preparing and editing this manuscript.

CONTENTS

Preface   vii

ONE

Long Ago and Far Away   3

TWO

The Process of Education at the Beginning of the Twentieth
Century   16

THREE

Some Irrelevancies Relating to the First World War   23

FOUR

Law and Politics in Wyoming, and Why I Left   30

FIVE

The Crash—and What It Meant   38

SIX

The Changing Jurisprudence of the Great Depression   54

SEVEN

Saint Thomas Aquinas Still Lives   71

EIGHT

Why the Full Employment Act of 1946 Became a Dead Letter   76

NINE

The Change from Fundamental Principles to Practical Expediency in
International Affairs from the First World War to the Present
Cold War   82

TEN

The Fundamental Economic Principles That Were the Basis for Political
Action during the Administration of President Eisenhower   88

ix

ELEVEN

The Power of Private Credit Organizations to Provide Consumer Purchasing Power, Which Started with the Wildcat Banks at the Time of Andrew Jackson, Has Not Since the Depression Been Sufficient to Absorb the Productive Capacity of the Twentieth-Century Revolution 98

TWELVE

The Rise and Fall of the Blue Eagle 109

THIRTEEN

"An Idiot in a Powder Mill" 113

FOURTEEN

The Sherman Act as a Charter of Economic Freedom 120

FIFTEEN

My Career in Government 131

SIXTEEN

Why Government Service Is a Dubious Career 147

SEVENTEEN

A Brief Career on the Federal Bench 156

EIGHTEEN

The Puzzling Problem of Obscenity in American Law 160

NINETEEN

The Law Firm of Arnold, Fortas & Porter 188

TWENTY

The Use of Legislative Hearings for the Purpose of Exposing Undesirable Characters 196

TWENTY-ONE

The Un-American Activities of Government Organizations to Suppress Un-American Activities 204

TWENTY-TWO

The Criminal Trial as a Symbol of Public Morality 228

TWENTY-THREE

A Lady from Colorado 246

TWENTY-FOUR

The Practice of the Law Is a Profession of Great Dignity the Pursuit of
Which Requires Great Learning 252

TWENTY-FIVE

The Education of the Educated Voter 272

Index 287

Fair Fights and Foul

CHAPTER ONE

Long Ago and Far Away

Laramie, Wyoming, is where I was born, on June 2, 1891. I lived there until I went to college at the age of sixteen, and I will never get over my love for that wild semiarid country.

How did I come to be born in the Far West? Perhaps I should go back to my ancestry, which, though it seems somewhat irrelevant for this book, I have been informed is proper, and it is my habit to follow the advice of experts because there is always one chance in a thousand they may be right.

My father's first ancestor in this country was John Arnold, who came here from Cambridge, England, in 1634. He landed at Newtown, Massachusetts, and was later one of the petitioners for land farther west and went with Thomas Hooker to Hartford when that colony was founded. His name is on the ancient memorial stone in the old First Congregational churchyard in Hartford as one of the original proprietors.

Six generations later my great-grandfather John Arnold and his wife, Sophie Lord, left Connecticut with the great Western Reserve emigration to Ohio. En route my grandfather Carl Franklin Arnold was born at Parma, New York. Reaching Ohio they settled in Ashtabula, and there my grandfather grew up. After being graduated from Oberlin College, he went to Africa as a missionary. While in Africa in 1850 he met and married Elizabeth Ramsauer, the daughter of Johannes and Maria Schultless Ramsauer. Her father, my great-grandfather Johannes Ramsauer, was the son of a Swiss silk manufacturer. The family story is that in a revolutionary uprising Johannes's father was killed and his mother left destitute. Along with many other children young Ramsauer was sent to Zurich, where it was hoped that he and waifs like him would be adopted. He was a homely little boy and he found himself finally standing alone after all the other children had acquired foster parents. A lady came up and asked if he could read the Latin inscription on the clock tower. He did, and she took him home with her.

At that time Johann Heinrich Pestalozzi was conducting his great school. Ramsauer was enrolled and became Pestalozzi's favorite pupil. After he was graduated, he was employed as a tutor at the Imperial Court at Württemberg, presided over by the Grand Duke Peter Constantine of Russia.

My Arnold grandfather and my Ramsauer grandmother became acquainted and married under peculiar circumstances. When Carl Franklin Arnold arrived in Africa as a missionary, he found Johannes Ramsauer's son there seriously ill. He wrote a letter to the young man's parents in Oldenburg, Germany, telling them that they had better send someone out to care for him. His sister came out, but the journey in those days was very long, and before she arrived her brother had died. It was under these circumstances that my grandfather and grandmother met. Later they were married, and remained in Africa as missionaries.

Two children were born. Then my grandparents decided to leave Africa and come to the United States. It was my grandfather's intention to become a missionary in the Far West. On their way they visited my grandmother's parents in Germany. The Ramsauers would not hear of their taking the children with them to the United States. They were wealthy people and would be able to give the two children the benefit of a good education. So my grandfather and grandmother left the children with them.

In the United States four more children were born, of which my father was the third. My grandmother named him Constantine Peter, after the Grand Duke Peter Constantine. The name was a constant affliction, because everyone called him Connie. He used to tell me how disappointed he felt when a box of clothing would come to the missionaries from the east containing girl's clothes for dear little Connie.

My grandparents were too poor ever to get to Germany, and so they never again saw their two elder children. It was only after my father was forty years old that he and my mother paid a visit to Germany and met his two older brothers for the first time.

My grandfather went to Laramie, Wyoming, as a missionary pastor. He founded the first Presbyterian church there. I remember him vividly when I was a boy. He was a tall and stately man, about six feet two, with a long white beard. He habitually wore a frock coat and high silk hat. In addition to his pastoral duties he was chosen to open each session of the District Court with prayer, an activity that since then has become unconstitutional.

He was a kindly man, and I was very fond of him. However, he did have his foibles peculiar to the Presbyterian faith of those times. For example, the Sabbath began at six o'clock Saturday evening and lasted until Monday morning. During that period there was no levity permitted, no games and no amusements. He taught us that playing cards was a sin. I once asked him why, and he said that it was an addiction that inevitably brought one in contact with gamblers and other undesirable associates. There was one form of cards, however, that he was willing to play—a game called Flinch. On each card there was a number instead of the pips that decorate the ordinary playing deck. The cards were dealt one at a time, and the object was to get rid of a stack of numbers in a complicated way that I have long since forgotten. I was unable to understand why it was a sin to play cards with pips on them and not a sin to play cards of the identical size with numbers on them. My grandfather explained that this was because no gambler knew how to play Flinch. This seemed plausible, because the game was so dull that I was sure no one but a preacher would ever try to learn it.

There was another distinction I was unable to swallow. Like all the boys in Laramie, I had a pony. He was a remarkably fast little horse, and I wanted to enter him in the race at the county fair. My grandfather put his foot down; he explained to me that race tracks were frequented by undesirable characters and that people gambled on races. This I could not understand, because we were permitted to go to the races and sit in the grandstands where the actual gambling was going on, and I knew that it was impossible to gamble while going at full speed on a race-track. I was bitterly disappointed, but all my pleas were over-ruled. This incident planted the seeds of skepticism about the old-time religion that have plagued and tormented me ever since.

My father was a prosperous lawyer who combined the practice of law with ranching. His ranch covered thirty square miles, not large for that area. It spread from the meadowland on the Little Laramie River to the dark pine timber that covered the foothills of the Medicine Bow Range, with its perpetual snow. The only way to get to the range was by pack animal, which took two full days. Once there you could get that feeling of beauty and loneliness and adventure that has gone forever from the mountains, now infested with roads and automobiles. Today one can get to the foot of the snowy range from Laramie in an hour. Indeed, apart from the fact that they still speak the English lan-guage in Wyoming, its atmosphere and culture are completely changed from what I knew as a boy. The small towns from Chicago to the Pacific Coast are carbon copies of each other. The wide-open spaces have shrunk until journeys that then took days now take only a few hours. The people no longer are isolated. They dress alike, look alike, and talk alike. Life in the West has lost its pic-turesque quality and its sense of adventure.

A few stories may illustrate the tremendous change that has taken place. When I was twelve I worked for one of my father's clients, Colonel E. J. Bell. He owned large ranches and put up over two thousand tons of hay. I proudly drove a rake. The Colonel had a hay crew of about fifty men, which made it expensive when rain stopped all haying activity until the grass was dry. One Mon-day it started to rain. Tuesday it was still raining; Wednesday the same. But Thursday was bright and sunny and the hay dried and the mowers went into the field. Friday morning the rakes and the stacking crew were called out. But at noon on Friday it began to rain again.

I remember the scene as if it were yesterday. I was unhitching my horses from the rake. The rest of the crew were doing the same. Suddenly there appeared from the direction of the ranch a tiny speck. As it grew larger we could see it was a man on horse-back. Then we could see that it was Colonel Bell, riding toward us at a dead run. When he reached the haystack where we were un-harnessing, he pulled his horse back on its haunches, drew his revolver, and began to shout at God. "I see the bald-headed old S.O.B.," he shouted, "and I'll get him." It seems funny now, but it didn't at the time. Everyone there believed in a personal God and in a hell of fire and brimstone. The awful effrontery of Colonel Bell chilled us to the bone. We confidently expected him to be struck by lightning, and were surprised when he wasn't. It was a daring gesture of rebellion against a world of injustice.

Today the noble art of profanity which flourished in the Old West is dead. You can't have real profanity unless you believe in a personal God who will be offended by it. Another story illustrates this point.

To reach Colonel Bell's Millbrook ranch you could ride a horse for four hours or take the Laramie, Hans Peak and Pacific, a railroad that meandered over the Medicine Bow Range to North Park, Colorado. It carried cattle and soft coal. Starting out from Laramie at noon and proceeding at a rate of about sixteen miles per hour, the train would reach the foothills just about dusk. Then it would stop, and the fireman would get out to light the acetylene headlight on the old locomotive, which had been discarded by the Union Pacific.

One evening when I was riding the train to Colonel Bell's ranch the wind was howling across the Laramie plains at the rate of about forty miles an hour. The train stopped as usual, and the fireman got out to do his duty. The engineer was one who had been fired from the Union Pacific for drunkenness. He waited for the fireman to light the headlight until his patience was exhausted. Then he went out in front and took over the job himself. The wind kept blowing his matches out. Finally, he climbed down from the cowcatcher, threw his hat in the middle of the track, and began jumping on it. After a few minutes of this he paused and shook his fist at the western horizon. "If I was God," he shouted, "I'd be a just God. I'd not be an S.O.B. and blow out a poor man's head-light." I stood there frozen with horror at this blasphemy.

Colonel Bell was greatly interested in the Department of Agri-culture at the University of Wyoming, which was located in Laramie. One year he decided to give a silver cup as a prize to the winner of the annual stock-judging contest. He made it a condition that he present the prize himself. I was a student at the University of Wyoming preparatory school, which at the time was the only high school in the state except for one in the capital city of Cheyenne. As I recall it, there were only eight students in the graduating class that year.

The time for presentation of awards arrived. The president handed out most of them, but when the stock-judging prize came up he called on Colonel Bell. The Colonel was a short fat man and he was visibly nervous. He stomped out on the platform in his high-heeled cowboy boots with the cup in his hand. He began, "Mr. President, Ladies and Gentlemen." Then he froze. He started a second time with the same phrase, and froze again. Finally he thrust the cup at the amazed prize winner and said, "Here, take the God-damn thing," and stalked off the stage. In one respect, at least, Colonel Bell's remark was like Lincoln's Gettysburg Address. It will be remembered long after the other speeches made on the occasion are forgotten.

Since Wyoming was a land-grant college, every student had to take military training under an officer assigned by the United States Army. The entire training consisted of learning the Manual of Arms and the rules of close-order drill from 11:00 to 12:00 each morning. Close-order drill in those days was a complicated science, requiring close study and intensive training. For example, I remember the command: "On left, into line of platoons, in columns of fours." At that command, officers in charge of platoons gave subordinate commands, and the battalion which had been marching abreast in a long extended line whirled and wheeled until the platoons were marching in the same direction in parallel columns of fours. Today, close-order drill is a lost art. The ROTC at Wyoming, I am told, has today an entirely different training program, probably just as useless with respect to the next World War as our close-order drill was in my time and not nearly so spectacular.

When I entered the Wyoming Preparatory School, I was only twelve years old and smaller than most of my classmates. Captain Yates, the cavalry officer assigned to Wyoming at the time, looked me over and developed the extraordinary theory that if I carried one of the heavy Springfield rifles left over from the Civil War, which were supplied to us for training purposes, it would eventually make one of my shoulders permanently lower than the other. This he conceived to be a disadvantage. I don't know why. It was probably because, with this handicap, I would never be able to carry water on both shoulders, a very necessary skill for a career in either law or government.

Whatever the reason, Captain Yates decided to issue me one of the wooden guns which the girl students of Wyoming drilled with. The wooden gun made me conspicuous. No doubt Captain Yates was a well-intentioned man. However, my resentment was such that I entertained the ambition that some day I would rise to a position that would enable me to get even with him. I have never achieved that ambition. Somehow or other, the pressure of other affairs and the necessities of earning a living and supporting a family diverted me. Now it is too late. Captain Yates is dead. I will always be a frustrated man. I will never be able to put him in his place, as he put me in mine back in the Year of Our Lord 1907.

Speaking of wooden guns recalls a custom of the University of Wyoming which has long since been abandoned. In those days the girls as well as the men were required to learn the Manual of Arms and the fundamental principles of close-order drill. There were two companies of girls and two companies of men parading around and doing fours right and left on the parade ground back of the Main Building from 11:00 to 12:00, five days a week. The girls drilled with wooden guns.

What effect this training of the girls had on our problem of national defense is still somewhat obscure. However, I have no question that it improved the character of the University women. It imbued them with the notion that it is a woman's duty to march forward and backward, to turn right and left, to carry a wooden gun on her shoulder or present arms, at the sharp command of a man. I think this training must have had a beneficial effect on domestic life in Wyoming in 1904. It is significant to note that since the training of women in close-order drill and the Manual of Arms has been abandoned in Wyoming, the divorce rate has increased by leaps and bounds.

Among the distinctive characters that adorned the local society of Laramie was the famous humorist Bill Nye, the editor of the

Laramie *Boomerang*. He was before my time, but his legend still flourished. His editorial offices were on the second floor of the principal livery stable. The stairway was opposite a stall inhabited by a gray mule. At the foot of the stairs Nye had posted a sign: "Twist the gray mule's tail and take the elevator." Just after Nye married and brought his bride to Laramie, his house was robbed. The next day the headlines in the Laramie *Boomerang* read: "Editor's house robbed and all his wedding presents stolen. We were able to trace the robbers thirty miles by the stuff they had thrown away."

Characters like the engineer, Colonel Bell, and Bill Nye were indigenous to the West. They have disappeared with the peculiar culture of that original society. How original and fascinating it was is attested by the popularity of Westerns today, not only in the United States, but all over the world. There is little resemblance between the modern Western and the old West as I knew it, excepting the wide-open spaces, the sense of adventure, and the belief that the good guys always win out over the bad guys. But there is enough nostalgia in Westerns today, and I never tire of watching them in movies or on television.

A Wyoming ranch in those days was isolated. One summer I was working on a ranch owned by a man named Knudson. A large part of the Laramie ranching community was owned by Swedes. It was haying time, and my particular job was that of horse wrangler. My duties required me to get up at five in the morning and drive the horses from the field into the corral. One morning as I was riding out just as the dawn was breaking my horse shied and started to bolt. There, right in front of me, were five elephants. They had broken the fence of the hay corral and were eating hay from a freshly made stack. I rode back to the barn at a dead run and told Knudson there were five elephants in the hayfield. He said I was crazy, but agreed to saddle his horse and ride back with me. When he saw the elephants a look of utter incredulity spread over his face, and he said, "Yesus Christ."

We learned the explanation later. Ringling's circus had played in Cheyenne the day before. After leaving Cheyenne some accident had happened to the train, compelling them to stop in Laramie. They decided that rather than waste the time they would give

Laramie a performance. But when they took their ten or twelve
elephants down to the Laramie River for water, the elephants took
fright at something and stampeded in all directions over the Laramie plains. A few days later the Ringling men came out to the
Knudson ranch and retrieved their elephants.

Outside Laramie the level grassy plains stretched to the horizon
or to the dark blue timber on the slopes of the snow-crested peaks
of the Medicine Bow Range. It was cattle country. There were no
fences except those around the meadows along the river. The cattle
were turned loose to graze. In the spring there was a roundup to
brand the new calves, and there was another roundup in the fall to
bring the cattle to market. No experience in my life has been so
thrilling and enchanting as those roundups. Every evening the cowboys would gather around the chuck wagon. There was always somebody who could play the guitar, and this music still seems to me the
most beautiful I have ever heard. It had only one fault: there were
never enough basses to offset the numerous tenors.

The Old West was a place of exaggeration and individualism.
Rawlins, Wyoming, was a windy town. To measure the velocity of
the wind a heavy long chain was hung from the Ferris Hotel. When it
extended out at an angle of forty-five degrees it was a comparatively
calm day. Only when the chain projected itself at a right angle
to the wall did the citizens consider it windy. One day the wind
stopped blowing for a moment, and everybody in town fell down.

The art of dramatic oratory was highly regarded. In this field
exaggeration knew no limit. I recall my father arguing a case in
the United States District Court as follows: "Rather than be in the
position of the defendant in this proceeding I would prefer to set
sail on a sea of storm, in a boat of stone, with oars of iron and
sails of lead, with the wrath of God for a gale and Hell for the
nearest port." I remember another of my father's arguments. It
was in a water rights case in which the government sought an injunction to prevent my father's clients from diverting irrigation
water from an Indian reservation. My father was arguing that the
federal court lacked jurisdiction. He concluded his remarks in this
way: "And finally, your Honor, the government wants this Court
to send its commissioners up to the Shoshone Reservation, and then
to report back to this Court in this beautiful courtroom with the

mud of the irrigation ditches on their boots and the red sand of the desert in their hair." The judge laughed and said, "The Court won't do it." And my father won his case.

Another occasion that I remember occurred years later, when I was practicing law with my father in Laramie. It was in the days of Prohibition. A popular local rancher was found on the highway in his car with a bullet in his head. Investigation showed that two Prohibition agents had been on the road looking for a prominent bootlegger who drove the same kind of car. They had been hired by the state of Colorado and had driven into Wyoming the night before. This was about all the evidence against them.

Feeling in Laramie ran so high that the county commissioners retained my father and me to assist the prosecuting attorney. The defense employed a prominent criminal lawyer from New York. Because of the strong feeling in Laramie, the case was moved to Cheyenne for trial. The defense called a number of character witnesses, among whom was the governor of Colorado. At the end of his testimony my father asked me what to do with him. "Drop him like a hot potato," I advised. "No, I think I'll try something," said my father. Rising slowly to his feet and in a voice dripping with sarcasm, my father asked, "What . . . state . . . did . . . you . . . say . . . you . . . were . . . governor . . . of?" The governor angrily retorted: "Fortunately, I was elected governor of the great state of Colorado." "Fortunately . . . for . . . whom?" said my father, and sat down.

You could not do that today in a courtroom without a reprimand. It was part of the drama that people in the Wild West thought they were acting in. Nowhere in this dull modern age can such arguments be made or such oratory heard. People today do not have enough reverence to enable them to compose inspired impertinence or to use magnificent profanity.

Laramie's local theater has long since passed away. *Uncle Tom's Cabin* is no longer played. No longer does the heavy villain tie the unfortunate heroine to the track in front of the advancing locomotive; no longer do the hardhearted parents turn their daughter who loved not wisely but too well out into the blinding snowstorm. Apart from the theater, which was of doubtful respectability, the town was a hotbed of culture. Rosa Bonheur's "Horse Fair" was looked upon as the highest achievement of the painter's genius. There was a Browning circle which met every week to wade through and decipher "Pippa Passes." Owen Wister's *Virginian* was considered one of the greatest novels. Itinerant lecturers drew tears from the citizens with lectures bearing titles like "Mother, Home and Heaven."

When I was a boy in Laramie there were a number of houses of prostitution on Front Street. The girls would be rounded up and fined before a justice of the peace every month. This was a sort of license fee for carrying on their profession. There were also about ten saloons with old-fashioned swinging doors. On Sunday it seemed as if half the citizens were in church and the other half getting drunk in the saloons. A casual view of Front Street on Sunday (weekdays were different because the cowboys were at work) would disclose at least half a dozen drunks. Being reared in such an atmosphere would today be cited as a cause for juvenile delinquency. We boys were avidly curious about the strange goings on in Front Street, yet I never heard of a case of juvenile delinquency among the families of the God-fearing citizens of the town. Indeed, the morality of the time was strict and rigorous. My grandfather, a thorough student of Presbyterian theory, would have strenuously opposed any attempt to prohibit prostitution by enforcement of the law. It was his belief that God put sin into the world to test mankind. To prohibit any form of sin by law would be directly counter to the teaching of the Holy Bible. The church had exclusive jurisdiction over morality. It was the function of the church to see to it that its members did not commit sin. And, oddly enough, this simple philosophy still seems valid to me.

About the only resemblance between the Old West and the modern Western is the respect and admiration boys hold for the bad men. One of our local heroes was the fabulous Tom Horn, who has been called the last of the bad men. He had been an Indian fighter under General George Crook. When I was a boy he was hired by the Wyoming Cattlemen's Association to rid the country of cattle rustlers. These were generally small homesteaders who would ride the range between roundups and put their own brands on calves belonging to the large ranchers who composed the Wyoming Cattlemen's Association. Wyoming juries, which were largely composed of these same homesteaders, uniformly refused to convict. The large cattlemen in desperation hired Tom Horn. Every boy had heard of him and his fabulous exploits. But one summer he went beyond his instructions and shot a boy named Willie Nichols on a ranch in the hills about fifteen miles east of Laramie. He put two stones near the boy's head, which was his usual way of identifying one of his killings. The brutal murder was too much for the citizens to put up with. The sheriff in Cheyenne, T. Joe Cahill, got him so drunk in a hotel room that he began to brag about his exploits and finally admitted the murder of Willie Nichols as well as many other killings. The clerk of the federal court, an expert stenographer, had his ear glued to the crack under the door and was taking it all down.

Tom Horn was promptly arrested and indicted for murder. His trial, held in Cheyenne, is one of the high lights in the annals of Western bad men. After the news of his arrest was published, scarcely any of the large cattlemen got a good night's sleep. The question that worried them was whether Tom Horn would turn state's evidence. When the trial opened, there was present in the courtroom a complete roster of the leaders of the Wyoming bar. My father was one of them, representing Ora Haley, a large cattleman from north of Laramie.

Horn seemed completely undisturbed. He had confidence that his employers had enough influence to get him acquitted. He kept that faith during the long trial, in which every legal device was put to use to secure a dismissal. But these efforts were in vain. He was convicted, and the conviction was sustained on appeal. But he went to his death without turning informer, which might easily have saved his life. A grateful audience at his hanging wept tears of sympathy and gratitude for his keeping of the faith.

These are only a few glimpses of the Wild West at the turn of the century, but I hope that they convey some of its flavor. By 1910 the horseless carriage began to infest the great plains. My father was convinced that the horseless carriage would never replace the horse. But by 1915 even he had succumbed and had purchased one of Henry Ford's tin lizzies. No doubt he was impressed by the Ford booth at the annual auto show in Denver. All that was in the booth was a phonograph that played over and over again the simple refrain "It gets you there. It gets you back. It gets you there. It gets you back." The idea that an automobile was a status symbol rather than a means of transportation had not yet penetrated the minds of the citizens of that time.

Today the Laramie plains are all under fence. There is a great university in Laramie. The town itself is clean, respectable, undistinguished, and extraordinarily dull. Every now and then the Chamber of Commerce decides to hold what it calls a jubilee in memory of days gone by. Automobile drivers dress up as cowboys. Some citizens take the parts of the old-time bad men and famous prostitutes and gamblers. They furnish gambling halls in the old style and bet with paper money. This is because those were the only interesting times that Laramie ever knew. So it is fitting that I close this chapter with one of my father's more inspired flights of oratory, delivered on an occasion the character of which I have forgotten long ago. The title of his address was "The Wild and Woolly West." He concluded as follows: "If the West is woolly it is with the wool of which victorious flags are made, and if it is wild it is because death alone is tame."

CHAPTER TWO

The Process of Education at the Beginning of the Twentieth Century

My college days were spent at Princeton. I recall that my wife once informed Robert Hutchins that I was educated at Princeton. "You mean he *went* to Princeton" was the reply, which was a much more accurate appraisal of the actual situation. The reasons Princeton was selected are somewhat obscure. It was probably because it had Presbyterian leanings and was considered in the Far West to be a very high-class school.

The change from Laramie to Princeton in 1907 was to a different world. My Western clothes, mannerisms, and speech did not fit. I was immediately classified as a queer character. I was not admitted to any club; indeed, I was never admitted to anything at Princeton. Princeton had then and still has a hierarchy of undergraduate clubs rated in social importance from the dizzy eminence of Ivy to the youngest club at the bottom. Since about ninety per cent of the class were club members, my years at Princeton were chiefly remarkable for their loneliness.

These Princeton clubs were a reflection of the ideals of the world outside. Society with a big S had a tremendously important value. In a way the American public's reverence for Society was a reflection of England's reverence for their aristocracy. Our Constitution prevented us from having a House of Peers, but we filled the need for one with institutions like the Four Hundred in New York and the Court of Mrs. Potter Palmer in Chicago. This feeling permeated small towns as well as big cities. In the small frontier town of Laramie, the Ivinson parties were the acme of Society. Edward Ivinson was the most respected banker in town, and a street in Laramie has since been named in his honor. My father had run for Congress on the free-silver ticket of William Jennings Bryan, which gave us a handicap that excluded us from all really high-toned society in Laramie.

"Society" is dead today. Its ghost may still linger in the halls of the Princeton Ivy Club, but the phrase "He is an Ivy man" does not reflect the reverence it once did. And now that the authorities at Princeton, with the co-operation of the clubs, have arranged things so that every undergraduate can become a member of a club, some of the best students do not want to join.

A respectable college is the mirror of the values of the world outside. Had someone in 1911 formed a college patterned after the ideas of today, it would have had no prestige. Upton Sinclair would have sent his children to it, but the well-heeled God-fearing parents who were the backbone of the country at that time would not have. Today the world has changed, and the Princeton club system, after the requisite period of doubt and anxiety that always accompanies the passing away of old faiths, has changed with it.

Incidentally, we owe to the Princeton club system one of our greatest Presidents, Woodrow Wilson. He was in full revolt against the system. He wanted to abolish the clubs and establish colleges patterned after those of Oxford and Cambridge. He was forced to resign as president of Princeton, and so became a politician.

The curriculum at Princeton in my day was extraordinarily dull. Greek was a required subject, on the old theory, now happily passé, that it trained the youthful mind, much as the dull exercise of pulling chest weights trains the muscles. Latin was required in greater quantities than Greek. The ancient texts were studied as if they existed in a vacuum, wholly apart from the culture of the civilizations that created them. This process made them an intolerable bore. It was small wonder that social life at Princeton was considered much more important than study.

It is impossible to exaggerate the narrow intellectual horizon of both the students and the faculty of that day. It was an age of absolute certainties. Particular studies were good for you and made you a well-rounded man. You went to compulsory chapel three times a week to improve your spiritual outlook. In a course on Horace and Catullus you could pass with a good grade if you committed enough Latin poetry to memory. The one thing that had to be avoided at all cost was the discussion of new ideas. Such an enterprise was useless because there were no new ideas worth discussing. All the ideas that were worthwhile had been discovered long ago. Nobody went near the library. We stuck to the textbooks that we were required to purchase. Individual student research was unthinkable. There was only one exception. Professor E. S. Corwin gave a course on the Constitution in which we read Madison's notes, *The Federalist,* and other contemporary works. But, by and large, I can recall no other professor during my stay in Princeton who said or did anything that had any relevance to the development of the social institutions that existed outside the college walls.

I was interested in abstract philosophy. Here was where the search for the truth that lies at the bottom of the well began, according to the thinking of the time. We read extracts from the philosophers from Plato to William James, though we read them not as part of the thinking or the values of the time in which they wrote but as seekers for abstract truth which had no relation to time or place. The effect of Rousseau's social contract, his justification for adherence to a king whose divine right was beginning to be doubted, was not part of the course. The question was whether Rousseau was right or wrong. In the same way, the effect of Hobbes in providing a theory to support the monolithic nation-states of the seventeenth century was not considered, nor was the liberating influence of Locke in the eighteenth century. The question was simply were these gentlemen right or wrong. Kant was considered the greatest philosopher. But Hegel and Spinoza were also top-drawer truth seekers. We learned a lot of formulas, such as the "being is becoming" of Spinoza and the "thesis, antithesis and synthesis" of Hegel. The pragmatism of William James was suspect because it seemed to deny fundamental truths.

I have lost touch with the philosophical pundits of today, but I doubt if many areas still exist where a search for abstract truth is carried on. Professor F. S. C. Northrup, of Yale, whom I admire greatly, is, I think, typical of the modern philosophical approach. Instead of thinking in a vacuum, he has become a member of the

Yale Law School faculty. He is writing and lecturing about the underlying philosophical ideas in the law and their psychological effect on contemporary social organizations.

Today a liberal college education is considered a necessity, whether a man is to become an engineer, a scientist, or a lawyer. We believe that technical training without a knowledge of the history and literature of the past may destroy a man's freedom of thought and narrow his outlook. When I went to college in the early days of this century a college education was a luxury few people could afford. It was not supposed to be of any utilitarian value. Its purpose was to endow its students with what we then called "culture." Culture was apart from the dynamic industrial development of society. Being a cultured gentleman was an end in itself. The old attitude is illustrated in the autobiography of Henry Adams where he notes that he never met an important businessman who interested him in the least. Yet the people whom Henry Adams chose to ignore were nevertheless the dynamic social forces of their time. Today the word "culture" is seldom used to describe the benefits of a college education. The idea is, rather, that in both industry and government a broad understanding of the history and literature of one's own society makes a man a better business manager. This idea has taken such root that great corporations are sending their executives to attend graduate liberal-arts seminars. The change may be noted, too, in the fact that the same kind of women who joined Browning circles to obtain culture when I was a boy, and met to discuss the hidden meanings of that great but forgotten poet, are now joining political parties, the League of Women Voters, and similar groups.

Today when I go back to Princeton I can recognize the buildings but otherwise it is a different university. Students are interested in ideas. If you lecture there, they ask you intelligent questions. Just as the old Princeton reflected an age of certainties and conventions, so the new Princeton and other educational institutions reflect an age of questioning and discovery.

When I went back to Laramie the summer after my graduation in 1911, I met Colonel Bell in my father's office. He patted me on the shoulder and said to my father: "Connie, I congratulate you. I'd rather have one son graduate from Princeton than have a thousand sons in the penitentiary." It sounded funny at the time, but reflecting on it at this distance I am convinced that the Colonel made an accurate summary of the intellectual value of a Princeton education at that time. None of us ever saw any faults in the educational process to which we were exposed. There was no criticism or skepticism. Such things had no place in a world of certainties.

In the fall of 1911 I entered Harvard Law School. It was a new and exciting experience. Enough of my Western manners had rubbed off so that I was no longer lonely. The professors at Harvard, compared with the Princeton faculty, seemed intellectual giants. The narrow logic of the law, the building of legal principle on the solid basis of a long line of precedents, and the analysis of cases in class by the Socratic method were fascinating. It was also fun to have to work hard, which one never did at Princeton. But the world of the Harvard Law School was as much a world of eternal verities and absolute certainties as it had been at Princeton. The study of human society was divided into fields in which scholars could work without having to acquaint themselves with what people were doing in other fields. The principal fields were law and economics. Then there was another field called the social sciences, though real scholars were dubious about whether this field was truly a science. It was felt that only superficial scholars would be content to work in the field of sociology. The study of psychology was something no sound scholar would care to be caught dabbling in. The idea that thinking was a form of human behavior lay far beyond the horizon. The writings of Freud were completely unknown to properly educated men.

The field of law in turn was carved up into many separate fields: contracts, agency, corporations, real property, personal property, and so on. The workers in these separate fields had little to do with the workers in other fields. They were joined together at the top by the brooding omnipresence in the sky called the science of jurisprudence. Through the wise application of this science, the accidental inconsistencies of the minor fields were ironed out and the law was made into a seamless web.

Professor Thomas Reed Powell, one of the few rebels on the Harvard faculty twenty-five years later, said: "If you can think of a subject which is interrelated and inextricably combined with another subject, without knowing anything about or giving any consideration to the second subject, then you have a legal mind." The mental process by which this was accomplished was as follows: Each individual endowed with free will by his creator had two little men in the top of his head. One was called Reason, the other Impulse. Reason was a highly reliable little man. Impulse, on the other hand, was completely unreliable and untrustworthy. He was unable to follow any logical and consistent course of conduct. He was prone to be influenced by the blandishments of demagogues. He was a pushover for unsound schemes. It was, therefore, the duty and function of the little man called Reason to put his foot squarely on the back of the neck of Impulse whenever that individual began to err and stray like a lost sheep, as was usually the case. The law was the quintessence of human reason.

The result of this method of thinking I tried to express in a poem written at the Harvard Law School in 1914 about a typical lawschool course:

CONFLICT OF LAWS

CONFLICT OF LAWS with its peppery seasoning,
Of pliable, scarcely reliable reasoning,
Dealing with weird and impossible things,
Such as marriage and domicil, bastards and kings,
All about courts without jurisdiction,
Handing out misery, pain and affliction,
Making defendant, for reasons confusing,
Unfounded, ill-grounded, but always amusing,
Liable one place but not in another,
Son of his father, but not of his mother,
Married in Sweden, but only a lover in *
Pious dominions of Great Britain's sovereign.
Blithely upsetting all we've been taught,
Rendering futile our methods of thought,
Till Reason, tottering down from her throne,
And Common Sense, sitting, neglected, alone,
Cry out despairingly, "Why do you hate us?
Give us once more our legitimate status."
Ah, Students, bewildered, don't grasp at such straws,
But join in the chorus of Conflict of Laws.

Chorus

Beale, Beale, wonderful Beale,†
Not even in verse can we tell how we feel,
When our efforts so strenuous,
To over-throw,
Your reasoning tenuous,
Simply won't go.
For the law is a system of
wheels within wheels
Invented by Sayres and Thayers and Beales ‡
With each little wheel
So exactly adjusted,
That if it goes haywire
The whole thing is busted.
So Hail to Profanity,
Goodbye to Sanity,
Lost if you stop to consider or pause.
On with the frantic, romantic, pedantic,
Effusive, abusive, illusive, conclusive,
Evasive, persuasive Conflict of Laws.

* (Brook *v.* Brook)

After my graduation from Harvard, in 1914, I went back to Laramie for the summer. On a visit to Cheyenne I called on Attorney General Walls, who had been an old cowpuncher. He asked me whether I had taken a course in legal ethics at Harvard. I replied that I had not. "That's good," he said, "because I can tell you all the legal ethics you will ever need to know in a single sentence." "Go ahead, General," I said. He replied, "If in the course of your practice you become involved in difficult and protracted litigation, and if in the course of that litigation it becomes apparent that somebody has got to go to jail, be sure that it's your client." That completed and rounded out my legal education.

† Joseph H. Beale was Professor of Conflicts of Laws at Harvard at that time.
‡ Sayre and Thayer were distinguished professors in the Harvard Law School.

CHAPTER THREE

Some Irrelevancies Relating to the
First World War

This chapter is inserted merely to preserve a chronological sequence. My experiences in the First World War have little to do with the theme of this book. Therefore, I will attempt to make it brief and confine it to a few incidents.

When I left Harvard in 1914 I decided that my future lay in Chicago. War had broken out in Europe but no one dreamed that the United States would be drawn into it; indeed, it was the opinion of many sound economists that the war would not last three months because modern war was so costly that no nation could afford to fight longer than that. A great man in Chicago at the time was William Hale Thompson, the mayor. He gained nationwide fame by saying that if King George of England ever came to Chicago he would punch him in the snoot.

After a brief period as an employee of a large firm which paid me the munificent salary of ten dollars a week, I decided that I could improve my station in life by forming a firm of my own. And thus the great but short-lived firm of O'Brian, Waite & Arnold was born.

My cash resources were so low that I was forced to live in a cubicle at the local YMCA in Ravenswood, from which I would take the elevated every morning to my office. The rules of the YMCA forbade smoking in the building. The commanding secretary had a nose like a bird dog and could detect cigar smoke through closed doors. For that reason I was constantly in trouble. My impressions of the YMCA I expressed at the time in the following poem:

HOME OFF THE RANGE

I do not smoke, I do not chew,
I never drink a single thing,
And so whene'er I'm feeling blue
(And generally I find I do),
I lift my plaintive voice and sing:

Oh, I live in the wonderful Y.M.C.A.
And my comrades are faithful and true,
    I eschew the narcotic,
    and shun the erotic,
As every respectable young man should do.
    And hereby take warning,
    I pray night and morning,
And the cuss words I use, they are mighty damn few
(An occasional "hell" and a "goddam" or two,
Is just about all the cussing I do).
And this regeneration, I'm happy to say,
Is due to the wonderful Y.M.C.A.

Shortly after the birth of O'Brian, Waite & Arnold, a National Guard battery of field artillery was organized with headquarters at Fort Sheridan. It was an extremely high-toned outfit. Its members were mostly sons of prominent families of Chicago's North Shore, and it had a long waiting list to get in, though I did. Somewhere in the background there was a vague notion that we were adding to the military strength of our country. But in the foreground there was the pleasing idea that it was fun to go out to Fort Sheridan and ride government horses in the atmosphere of an exclusive club. Fred McLauchen, a famous polo player, was a member. John Richardson, the youthful vice president of Marshall Field; Lawrence Houghteling, a partner in the financial house of Peabody, Houghteling; and Joseph Patterson, then with the Chicago *Tribune* and later to become editor of the New York *Daily News*, were among the group. This is enough to give the flavor of the little gathering.

On March 9, 1916, Pancho Villa, the notorious Mexican general, in retaliation for our country's recognition of President Carranza's government crossed the United States border with some four hundred men and raided Columbus, New Mexico, killing sixteen Americans and partially burning the town. The next day President Wilson ordered Brigadier General John J. Pershing to pursue Villa with United States cavalry into Mexico and capture him and his band. Shortly afterward Wilson mobilized the National Guard and sent it to the border as a precautionary measure.

This came as quite a shock to that exclusive little group known as Battery C. I remember the telephone call I received from Pompey Howe, our top sergeant. He said, "Report out to Fort Sheridan by noon tomorrow. The National Guard has been mobilized." I replied, "I can't possibly do it. I've got an argument in Municipal Court tomorrow morning." He said, "If you don't show up, you will be arrested." I showed up.

When I got there everything was confusion and consternation. Today I imagine that a man who joins the National Guard knows that he is taking a risk of being called into service, but in those days such an event was not even considered a possibility. We had not been at war since the fighting in the Philippines. There were no race tensions or race riots or anything else requiring military intervention. Therefore, an atmosphere of outrage pervaded the whole assembly as we were herded onto a train and sent south. Exclusive Battery C still had a long waiting list, but this particular waiting list, unlike the former one, was headed "out" instead of "in."

The period of three months I spent on the border was both an amusing and an educational experience. At the beginning a large part of our time was spent with picks and shovels in the broiling Texas sun digging latrines and trenches for our water system. As a result of that our battery song went as follows:

> The poster showed me a horse to ride
> But it didn't show the shovel on the other side,
> I don't want any more Texas
> Lordy, how I want to go home.

The most useful information I acquired was the fact that if you were called out on a pick-and-shovel detail, you should select a pick instead of a shovel. That was owing to my discovery that you can shovel practically all the time whereas a pick can be used only at intervals. Today, however, automation and improved digging machinery have rendered this information obsolete.

Toward the end of our service on the border the War Department decided it would have the whole National Guard division of twenty-five thousand men march from San Antonio to Dallas and back again. This was the largest body of men that had been moved as a unit since the Civil War. The march took two days and two nights each way. It proved the inexperience of the National Guard staff. We rode all day through choking dust so thick that the caisson just ahead could not be seen. This was not the fault of the staff, but when we camped on the San Marcos River the only way to water about three thousand horses was to go through a narrow little approach. It was three o'clock in the morning before the last horse had his fill. This seemed to indicate to us some lack in the staff somewhere.

To summarize this episode of glory, Pershing and his cavalry never did catch up with Pancho Villa. They finally gave up and came trooping back. President Wilson released the National Guard, and I returned safely to Chicago to resume the practice of law—though not for long.

On April 6, 1917, the United States declared war against Germany, and I promptly entered officers' training camp at Fort Sheridan. The lease on my office in the New York Life Building on LaSalle Street had several years to run, and the rent was due about two weeks after I reported to the training camp. I had no cash. I don't know whether the rent ever got paid or not. In any event, when I go to Chicago today I go around the block so as not to pass in front of the New York Life Building, because of the fear that if I do, someone will dash out of the lobby and serve me with a summons.

The great crusade to make the world safe for democracy was a thrilling and inspiring experience to many. We were not in the war long enough to acquire any general appreciation of its horror. But the seriousness with which training camp was taken can be illustrated by an incident that occurred in another battery in our battalion. The candidates were all in the barracks polishing shoes and what not during a rest period. An officer suddenly appeared in front of the building and blew a whistle. Everyone piled out.

He gave the command "Fall in," then "Squads right." He conducted them to the main road passing by Fort Sheridan. Down the road they went, their ranks in perfect alignment. Usually after half an hour of marching, the column would be halted and the men given a brief rest. This time it didn't happen. The column kept marching, eyes fixed to the front, with flawless discipline for over an hour before they discovered that no officer was with them.

I remember another incident that illustrates the seriousness of some. A number of us had been in the Illinois National Guard, which was camped a short distance from our battery headquarters. We would explain to our new comrades the necessity of getting a saddle that would fit them, that a poorly fitting saddle would cause chafes and burns and intense discomfort on the march. We would then tell them that Charlie Vokel, stable sergeant of our old National Guard battery, was an expert in measuring people for saddles and that we would get him to measure them as a special favor. Not many people fell for this, but there were a few who did. We would conduct such candidates to the stables of our old battery, get them to bend over, and Charlie would take their measurements from one of the various important points to another, while someone else would write them down. Then one of us would hit the victim with a large paddle. He usually took it in good nature and joined in the laughter. But there was one candidate who required special treatment. After he had been measured and hit with a paddle, he laughed with us and then became serious. He said, "Come on, fellows, cut out the kidding and really measure me." And so we had to do it all over again before he got the point.

I came out of the training camp a first lieutenant and was assigned to depart for France within two weeks. The girl to whom I was then engaged decided that we had better get married before I sailed and wired me that she was coming to New York for that purpose. Unfortunately, I did not get the wire. I had gone to see a friend at the training camp at Plattsburgh, and had thriftily checked out of my hotel in the interest of balancing the budget. When my future wife reached New York, she called the hotel and was, of course, told that I had checked out and left no address. She left a note there, however, and the next morning I returned and found it, and then her. Needless to say, she appeared glad to see me. I then discovered that I had left all my money in my Pullman berth. This was most disturbing, but she had a blank check signed by her father. She filled it out for a generous amount. In spite of the fact that her father's credit was good at the hotel, they declined to cash it, giving as a reason some obscure provision in the law of negotiable instruments. So I was forced to panhandle from some of my friends before we finally got the wedding financed. I sailed for France the week after.

In France I was assigned to the French Artillery School at Saumur. On completion of that course I was sent to the 101st Field Artillery of the 26th Division, commonly called the "Yankee Division," which moved to the front in February, 1918.

Life at the front was an exciting experience. There was the noise of shells exploding and gas attacks too frequent to recite in detail here. But the artillery was far enough behind the front lines for our casualties to be relatively light. The chief discomforts were the cold and the wet, which I will never forget.

I can think of few incidents worth telling, but one is about how I failed to get promoted to captain, although I richly deserved it. Our battery was located just behind a road under heavy camouflage. I had been transferred to battalion headquarters, where my duties were to write out the orders of the major and distribute them to the battery commanders. One day I received a memorandum circulated by General C. R. Edwards, who then commanded the 26th Division, which said in effect that the General had inspected our brigade and found the horses in terrible condition. He had also noticed that some of men were riding the horses at a gallop around the rear echelons of the brigade. He said that he didn't want any horse ridden faster than a walk. He concluded: "This is only a suggestion but a suggestion in my present frame of mind is equivalent to a command." I immediately sat down at my typewriter and composed a similar memorandum. It stated that General Edwards had inspected the brigade and discovered that the woods behind the three batteries were filled with cuckoos without any clocks. (This happened to be a fact.) The General suggested that all battery commanders purchase clocks for these cuckoos as soon as possible. I concluded: "This is only a suggestion but a suggestion in my present frame of mind is equivalent to a command." Somehow or other, my memorandum got to general headquarters, and I was told that it was not favorably received. When the promotions to captain came out at the end of that month, my name was not on the list. I have always suspected that the memorandum had something to do with this, but there are those who believe that there were other reasons.

There is another incident I remember vividly, though after forty-seven years I cannot precisely recall when or how it happened. One rainy night in March or April our regiment replaced another American regiment—I think one from the First Division, a better-trained battle outfit than ours—which was going somewhere else to more serious work. I was at the head of my battery. We moved for hours in the cold rain, and everyone was wet and discouraged. We came at last to a little French village that had been battered by artillery fire; this was to be our rear echelon. The road was jammed with my regiment's artillery moving in and the other artillery moving out. There was a light in the basement of a house that had been partially destroyed by shellfire. A wagon from the regiment that was moving out was in front of the house. I heard someone call from the basement to the wagon driver, "Hey, Bill, you've left an officer's bedroll." The wagon driver called back, "Whose bedroll?" "Lieutenant ——," said the voice from the basement. "He's an S.O.B.," said the wagon driver. "Giddap." And off the wagon went. I was tempted to interfere, but I was too tired and cold and wet and unsure of my authority. I can imagine the scene the next morning, though: "I looked everywhere for it, sir; I hunted and hunted. Somebody must have stole it." It did not pay in those days for an officer to be unpopular with enlisted men.

In August, 1918, I was ordered back to the United States, with a number of others, to serve as an instructor to new divisions about to sail. Mine was the 35th Field Artillery. In November, this division was ordered to the front. Our advance party did sail for Europe, and the rest of us were preparing to follow them. Then the Armistice was signed, and we stayed at home.

The net result of all this with respect to my wife was this: She had married me a week before I sailed, betting everything in the hope that she would collect $10,000 in war-risk insurance. She lost.

CHAPTER FOUR

Law and Politics in Wyoming, and Why I Left

After the war I returned to Laramie to practice law. It was then a wild and woolly town of about eight thousand. My practice was a general one, with many interesting cases, though a bit heavy with divorces and collections.

Two of my cases may be of interest. In the first one my wife was my client. A door-to-door salesman had worked his way into the house. He told my wife that he was privileged to bestow a great honor on her. He was selling an encyclopedia which his publishers were introducing for the first time into Wyoming. They had authorized him to determine who the most prominent women in the state were and to present to them a free copy of the encyclopedia. The recipients could then recommend it to their friends. There was no obligation involved, but she would want, of course, to keep the encyclopedia up to date by purchasing the loose-leaf supplements. She felt elated and quickly signed a piece of paper which she did not read.

Later there came a series of bills for the loose-leaf supplements which arrived every month and which were promptly sent back. This treatment caused the publishers to lose patience with us. Finally, one day when my wife was away on a visit to New York, we received a letter from the publishers. The letter expressed entire lack of comprehension as to why we were ignoring the bills. It went on to explain in an eloquent and persuasive way that we lived in a world of credit and that the most precious asset a person could have was his credit. They hoped that it would not be necessary for them to give my wife's name to the National Credit Rating Agency and thus ruin her credit everywhere. They would hate to do this, but if she continued to ignore their bills they would have no alternative.

The idea intrigued me. I wrote to the publishers and informed them that my wife had apparently unlimited credit in Denver, Chicago, New York, and perhaps many other places. As a result, I was continuously broke. I therefore urged them to turn my wife's name in to the National Credit Rating Agency as soon as possible. I concluded: "If you will keep up the good work on a national scale I will see what I can do on the local level." To this date I have not received a reply.

The second case concerned three neckties. There was a sales device current then of sending out neckties through the mail. The recipient was informed that if he liked the ties, he could remit a dollar apiece for them, otherwise he must return them.

I happened to like the ties, so I sent three dollars. A friend of mine who was a doctor was not so well advised. He wore the ties but did not remit the money. Thereafter he received a series of threatening letters and came to me for advice. I told him that the law was pretty clear that he did not have to return the ties, that he could throw them in the wastebasket, but if, instead of doing this, he wore them, he was liable to the seller. He did like the ties, so I composed a letter for him to sign. In it he said that he thought the ties were such a magnificent bargain that three dollars was inadequate compensation. He was therefore enclosing three pills that were good for any disease to which either horse or man is heir. The pills were worth ten dollars apiece, he wrote, but he was making a special offer of six dollars. He suggested that the tie company either send him three dollars, the difference between the value of the ties and the pills, or else return the pills.

A week later he got a letter returning the three pills and indignantly demanding three dollars for the ties. I wrote a second letter for the doctor to sign, in which he said that he was sorry that the tie company had not availed itself of this magnificent bargain. Nevertheless, he would be very glad to mail back the ties. There was only one minor obstacle. The ethics of the local medical association required him to charge five dollars for every call, and he had learned to his regret that a call to the post office was just like a call anywhere else. Therefore, if they would send him two dollars, he would immediately mail the ties back with no charge for packaging or postage. He never received an answer.

One of the things a young lawyer in practice in a small town must do is enter politics. It is necessary for his influence and reputation. It was for this reason that I ran for mayor of Laramie —not a remunerative job, since it paid only twenty-five dollars a month, but nevertheless one of high prestige. At the time I ran, for reasons obscure to me at the present time, I was an ardent Prohibitionist. My opponent on the Republican ticket owned a paint-and-paper shop. Ovi Burris, of our local newspaper, announced that between a paper hanger and a crepe hanger he would pick the paper hanger every time. In spite of this sound and logical anaysis, I was elected.

Shortly after I had taken office the phone rang one evening in my home. A lady's voice inquired, "Is this the Mayor?" I replied, "Yes, it is." She said, "Isn't it the duty of the Mayor to suppress these cat and dog nuisances which are so annoying to the taxpayers?" I answered, "I so understand it, madam." She said, "For the last three nights there have been cats squalling on my back fence." I said, "I will take care of it immediately, madam," and dismissed the matter from my mind. A week later she called up again and said, "Mr. Mayor, I want to thank you for taking care of those noisy cats." I said, "Don't give it a thought, madam, except I wish you would remember it when I next run for office."

Another adventure into politics was my election to the Wyoming state legislature. This was in 1920—the year that Warren G. Harding swept the country, and when the smoke all cleared away I was the only Democrat elected to the Wyoming House of Representatives. When I got to Cheyenne the Republican representatives were in a great dither about who was to be elected speaker. The deadlock lasted for days. Finally one faction won the controlling vote, but the price was that a ranchman from Big Piney was made speaker pro tem.

On the fateful day the legislature assembled to elect a speaker, there were a number of flowery speeches made for the leading candidate. After they were over and the question was about to be put to a vote, I rose and said, "Mr. Speaker, the Democratic party caucused last night, and when the name of Thurman Arnold was mentioned, it threw its hat up in the air and cheered for fifteen minutes. I therefore wish to put his name in nomination for speaker of this House." I then sat down, but I got up immediately and seconded the nomination. I said, "I have known Thurman Arnold for most of my life, and I would trust him as far as I would myself."

Everybody laughed except the Speaker pro tem. My nomination was not on his carefully prepared agenda, and he did not know what to do. People were waving at him from all directions. So I rose a third time, and said, "Mr. Speaker, some irresponsible Democrat has put my name in nomination and I wish to withdraw it." After that, the train got on the track again.

As the years went by it became increasingly apparent that the West and the South were becoming afflicted with an economic blight known as absentee ownership. In the period of the 1920's the antitrust laws were, in practical effect, suspended. It was a period of rapid growth of nationwide industrial combinations. These great enterprises would use their control over a product local enterprises had to have to force the latter to sell out at a distress price. The motion-picture industry is as good an example as any. The major distributors controlled the vast majority of feature films. They would supply them only on such terms as would bankrupt a local theater, after which the major company would buy the theater at its own price.

It was plain murder of small business, but nobody seemed to mind. Local lawyers were as ignorant of the antitrust laws as they were of the laws of the Medes and the Persians. Respectable and sound economists might have heard of the Sherman Act, but they did not believe in it. Concentration of economic power in Eastern cities was the sign of a strong economy. Further evidence of a sound economy in the 1920's was the spread of stock-market speculation to every small town in the land. The market kept going up, and everybody was making money. The economist Irving Fisher, of Yale, threw the weight of his prestige behind the prediction that the United States had reached a permanent high level of prosperity. Practically no one in the year 1927—when I left Laramie—had any notion of the financial catastrophe that lay so close ahead. Illegal merger followed merger. Giant corporations continued to absorb local industry, draining off to the big cities the purchasing power of the West and the South. But the money taken out by absentee ownership of local enterprise was being put back into the small towns through their local stockbrokers. This iridescent bubble constituted the sole balance of payments between the city and the small town.

A practicing small-town lawyer could easily sense what was happening. The local motion-picture theater was about to be taken over by Fox. The local plaster mill was being purchased by Celotex. The local oil refinery was being absorbed by Standard Oil of Indiana. There went three of the big local clients. Divorce cases and collections grew to be the major source of revenue for the local lawyer.

And then, to add to the economic troubles, there came the agricultural depression of 1925, from which the farmer has never recovered. He had been prosperous for a few years after the war. The cattle business was booming, and land values were going up. Everything the ranchman had was mortgaged, but the banks had been cautious, or thought they had, and there seemed plenty of margin. Then agriculture in the rest of the world caught up. Agricultural prices fell. Mortgages had to be foreclosed. The banks could not get rid of the land, and began to topple in agricultural communities. The only thing they could do was decline to foreclose, keep advancing money to the ranchmen, and hope for the best. The principal banks in Wyoming were closed in 1926.

I recall a conversation of about that time that a client of mine, who ran ten thousand sheep on about a hundred thousand acres of land, had with our local banker, whose bank was still open. He said, "John, I want to buy a new car and have come in to borrow the money." The banker was stupefied. He said, "Fred, you don't need a new car. And besides, you already owe us about a hundred thousand dollars. Go back to your sheep and forget about it." My client replied, "John, have you ever been in the sheep business?" "No," replied the banker. "Well, you're in it now," said Fred, and got up to walk out. Needless to say, he didn't get to the door. The next day he drove back to the ranch in a new car.

I saw no future in Laramie under these conditions. And so in 1927, when, out of a clear sky, I was offered the deanship of the College of Law at West Virginia University, I packed my family in our car and drove away, never to return except for casual visits. How we hated to leave that wonderful combination of rolling plains and blue, snow-capped mountains that we knew as Wyoming! My wife wept continuously for the first thirty miles, and the children looked as if they thought I was selling them down the river into slavery.

In 1930, after two years as dean of the West Virginia University College of Law, an excellent school, I accepted an appointment to the law faculty of Yale. The years that followed were among the most interesting and exciting of my life. Dean Charles E. Clark was the greatest educator I have ever known. He had assembled around him a remarkable faculty. There was William O. Douglas, now a justice of the Supreme Court of the United States; Walton Hamilton, an economist who had been head of the Brookings Institution in Washington; Arthur Corbin, the author of the leading book on contracts today; Wesley Sturges, and Underhill Moore. There was also a more conservative group of scholars, among them John Edward Vance, Edwin Borchard, and Ernest Gustav Lorenzon. It was altogether a formidable assembly of legal talent, and its general attitude was against dogma of all kinds.

Under former Dean Robert M. Hutchins, the Yale Law School had taken off on a new tack. It adopted a policy of limiting the enrollment to one hundred in each class, who would be carefully selected from a larger group of applicants. There was a certain amount of fraud in the initial application of this policy, because even previously there had never been more than a hundred in each class. Nevertheless, it was a bold announcement to the world and particularly to Yale's competitor, the Harvard Law School, that Yale intended to remain a small school, not because few students applied, but because it had voluntarily resolved to remain small. Under the leadership of Dean Clark, it was not long before applications increased so heavily that the selective-admission policy became a reality instead of a false front.

I recall Harvard's Professor Thomas Reed Powell discussing the matter with Dean Clark. Powell said, "Charles, I think your policy of limited enrollment is a great mistake." "How come?" said Dean

Clark. Powell replied, "At Harvard we have been conducting experiments with large and small classes, and they have demonstrated to my satisfaction that the students themselves prefer the larger classes." "I don't believe that," said Dean Clark. "Well," said Powell, "we have made a careful count at Harvard under our free elective system and have found that there are always more students in the larger classes than in the small ones."

It turned out to be a lucky guess that I had decided that the growing system of absentee ownership made economic advancement in the West impossible. I had had some interests in ranches in Wyoming. I had also been a conservative investor in the stock market. Instead of buying stocks on a ten-per-cent margin, which was permitted at that time, I had been conservative and bought nothing at lower than a twenty-five-per-cent margin. Between livestock in Wyoming and stocks in New York, the small capital I had taken with me into the teaching profession was wiped out in the stock-market crash. But I rode out the Depression secure with a good salary at the Yale Law School.

My friends in Wyoming, however, faced bankruptcy and ruin. Sheep, which had been worth thirteen dollars a head prior to the crash, dropped to three or four dollars. Mortgages that seemed to have a safe margin on the former figure were not bankable loans on the latter. A rash of foreclosures took place. Farmers in the Middle West rioted, uselessly, against this confiscation of their entire savings. And after the foreclosures the banks and finance companies faced the problem of what to do with the land.

I remember talking to a social worker in New York who had been approached by a large mortgage or insurance company to see if she could get some of the unemployed in New York to go out and farm these lands. She explained that they would have to be trained in agriculture and provided with capital before they could take the place of the farmers who had been driven off by foreclosure. She asked, "Why don't you get the old owners, give them the necessary capital, and restore them to the lands they used to own?" Her interviewer looked blank. He thought for a moment, and said, "We don't know where they are."

There was a further, psychological, deterrent to the social worker's proposal. To put a man who has been foreclosed back on the land and refinance him would be to give him a handout. It would ruin his character. From then on he might believe that nobody had to pay his debts.

The economic conditions of this period were completely avoidable—if men had only understood the economic world in which they were living. Some recognition of the possible use of national planning to avoid economic catastrophe had, indeed, arisen out of the war. Never before in our history had the economy been so completely planned and mobilized as during the First World War. Many who had had a hand in successful government planning then thought that the same principles should be followed during the period of adjustment from a wartime to a peacetime economy. But Woodrow Wilson would have none of it, and when Harding was elected, *laissez faire* under the name of Normalcy reached its zenith. When the stock market crashed, no one had ready money left, and the disastrous spiral of the Depression took over. A third of the money spent during the Second World War might have brought about recovery had it been poured into the economy at the beginning of the Depression. And the enforcement of the antitrust laws already on the books might have corrected at least to some extent the imbalance of payments caused by the growing curse of absentee ownership during the 1920's.

CHAPTER FIVE

The Crash—and What It Meant

The Depression was the result of faith in an obsolete economic creed that was unable to adjust itself to the facts of the twentieth-century industrial revolution. I would like to describe it by reprinting most of a chapter I wrote for *The Aspirin Age, 1919–1941,* edited by Isabel Leighton and published in 1949.

1.

An event now and then reveals a society in crisis. The year 1929 is such a landmark in economic history. It is the year of the stock market crash, of the beginning of the Depression, of the great toboggan ride. In the past our economy had experienced other panics; but it had always taken the shock and bounced back. But the crash of 1929 was different. It was not a mere attack of economic indigestion curable by liquidating uneconomic ventures, bringing wild prices down where the consumer could reach them. Instead it turned out to be the first outbreak of a wasting economic fever which, through long years of depression, debilitated an entire nation, deprived it of the use of its productive strength, and created want in the midst of plenty. The public discovered that "sound" business thinking had been mostly superstition. Respectable theories of the functions of the state had to be abandoned. A hesitant Federal Government was forced, step by step, into a dominant role in the operation of our economy, against every American habit and tradition.

In 1928 no one dreamed we were on the verge of a catastrophic depression. It had been a glorious year. Stocks had made a gain of $11,385,993,733. The New York *Times* wrote in its New Year's editorial of January 1, 1929: "But it will go hard to get people to think of 1928 as merely a 'dead past' which we must make haste to bury. It has been a twelvemonth of unprecedented advance, of wonderful prosperity—in this country at least. . . . If there is any way of judging the future by the past, this new year may well be one of felicitation and hopefulness."

The note of hope was sounded everywhere in that New Year edition of the *Times*. Big businessmen made their usual yearly forecasts, all of them rosy, with only here and there a note of skepticism. There were a few stories and comments of an uneasy nature, but only a few. For example, one article told of the disappointing year which England had just gone through. There was a story that the state guarantee of bank deposits in Nebraska was inadequate to meet the pressure of mounting bank failures. But the stock market was up. Most people thought it was up permanently. And anyway sensible conservative people did not believe in guaranteeing bank deposits. It was an assault on free enterprise. It was a penalty put on good bankers for the benefit of poor ones.

There were many reasons for optimism so far as the real wealth of the country was concerned. In the beginning of 1929 national income was still going up in terms of the production of physical goods. It was the end of a ten-year period which had shown the greatest increase in national income this country had ever known. Between 1910 and 1919 the increase in the national income in terms of physical goods was about 10 per cent. During the period from 1920 to 1929 the increase was 93 per cent. We had practically doubled our national production of goods and services. Since in the long run real wealth consists only in ability to produce goods and services, we appeared to the casual observer on New Year's Day of 1929 to be richer by many times than ever before in our history. And the curve of increased production was going up at a more rapid pace than ever before.

We had become more efficient industrially than any other country in the world. Output per man-hour in manufacturing industries had doubled in the twenty years between 1909 and 1929. In coal mining and railroads the increase in output per man-hour had not been so great but it was nevertheless large. As a result, on New Year's Day of 1929 both weekly cash wages and real wages were at the highest point in our economic history. Real wages had more than doubled since 1914.

Mr. Hoover, who was then President, was an engineer with an engineering mind. He shared with everyone else, including our best economists, a lack of vision with respect to the defects in our social organization. But he saw better than most old-fashioned business-men and bankers the technical possibilities of an industrial revo-lution in methods of production which had begun in the nine-teenth century and was moving toward fruition in the twentieth. During the 1928 election campaign, he had informed the American people that they could expect two chickens in every pot and two cars in every garage as part of the normal standard of living for every family.

Wall Street was fully in accord with such sentiments. During May and June, 1928, stocks wavered, but as Election Day approached, the market advanced. And when Hoover rolled in by twenty-one million votes to Al Smith's fifteen million, the Dow-Jones industrials soared to 300. The "New Era" had arrived. A new school of economists argued that when you buy common stocks, you buy the future, not the present. Imaginative projections of earnings, five and ten years ahead, flourished. Radio went up to 500, was split five for one. Names like Auburn, Grigsby-Grunow, Kolster, Radio—names you no longer hear of—flashed across the ticker tape. Blue chips, like U. S. Steel, American Telephone, and Eastman Kodak, reached all-time highs.

Inauguration Day—March 4, 1929—found Wall Street even more ebullient. The Dow-Jones industrials were up another 20 points. When stocks faltered in April, Wall Street seers regarded it as a "buying opportunity." And so it proved for a few months. By August the Dow-Jones industrials hit 380. But somehow, some-where, the old zip was lacking. Pools worked valiantly, but stocks thrashed about getting nowhere. The first week in September stocks climbed to 381, the highest they had ever been.

The break came early in September. There was a mid-month re-covery, but it was the last gasp. Liquidation increased. Brokers' clerks worked long hours sending out margin calls. Came Thursday, October 24. Panic. U. S. Steel, which had been as high as 261¾, opened at 205½, crashed through 200, and soon was down to 193½. General Electric, which only a few weeks before sold above 400, opened at 315, dropped to 283. About noon, Charles E. Mitchell, head of the National City Bank, slipped into the offices of J. P. Morgan and Company. So did Albert H. Wiggin, head of the Chase National, William Potter, head of the Guaranty Trust, and Seward Prosser, head of the Bankers Trust. They, with Thomas Lamont, of Morgan, and George F. Baker, of the First National Bank, formed a consortium to shore up the market.

Toward 2:00 P.M., Richard Whitney, known as the Morgan broker, bid 205 for Steel. The market rallied. There was in that rally no hint that Whitney, then vice-president of the Exchange and subsequently its president, would ultimately go to Sing Sing for peculations as head of the firm of Richard Whitney and Company —a Depression casualty.

Came Black Tuesday, October 28. Buy and sell orders piled into the Stock Exchange faster than human beings could handle them. The ticker ticked long after trading closed. A record 16,410,000 shares changed hands. The climax came November 13, 1929. The Dow-Jones average dropped to 198.7. And how the high and mighty had fallen! American Can was down from 181⅞ to 86; American Tel. and Tel. from 304 to 197¼; General Motors from 72¾ to 36; New York Central from 256⅜ to 160; United States Steel from 261¾ to 150. "The Big Bull Market was dead." And Coolidge-Hoover Prosperity was dead with it.

Yet the end of the epoch did not destroy the basic vision. From an engineering point of view Mr. Hoover's guess about the two chickens in every pot was entirely too conservative. In 1929 we had no adequate idea of the industrial revolution of the twentieth century. We did not realize the vast power development which scientific research was to bring forth, or the cheaper transportation, the light metals and chemicals, the untold resources of the new age. Almost twenty years later agricultural experts were saying that, so far as physical capacity is concerned, the world might be raised to an American standard in a matter of sixty years. And Mr. Charles Luckman, then President of Lever Brothers Company, was saying:

"My first and only factual statement about the future of your business is that it can and should double during the next generation *if the leadership of American business is willing to establish as its objective for 1970 a standard of living for the American wage earners which is at least 100 per cent higher than the level of today."*

Mr. Luckman made this remark in the year 1946, when industrial production had doubled that of 1929.

2.

On the foreign front in 1929 unrest could be seen, but we watched it with comfortable indifference. The slogan of the returned soldiers, "We've paid our debt to Lafayette; who the hell do we owe now?" had been accepted by the nation. The Senate had turned down the peace treaty. The people had voted that Europe was not our affair. In a grandiloquent "return to normalcy" we had turned our back on the world.

Behind the façade of isolation, however, our commerce was entangled in a world economy that we did not understand. Our ignorance had been of long standing. In 1919, ten years before the crash, statesmen of the Big Four had met at Versailles to make the world safe for political democracy. At the same time a corporate congregation from Britain, the United States, and Germany assembled at Baden-Baden for a different purpose. The statesmen were busy giving to a quaint and outmoded nationalism a last fling. The businessmen were concerned with seeing that their far-flung opportunities for investment were not shut off. As the statesmen carved out a revised version of the old map of Europe, the corporate conclave studied ways and means of building vast business empires that ignored political frontiers. When the shooting war ended, the economic war began.

We know now, as we look back, that Versailles was a foolish sort of thing. It was noble in intent and aspiration. But the little fact that had been overlooked by the big statesmen was that the world of the individual free trader operating under the laws of an independent nation was gone. Large-scale production and mass consumption had changed the world into one in which man could not live alone on isolated farms, in self-sufficient communities, or in independent countries. It took a whole aggregation of closely related industries to supply the wants of a single family. If such an economy were really to work it had to have area, resources, and world markets. The great factory assembly line had created establishments in which the necessities, comforts, and even the frivolities of life were first standardized and then turned into volume by "quantity methods." Such plants to operate successfully had to run at capacity. To run at capacity they needed outlets for their whole output. Political boundaries were not drawn with that kind of market in mind.

Prior to the first World War, the separate national sovereignties had done fairly well, even though some of them were bursting at the seams with the pressure of populations which required more resources than were contained within their boundaries. This was because we had developed the doctrine of complete separation of government and industrial economy. Under this slogan business could jump over national boundaries easily enough. Governments had not interfered with this process to any alarming extent when Britain was developing her empire. In the days of Queen Victoria tariffs that were so high as to stop trade were not tolerated. In the early days of the century America, though it showed evidences of a growing desire for economic isolation, still had a frontier. Tariffs were to encourage infant industry. Some of the infants were pretty big, but the robber barons, for all their faults, were gamblers and builders. The least of their worries was the protection of public investment against risk. This may or may not have been hard on the public, but at least wheels turned, railroads and industries were built. Economic expansion went on at a terrific pace. Panics came and went, but never stayed. The process of bankruptcy wiped out the claims of obsolete capital and price lines that were too high. Monopolies were started. Nevertheless, though in an imperfect and disorderly way, the most efficient businesses survived, in both domestic and world trade.

In the twentieth century, the lords of industry had settled down to a more humane and more comfortable bankers' philosophy. Morgan had taken the competitive risk out of the steel industry. He had to pay Andrew Carnegie four hundred million dollars for about eighty million of actual assets. But Andrew Carnegie was a price cutter, and it was worth that to get rid of ruinous competition in the steel industry. Morgan created an industry that could not fail as ordinary industry had failed in the past. It was big enough to protect itself against competition, and to saddle on the American public the vast financial burden of its capital structure forever.

The example of steel was followed in other industries. After World War I this process continued at an increasing tempo. Economists began to preach the advantages of administered prices, controlled by wise businessmen. The idea that industry must be planned by a hierarchy of corporate executives was accepted by the American people. They cheerfully bought stock in bigger and bigger mergers, and happily watched that stock rise. Men began to dream of a new world order in which both panics and wars could be eliminated. Panics would be impossible because all industry was regulated by sound banking houses, which would come to the rescue when danger threatened. Wars would be impossible because international business, which had everything to lose and nothing to gain by war, would prevent any powerful and civilized nation from aggression. Uncivilized nations which bankers did not dominate were too weak to count.

There is an interesting parallel between the great sprawling corporate bureaucracy which had reached its height just before the stock market crash and the medieval Church before the Reformation. Both were institutions that were held together not by political force but by accepted beliefs in established truths. Neither the Church nor the industrial bankers had troops at their command. But each thought they had the power to excommunicate competing organizations. The weapon of the Church was to refuse access to the sacraments. The weapon of international business was to refuse access to financial support. In the nineteenth century the banking power of England ruled the civilized world. If someone in an undeveloped country wanted to build a factory he took a collection of paper documents to British bankers. If these gentlemen said that the documents represented money he could build. It they thought otherwise he could not.

Since England had both the goods and the control over the seas, her power was real. But it was a power that diminished with industrial development in other countries. Nevertheless, long after the real power was gone, the symbol remained. Many believed that some mysterious economic law made a nation grow weak and infirm if it violated the theories of British bankers. American businessmen believed with a religious faith that the world was composed of independent civilized states, whose function was to keep order at home so that international finance and investment could be free. In 1929 this kind of world no longer existed. But the symbols still remained and were mistaken for the reality.

This faith had been so strong that before the First World War many economists were able to prove that a prolonged war in the twentieth century was impossible because no nation would be able to finance it. When World War I began, articles were written explaining that it could not last longer than a few months because Germany would run out of money. After World War I, men realized that the rules of business did not apply in war. But certainly, the believers in the old religion still maintained, no nation could grow to the industrial strength necessary to fight a modern war if during its periods of peace it disregarded the rules of sound finance!

3.

And so, even after the Great Crash of 1929, we were sure that the wisdom of our bankers and industrialists would save us, if we pursued our traditional course and did not yield to the temptation of invoking government controls. Our great businessmen responded nobly. John D. Rockefeller announced to a public eager to follow his leadership, "My son and I are buying sound common stocks." On New Year's Day, 1930, the New York *Times* was still optimistic, relying on the assurance of the leaders of industry and finance. Andrew Mellon, who combined the authority of Secretary of the Treasury with the prestige of controlling the aluminum monopoly, predicted speedy business recovery. Bankers announced their confidence in the industrial future.

However, as one reads the press of that day, one discovers an uneasy note. It recalls the atmosphere of a prayer meeting held to bolster up the wavering faith of a congregation sorely troubled by doubt. Just as the medieval Church in times of trouble stressed the necessity of faith as an end in itself, so our business leaders decided that "lack of business confidence" was the cause of the continued depression. The remedy was to preach business confidence, whether in your heart you believed it or not. This attitude reached a high note in 1932. Men like Nicholas Murray Butler issued statements that "courage will end the slump." The nation, in effect, was called to gather in a giant prayer meeting to reaffirm its faith in business leaders.

In spite of all this, President Hoover was slipping. The stock market refused to respond to his sermons about prosperity being just around the corner. A worried electorate put a Democratic majority in Congress.

The Democratics knew just what to do. They thought they had discovered where the trouble lay. The budget was not balanced. Statistics showed that in 1911 the entire expense of the government had been less than a billion dollars. Hoover had spent over four billion in 1932. And so the Democrats proposed to slash government payrolls and thus restore prosperity. They succeeded to the tune of a few million for a short time. But still the Depression continued.

To the actors the drama of the great slump was as strange as it was terrible. It came to them out of the blue; they rode it as they would ride the wind. They were carried along by a course of events they were powerless to direct. Business executives, economists, and the public alike knew little of the industrial system they were operating; they were unable to diagnose the malady; they were unaware of the great forces operating beneath the surface.

The response of the business community was to hope and to go it blind. Its policy—if playing-by-ear is a policy—was to hold fast to familiar landmarks and to hope for the best. Investments had to be protected. Therefore, prices must be maintained. Sales were falling off. So costs were to be reduced at the expense of labor and groups least able to fight back. The case of American Tel. and Tel., no more enlightened and no more foolish than a hundred other corporations, tells the general story. Rates were not lowered to the capacity-to-pay in a depressed economy; instead, they were maintained. Families gave up their phones. The range of service was greatly restricted. Workers were laid off and wages cut, thereby impairing the power of Bell employees to purchase the goods of other industries. Dividends had to be kept at predepression figures to restore business confidence even if surplus had to be dug into. Security was sought for the chosen few; the interests of other groups were neglected; the public interest was utterly forgotten.

The judgment was based not on a realistic or common-sense appraisal of the situation but on values which were inherently moral or religious. The decrease in goods and services impaired the efficiency of the whole economy. Keeping up prices did not protect investments as was intended. Instead, it destroyed the market for goods, because workers who were laid off could not buy. No better policy to keep the depression going could have been devised. Yet any other policy seemed to be an admission of lack of faith in the stability of the system of high prices and sound investments which had been ordained by our industrial priesthood. These men were our leaders. If they wavered and fell we were lost.

When it became clear to President Hoover that government had to do something, it seemed axiomatic, according to the faith of that day, that capital had to be encouraged and stimulated by government aid. To give similar relief to labor would destroy the self-respect of American workmen. On the other hand if the powers at the top, both corporate and individual, were made affluent, prosperity would trickle down through the whole financial structure. Accordingly Hoover put three magic words together, and the Reconstruction Finance Corporation resulted. It seemed impossible that three words of the appeal and potency of these could not lure prosperity from its hiding place around the corner. Yet the Depression continued.

The shock of the universal bank failure brought a new group to Washington under the Roosevelt regime. It was composed of men with all sorts of theories. They were united on one thing only: Government must directly intervene and do something to relieve national distress. People had to be fed. The business hierarchy was not up to the task. Government must take over. This program represented a tremendous shift in the objectives of government assistance. The top dog was no longer the chief concern of economic policy. The underdog, the Forgotten Man, had come into his own.

There was wisdom in Roosevelt's "Re-employment Agreement"; for, if assembly lines were to be kept moving, mass purchasing power had to be restored—and only employment and wages could do that.

There was a look to the future in his advocacy of the Tennessee
Valley Authority. There was help for groups at an economic disadvantage in the Agricultural Adjustment and the Labor Relations
Acts. And there was, in the banking and financial measures, quite
a bit of tinkering with antique mechanisms which could no longer
operate on their own.

But, in general, measures were improvised and hurled at symptoms. There was no probing diagnosis which got beneath the surface of things, no surgery which cut to the root of the disease. There
was a magnificent opportunity to do something. Effective measures
could not have stirred up more opposition than did the halfway
ones which were employed. The cry was for economic reform; the
administration settled for a handful of palliatives.

The measures taken did not lack merit, but they did not rise
above the plane of expediency. Labor was granted a bill of rights
long overdue, but no attempt was made to link its interest with that
of the public. An installment of security was provided to the worker
for wages against industrial accident, unemployment, old age; but
health was timidly omitted, and little was done to reduce these
great hazards of life to a minimum. Provision was made for the
family to finance and to own its own home; but this did not extend
to a continued abundance of jobs, which is the only adequate un-
derwriting of a mass home-ownership. The unemployed, according
to their several trades, were gathered into a Works Progress Administration, so broad in its scope as to admit even actors, painters,
and musicians. But the sums laid out, for all the cry about their
size, were pitiful—far too small to prime the pump of a lethargic
economy. At the same time the desire to maintain prices by creating
scarcity put its mark on administrative policy. Little pigs were
slaughtered that the price of pork might be high in the land. The
farmer was to be lifted toward plenty through scarcity. Hoover's
R.F.C. was now fitted out like U. S. Steel with a host of subsidiaries,
and continued its dole to industry.

4.

The underlying idea of the Roosevelt New Deal was conservative,
not radical. The idea was that people had to be fed while industry
got going again; that industry would get going as soon as it be-

lieved that prices were stable and investment safe. Nevertheless the program violated two basic tenets of the economic fundamentalists. The first was the one inherited from our Puritan forebears that the life of the poor must be made as uncomfortable and insecure as possible in order to induce them to work. The other was the nineteenth-century doctrine of the separation of business and government. Hence, except for a brief period during the first days of the NRA, the New Deal, instead of reassuring business, literally scared it to death. Class was being aroused against class, was the cry. The government was a peculiarly vicious sort of Santa Claus, because it distributed gifts to the undeserving. And on top of that it was destroying the Constitution, step by step. Property was no longer sacred. Business was being threatened by government competition. Socialism and Communism were on the march in the land of free enterprise.

The faith in old forms was nowhere better illustrated than in the complete confidence of many advisers of the administration that the Depression could be cured by the manipulation of currency and credit. Some thought that if the Federal Reserve would only buy enough bonds, all would be well. Others put their faith in abandonment of the gold standard. Looking back at the gold controversy today, we discover how naïve was the thinking of our economists and businessmen on both sides. Professor George Frederick Warren of Cornell and his followers thought that going off the gold standard would mean the immediate resumption of world trade. Professor O. M. W. Sprague of Harvard headed a group which predicted a disaster from which the country would not recover for years. Dissenting members of the Supreme Court seriously thought that it meant the end of the Constitution, the beginning of an era of lawless anarchy, the end of every conception of government morality and decency.

The trouble with the gold program was that it was only a minor treatment of a symptom. Its advocates and opponents were both wrong. It produced neither disaster nor recovery. Today it seems a sensible step to have taken. Few are now critical. The hysteria which accompanied it appears slightly psychopathic. One also wonders at the basis for the extravagant hopes.

The first frontal attack upon the national economy was the National Recovery Administration. A mandate went out from the White House through all the land that every industry should go up to Washington and be coded. And to Washington they trooped, oil and steel and nonferrous metals; aluminum, magnesium, and solid fuels; cast-iron soil pipe, paper and pulp; chemicals, heavy and light, ethical drugs and drugs not so ethical, lumber in all forms, sizes, and shapes, carboloy and lead pencils, matches, whether of the book, strike-on-box, or strike-on-pants variety, dog food and waste paper.

Fury, sound, and Hugh Johnson did succeed in establishing hundreds of codes and arresting the tail spin into which price systems had been driven. But as yet business was still too individualistic for such a drastic regimentation. The clash of interests within industry turned codes into compromises; those economists and lawyers who represented the public interest possessed a high nuisance value; against their vigilance codes were not easily instrumented; as times began to improve, businessmen found the necessary discipline onerous. Order, never established in outlying provinces, began to break down. And then, in the case of the dead chicken, the Supreme Court gave a last fatal blow to the crumbling empire of the blue eagle.

After the fall of the NRA in 1935, the economic philosophy of the administration was thrown into reverse. Two events brought a swing in the other direction. Alarmed over the trend toward the concentration of economic wealth and power, the President asked Congress to establish the Temporary National Economic Committee, with Senator Joseph O'Mahoney of Wyoming as chairman. The Department of Justice rediscovered in the statute books an old law against trusts called the Sherman Act, and actually set about enforcing it. The Act, a legacy from Populist days, was plain and strong in its language. It ordered members of an industry to compete with each other and decreed that prices were to be made in the free and open market. Its intent was that big boys were not to get together to fix their own prices and conspire away the rights of the public. It went so far as to make "restraint of trade" a crime and to enjoin courts to put a stop to all such antisocial practices. The TNEC revealed large and important areas of the economy in which business was being run in ways of which the law did not approve. The Department of Justice began a vigorous campaign to break up the corporate empires, to restore the free and open market, and to plant the feet of industry firmly on the road to competition.

. . .

We have long been a nation where local production and markets have been controlled by absentee owners. In 1909 two hundred industrial corporations owned one-third of the nonbanking corporate assets. By 1929 this was increased to about 50 per cent. By 1939 the share of this group increased to 57 per cent. This trend was observed by Adolf Berle, by the Temporary National Economic Committee, and by the National Resources Committee. The whole situation was described by President Roosevelt in his monopoly message of 1935. He said:

Statistics of the Bureau of Internal Revenue reveal the following amazing figures for 1935:
Ownership of corporate assets: Of all corporations reporting from every part of the nation, one-tenth of 1 per cent of them owned 52 per cent of the assets of all of them.
And to clinch the point: Of all corporations reporting, less than 5 per cent of them owned 87 per cent of all the assets of all of them.
Income and profits of corporations: Of all the corporations reporting from every part of the country, one-tenth of 1 per cent of them earned 50 per cent of the net income of all of them.
And to clinch the point: Of all the manufacturing corporations reporting, less than 4 per cent of them earned 87 per cent of all the net profits of all of them.

The apologists for this system of the concentration of economic wealth insisted even after the crash of 1929 that business had learned its lesson, that competition was wasteful, that great corporate empires were here to stay, and that prices and production would be wisely administered in the future by this financial oligarchy.

Against this philosophy the program of vigorous antitrust enforcement gained great headway. A *Fortune* poll in 1940 showed that it was the only policy of the administration endorsed by a majority of business executives. In the four years following 1939 over 50 per cent of all the antitrust prosecutions brought during the entire fifty years of the Sherman Act were instituted. There seemed hope at least for a policy to eliminate absentee corporate control over local industry by inexorable corporate empires.

5.

The beginning of the movement for industrial decentralization was suddenly stopped and then put in reverse by World War II. What might have happened to a government program of decentralization had there been no war is anyone's guess. The trouble was that war was already on us as the result of the underlying causes of the great stock market crash. The political and economic institutions of the nineteenth century were dying. The cement was falling out of social structures. Peoples and goods were hemmed in by obsolete national boundaries. When goods fail to move, armies march.

There was no formal departure from the administration's antitrust policy. But with military values dominant, all questions of the character of the economy were postponed. A range of commodities, as varied as the combined lists in a Sears Roebuck catalogue, had to be obtained—and in abundance. It seemed to military men easier to place orders—even if deliveries were not so certain—in large quantities than in small. It seemed most feasible to deal with the dominant concerns in each industrial field.

This general program was at least not hindered by the infiltration of representatives of big business into the War and Navy Departments, nor by formally recognizing business as a department of government for war, in the organization which went forward under a number of alphabetical permutations and came to rest as the War Production Board. And F.D.R., recognizing that he could have only one war at a time, was content to declare a truce in the civil struggle. Business gave him patriotic support—on its own terms. More than 90 per cent of all war contracts went to a handful of giant empires, many of them formerly linked by strong ties with the corporations of the Reich. The big fellows got the contracts; the little fellows were dependent upon subcontracts with the big boys. Methods of payment and an "accelerated depreciation" allowed many a concern to reconstruct its plants at the expense of the government. Though the government kept title, new and old were often so closely fused as to be inseparable; and the only practical disposition of many government plants was to the corporations which operated them during the war. And over all moved the trend to the further concentration of wealth and power—a trend which was given an impetus during the Second World War far greater than ever before.

CHAPTER SIX

The Changing Jurisprudence of the Great Depression

In the year of our Lord 1930 the world was standing on its head. All over the United States people were unemployed, bankrupt, and starving. The sound and learned men of the time had their faces set like flints against any sort of government plan to do anything about it. And the public followed them in their fear of innovation. Never in our history has the myth-making capacity of the American people flowered so splendidly as at the beginning of the Great Depression. For a while prosperity was just around the corner, and we would reach it soon if we did not fall for the blandishments of demagogues. But economic hell awaited us if we took any positive measures to relieve distress. All such measures, from the TVA to the regulation of the stock exchange, were unconstitutional. If we started to do unconstitutional things, we would be unable to stop before we had completely changed our form of government and embraced socialism. In a nation that was without enough purchasing power to absorb the goods its productive plant could turn out, and where everywhere one was greeted with the spectacle of idle plants and idle labor—poverty in the midst of plenty—the greatest fear that obsessed our learned economists and lawyers was inflation.

There were certain unalterable truths to which the wise and good could repair.

1. Relief of destitution ruined the character of its recipients by making them unwilling to work.

2. The unemployed could get jobs if they were forced to do so. If they were not, they would not even try.

3. The nation could pull itself out of the Depression by practicing thrift.

4. The real reason for the Depression was lack of business confidence. It could be restored only if the government balanced its budget and refused to reform even the worst business abuses.

5. Now was the time to stand by the Constitution in its hour of peril. Anything that interfered with states' rights or business practices or relieved distress would be a step toward the destruction of the Constitution. (Thus Al Smith was against child labor, but even he was certain that prohibiting it by law would irreparably damage the Constitution.)

These truths and others even more absurd were taught in our schools and faithfully followed by conservative lawyers, economists, respectable businessmen, editors of our leading journals, indeed all sound-thinking intellectuals. Skeptical of these principles were the New Dealers, but their support was limited to the uneducated voter.

The opposition to these ideas had little respectable theological support. There were Francis Townsend's movement for old-age pensions in California and the "Share the Wealth" notions of Huey Long. Father Charles Coughlin attracted a tremendous radio audience with inflationary proposals for a "living annual wage." Crackpots proved to be better prophets of the future than respectable learned men of the time. Their aims, though not their methods, are now generally accepted. But during the entire Depression our best-educated citizens clung desperately to the old-time legal and economic religions. They felt that the rapidly growing bureaucracy under President Roosevelt was bound to substitute the individual whims of government officials for the rule of law under the Constitution, which remained the sole safeguard of our liberty. And the majority of the Supreme Court of the United States agreed with them.

It is interesting to note that a recent announcement by Dr. George Gallup says that an analysis of his polls of the past seems to establish the fact that had the voters been confined to the educated class, every Republican candidate for President since the beginning of the

Depression would have been elected, including Herbert Hoover and Alf M. Landon.

Why have the better-educated members of the electorate been not only poor prophets, but also poor policy-makers in times of change? The obvious reason is that the great majority of educational institutions in the United States are devoted to teaching their students the traditions and principles of the past. They are, in the very nature of things, unfitted for the task of objectively examining either their own functions or the social organizations that have dominated our society.

From the rituals of savage tribes to the complicated logic of modern economics, the function of education has been to teach men to conform to tradition. That sort of training makes them more acceptable; it gets them ahead, unless some great economic change, such as has occurred in the twentieth century, makes the traditions of the past obsolete. In such a situation there is no pair of blinders so tight as a good American college education. At every commencement, on campuses located far and wide in this great republic, speakers inform the graduating class that the future of the country lies in their educated opinions on law, politics, literature, and so on. It is always the literature, the law, and the politics of the past that furnish the guidelines. There is little chance for the college-educated man to keep up with the present in times of rapid economic change. (It was at his own college, Harvard University, that Franklin Roosevelt was booed.)

Since Plato advanced the notion that philosophers should be kings, and on down through Burnham's managerial revolution, which predicted that our economy would soon be managed by the skilled control of the presidents of our largest corporations, the idea that government by an intellectual elite is the ideal government has had tremendous appeal. To allow persons uneducated in the principles of law and economics to have a large voice in government policies seems to invite demagogues to power through their ability to mislead the untutored masses. Yet throughout the Depression it was the uneducated voter who proved to be right, and the educated voter, caught in the traditions of the past, to be wrong. It was demagogues like Upton Sinclair, Townsend, and Long who, with their ideas that the productive capacity of the country was sufficient to help all citizens, started us on our present program of social security. In those days no conventionally educated economist could possibly have supported the idea of old-age pensions for everyone.

To distrust government by the elite does not mean it is necessary to accept government by practical humanitarians. Men live by formulas and principles. Take them away and there is no justification for government except the benevolent exercise of power. And those who achieve power under a humanitarian philosophy are never the humanitarians who started the revolution. A stable government is like a ballet. It requires a whole cast of characters, each with his particular role to play, dancing in opposition to each other. In this ballet the role of our institutions of higher education inevitably becomes one of supporting the traditions of the past.

Yet, though the conservatism in American universities might well, had it had the opportunity to do so, have frustrated every reform of the New Deal, now that time and experience with those reforms have demonstrated their necessity, our intellectual elite stands as a bulwark against the radical right wing of the Republican party. In the 1964 election campaign, Barry Goldwater advocated drastic change, and it is the great virtue of conservatism that it is opposed to drastic change. This was exemplified in the poll of students at Princeton, a poll taken during every Presidential election year. Most of these students come from conservative families, who formerly disliked any exercise of power on the part of a central government. Yet Goldwater's exhortations to return to the good old days and reduce government power fell on deaf ears at Princeton. The poll showed that about seventy per cent of the students favored Johnson and were opposed to Goldwater's philosophy. This was greater than the national average of less-educated people.

During the Depression, when our educated elite was buried in the myths of the past, the Yale Law School was an island of dissent. Dean Robert Hutchins, who had left Yale the year before I went there to become president of the University of Chicago, had started the Yale Law School on a new, and for those times radical, path. He knew that the traditional concept of the law did not fit our changing society. That generally accepted concept was that the law progressed through the process of abstract reasoning, the results of which became more and more certain through proper legal education. The law was a separate science, apart from other human institutions. The purpose of it as a science was to remove from its administration the element of fallible human judgment and to put in its place the process of inexorable logic. That, as I said earlier, was the theory of jurisprudence when I was graduated from Harvard in 1914. It was still the prevailing view in 1930 when I went to Yale.

That faith had given us comfort and stability for the preceding half-century. It had been responsible for the growth of our great law schools. Of course, the search for certainty in the law was not producing certainty. The cases pouring off the presses were increasing in headlong arithmetical progression. Some central institution had to be created to reconcile them. And thus was born the American Law Institute. Professors were recruited from all over the United States—principally from Harvard, which was then the high church of abstract legal theology. A restatement of American law was launched, with the end in view of analyzing the cases and providing the best principles for our erring courts. But the American Law Institute had its eye firmly fixed on the past and its heart full of faith that inexorable logic was the cure for all the law's imperfections.

The general attitude that pervaded the law at the beginning of the great Depression, as expounded by professors, lawyers, jurists, and judges, was that property was more important than human rights. This was expressed in the familiar phrase "Hard cases make bad law." It was a short way of saying that in a case where ideas of common sense and justice collided head on with established legal principle or precedent it was better to reach an unjust result than to disturb or modify the precedent. The idea that judges should not legislate was a necessary limitation on judicial power. But in the early days of the Depression this notion was expanded into the principle that judges could not correct their own mistakes; *stare decisis*—right or wrong the decision must stand. Only the legislative branch of government could correct the mistakes of the courts.

In that highest of all areas of the law, the United States Constitution, not even the legislature had power to act. Long after the evil of child labor had been recognized by the public, for example, no Congress was permitted to abolish it. The Supreme Court had decided that such legislation was unconstitutional. For that court to change its decision would mean that it had power to amend the Constitution.

At the beginning of the Depression almost every proposal, from the TVA to social security, had to face a long constitutional battle. In that struggle, to the liberals of the time the Supreme Court of the United States stood in the way of both human rights and economic progress. To the conservatives, the Supreme Court was the last defense against the destruction of the capitalist system and the establishment of a socialist state.

It was out of that struggle that a new school of jurists was born. It went under the name of legal realism. The principal shrine of this new school was located at Yale. Its high priest was Dean Hutchins. The clash between the new attitude toward law and the old is illustrated by an alleged conversation between Hutchins and Justice James C. McReynolds of the Supreme Court of the United States. The Justice is said to have remarked to the Dean: "I understand that at Yale you are teaching your students that the decisions of the Supreme Court of the United States are all nonsense." Dean Hutchins replied, "Not at all, Mr. Justice. We simply give them the decisions to read and let them judge for themselves."

In Hutchins's view the law was only part of a larger science, the science of human relations. With his characteristic energy and persuasive power, he obtained a grant to set up an Institute of Human Relations in which law and psychology, medicine, psychiatry, and indeed practically everything but the physical sciences would be studied together. Rooms were provided in the School of Medicine where members of the Institute could meet and discuss the interrelations of their fields. Seminars were organized in which psychiatrists, psychologists, and lawyers took part. A phrase was invented to describe these occasions: "the cross-fertilization of intellectual disciplines." I have found out since that what the phrase really means is getting everything all mixed up. In any event, it made the Yale Law School a hotbed of legal realism.

If you were a legal realist who wanted to find the true nature of the decision-making process in law, you might go to a psychologist and inquire about the nature of human reason. He would tell you that the ordinary conception of the application of reason involved the assumption that there were two little men in your head, one called Reason and the other called Emotion. Emotion was an unreliable little man, constantly swayed by irrational prejudice. It was the duty of Reason to keep his foot on Emotion's neck and thus reach decisions unclouded by any sort of bias. The psychologist would probably tell you that these two little men do not exist, and that all thought is simply a form of human behavior. He would inform you that there are two ways of so-called thinking. One is illustrated by a football player who runs through the opposing team for a touchdown. Every move he makes is logically the correct one, but if he ever stopped to "think" in the rational sense, he would be tackled. The other way of thinking, supposed to govern the application of logic and reason, is also supposed to govern the judicial process. But the psychologist might tell you that this, too, was an illusion. For example, suppose a student is debating with himself whether to quit work and go to a movie. He first says that he is behind in his work and had better stay home. He replies that a movie will freshen him up and enable him to work better the next day. He counters with the notion that if he goes to the movie he will inevitably meet Bill Jones, who will invite him to have a drink, and after several rounds he will feel worse the next morning. The answer to this is that he should be man enough not to take a drink, and to hell with Bill Jones. Whichever one of these premises is uppermost in his mind when he stops "thinking" will determine whether he goes out or stays in.

The point at which a judge stops thinking may be predicted from his background and environment. Thus, if you ask an Alabama judge to reason out the principles of law that should govern the problem of integration, you may as confidently predict the result as if you had asked an editor of the *Wall Street Journal* whether an unbalanced fiscal budget leads to inflation and eventually to socialism.

On less-controversial subjects, if you put a reasonable facsimile of the judge's training, background, and general social relationships with others into any good computing machine, it could predict his decisions. Indeed, at Yale Law School there is presently an experiment going on in collaboration with the American Bar Association to test the ability of computing machines to predict decisions.

These ideas about thinking and human behavior, familiar enough today, were new when Hutchins got his money for the Institute of Human Relations. They certainly have their utility in the understanding of judicial process. The fact that law schools today have sociologists and psychiatrists on their faculties is the outgrowth of the efforts at Yale to create a union between legal and social sciences.

Nevertheless, the Institute was short-lived. When you apply the principles of psychology to the law, you take away all dignity from the judicial process. The effectiveness of the law consists in the fact that there is a consensus that it represents a rational process, devoid of personal bias or prejudice. A society that does not believe in the rule of law above men, which can be discovered by a process that Professor Henry Hart, of Harvard, has called "the maturing of collective thought" through judicial conferences, cannot establish a respected judicial system. This is another way of saying that if you do not believe that men are endowed with the ability to exercise unbiased free will and are able to make decisions along the lines of inexorable logic, you will not make a good judge.

The effect of taking a realistic and psychological point of view in removing all dignity from human conduct was never better illustrated than by a Yale seminar I gave with Dr. Harry Stack Sullivan to a group of law students, though it had nothing to do with law. Sullivan was one of the most interesting characters in the world of psychiatry. He is dead now, but he remains a great and outstanding figure in his field. The seminar consisted of three lectures centering around the therapeutic value of mentally disturbed people becoming adults and forgetting their infantilism. This general idea would be understood by any educated person today, but in 1930 the basic ideas of psychiatry had not become part of our common knowledge. The whole concept of adult conduct and infantile conduct was new and exciting. At the end of the last lecture, after Sullivan had convinced the class that their salvation lay in adult behavior, he leaned back in his chair. "And now, young gentlemen," he said, "when you have lost your taste for adventure, when you have forgotten romance, when the only things worthwhile to you are prestige and income, then you have grown up, then you have become an adult." And thus he neatly turned everything he had been saying for the past week inside out and stood it on its head. The students walked out muttering to themselves in utter confusion. I said, "Harry, why on earth did you do that to those poor boys?" "What other possible way was there of getting across the idea that though a materialistic point of view may lead to success, it must be balanced by other values?" he replied.

Most of the projects for joint study planned by the Institute and the Law School came to nothing. One such was a seminar to be given by Dr. Eugene Kahn and me. Dr. Kahn was a noted psychiatrist from the University of Vienna. It was our purpose to examine before the seminar individuals who had committed crimes. In this way we hoped to learn more about the abstract concept of criminal responsibility. One of the characters who came before us was a woman of forty-five. She was in jail because she had severely burned her little girl's hand as a punishment for stealing a dime. Tests showed that she had a mental age of eleven. Dr. Kahn asked me, "Iss she criminally responsible?" I replied that she was, and added that the only way under Connecticut law to get free psychological treatment for her was to convict and sentence her. A look of horror spread over Dr. Kahn's face. "She iss not, she cannot be, criminally responsible. She iss only a little girl of eleven." "Hell, no," I said, "she is a great big woman of forty-five." This was the end of the cross-fertilization of intellectual disciplines so far as Dr. Kahn and I were concerned. It is an example of the almost universal human habit, common particularly to lawyers and psychiatrists, of classifying individuals and phenomena, and then looking at them through the lens of that classification. The result is that the observer cannot see what is before him at all. I have no doubt that Dr. Kahn actually saw a little girl of eleven sitting across the table. A large part of our legal and economic learning is made up of thinking of this kind.

Another venture in objectivity that failed to become a conspicuous success was the faculty's collaboration with the National Committee on Law Observance, known to the common herd as the Wickersham Commission on Prohibition. The Rockefeller Foundation had advanced some money for a statistical study of the law in action in the hope that it would shed a great white light not only on Prohibition, but also over the entire system of law enforcement. William O. Douglas, then my colleague at Yale, with me as his chief assistant, set up offices, engaged research assistants, and rented a Holorith Card Machine, the predecessor of the modern computer. We then proceeded to count everything that happened in courts in Connecticut. We found the exact number of demurrers and every other kind of pleading that had been filed over the course of a year. We counted the time it took to finish the cases. We learned how many cases were decided for the plaintiff and how many for the defendant. In addition, we counted everything else that we or anyone else could think of. All this information was transferred to cards with holes punched in them and run through the trusty old Holorith machine. The result was the most fascinating body of legal statistics that has been collected in this century. They had only one flaw. Nobody then and nobody yet has ever been able to think of what to do with them. They are presently enshrined in government archives awaiting the coming of the Prince who will awaken their true beauty.

Perhaps the greatest contribution of the Yale Law School to legal education in 1930 was made by Dean Charles E. Clark. He discovered a fact that was seldom admitted by the legal pundits of the day: that the law in action, the law that actually affected the conduct of people, was the law of procedure. The so-called substantive law, the law with the big L, was useful as a theology. Not that Clark did not recognize the value of legal theology. But he insisted that you could not understand legal processes or legal institutions by reading theology, any more than you could understand the Catholic church of the Middle Ages by confining yourself to its theology.

Procedure, Clark thought, should become the center of a law-school curriculum. It should be taught not as an abstract science, but as a practical way of managing litigation with the least inconvenience to the litigants.

And so procedure courses became the center of the Yale curriculum instead of being trivia around the perimeter, as they were at Harvard. Once this was done, the old so-called fields of the law—contracts, agency, torts, conflicts—lost most of their significance.

They became important only because they provided the vocabulary with which the lawyer talked, and their classifications were needed as a method of indexing decisions in relation to subject matter. But this vocabulary and this index had no reality or use except with respect to procedure in court.

This idea seems sensible today. At the time Clark changed the course in procedure it created a storm of protest. Procedure as taught in law schools was a logical science that had evolved from ancient common-law writs dating back to immemorial times. Books had been written on the nature of a "cause of action in law," a "cause of action in equity," and a "cause of action in general." Lawyers would consult these books and then file a motion that the plaintiff should separately state and number his "causes of action." Then followed intricate briefs as to what his causes of action were. Were they in tort, were they in contract, were they in law, or were they in equity?

In the ancient days in England there had been separate courts of law and equity. Law courts applied the traditional language of the law; equity was an escape from this traditional logic where as a matter of justice the legal remedy was inadequate. You could tell in the nineteenth century whether an action was in law or in equity by observing what court it was in. But the Field Code in New York, in an attempt to simplify this complicated judicial system, had abolished separate courts of law and equity. There and in most other states the two courts had been merged. Nevertheless, in the legal thinking of the time the distinction between law and equity was such an important philosophical distinction that it was necessary to bring your case either on the law side or on the equity side. If you brought it on the wrong side of the court, it would be dismissed. You would have to start it again on the other side of the court. As a result of this, the New York procedure became a tangled and obscure set of abstractions. There were hundreds of cases wrestling with the philosophical problem of the difference between law and equity.

Every law-school curriculum had a separate course in equity. You learned the law side of contracts in a course on contracts. Then you found out how the law had been modified by equity in a course on equity jurisdiction. There was usually also a course in common-law pleading. This was because ancient common-law pleadings were the origin of the abstract principles of modern pleadings.

It is impossible for me to convey to the lay reader or even to the younger lawyer the abstract intricacies that governed procedure prior to Clark's revolutionary work. But perhaps I can give the reader a notion of these abstract procedural concepts, and of how easy it was for a lawyer to slip up, by describing a case I tried in Wyoming in the early 1920's.

At that time I had just started to practice law in Wyoming, and a large part of my practice was collecting small accounts from merchants on requests sent to me because of my membership in various lists of collection attorneys. I got fifteen per cent if the bill was collected without suit, and twenty-five to thirty per cent if suit was required. Most of these items involved from ten to fifty dollars. But one morning I received in the mail directions to start suit against a large corporation, the Holly Sugar Company. I think that the amount involved was thirty thousand dollars. How such a suit came to be referred to a collection attorneys list I do not know. But here was a piece of business that might give me eight or nine thousand dollars, which meant the difference between affluence and poverty.

The only trouble was that the Holly Sugar Company was not "doing business" in Wyoming. The Wyoming courts had no jurisdiction over it. The claim had apparently been sent to me in error. Nevertheless, I decided to take a chance. I sued the Holly Sugar Company in Wyoming and served it by publishing a notice in the newspapers, which was sent to the defendant in Salt Lake City by registered mail. This was called "service by publication." It was not effective service on a nonresident defendant unless such defendant had property subject to attachment in the jurisdiction in which the suit was brought. The Holly Sugar Company had none in Wyoming. Unless some procedural mistake was made by counsel for Holly, the service was bound to be quashed.

Holly immediately filed such motion to quash service of summons on the grounds that they were not doing business in Wyoming and had no property there. Then came the procedural mistake I had been hoping for. In addition to asking the court to quash the service of summons, counsel for Holly added the words "and to dismiss the suit." By putting these words in, the defendant had appealed to the general jurisdiction of the court. It was no longer a special appearance; it was a general appearance, thank God. Holly had "voluntarily" submitted itself to the jurisdiction of the Wyoming court, and there was no way to pry itself loose. The moving finger had writ, and having writ moved on, showering down on me the largest fee I received that year.

Since the time of Dean Clark the way you can tell a special appearance from a general one is by determining the intent of the pleader. This attitude toward brushing aside a legal technicality seems sensible now, but at a time when procedure, like substantive law, was the application of logic to precedent, a failure to follow a procedural technicality was a mortal sin against the abstract science of pleading that had come down to us from the common law of England.

Another difficulty that made pleadings so complicated was the philosophical distinction between statements of fact and conclusions of law. Pleadings were supposed to contain no conclusions. Conclusions were to be argued before the judge. But the abstract difference between the two was so confused that no one could write a persuasive pleading without having a motion filed against him to strike out half of it because it contained conclusions of law. Today such a motion is unheard of. Under modern pleadings you can state your case persuasively without regard for this abstract distinction.

Clark also abolished the course in equity. He led the movement that resulted in the most significant reform of American legal procedure in recent times. Today there can be no fatal mistakes in pleading a case. Technicalities in the old sense have disappeared. The very first rule of the Federal Rules of Civil Procedure states that the rules "shall be construed to secure the just, speedy, and inexpensive determination of every action."

Another significant reform accomplished under the intellectual leadership of Clark was the establishment of modern pretrial discovery proceedings. Before Clark, if a plaintiff sued a large corporation, there was no possible way for him to find out who the witnesses against him were or the nature of the defense. Today he may take the depositions of any of the defendants or of anyone who he suspects knows anything about the case, before the trial, to find out whether the facts he has stated in his complaint as true to the best of his information and belief are really true. The depositions taken under the discovery rule do not occupy much of the court's time. Indeed, the court need not be bothered at all unless a dispute arises as to whether the questions go beyond the scope of a proper inquiry to bring out information on the plaintiff's case. And the rules here are very broad. Questions to elicit information that would not be admissible in court may, nevertheless, be asked if there is a possibility that they will lead to the discovery of admissible testimony. No other nation in the world gives this advantage to a plaintiff. The same advantage is given to the defendant. The art of springing surprises on one's opponent and leaving him confused and unprepared in the midst of a trial, which was an important legal weapon prior to Dean Clark, is gone.

Clark's reform movement ended in 1938 in the present Federal Rules of Civil Procedure, which were rapidly copied in state procedure, until now there is little procedural difference between state and federal practice. Prior to Clark an attorney not versed in federal practice would not dare bring a case in the federal courts, and vice versa.

Few lawyers today have any notion of the technical traps and procedural monstrosities that existed prior to the Federal Rules. It is impossible today to dismiss a suit because the complaint does not state a cause of action from a technical point of view. Thus legal procedure has been brought up to date after the centuries of of obfuscation that are so dramatically portrayed by Dickens in *Jarndyce v. Jarndyce.*

Needless to say, Yale was an exciting place in the days of the Depression. Harvard represented, to us at least, the conventional attitude toward the law, the traditional forces dividing the law into separate fields and the lack of emphasis on procedure. We at Yale were busy tearing up the old courses and devising new ones that we thought were far better adapted to the realities of judicial institutions. Wesley Sturges was writing his books on credit transactions, which threw together the conventional fields of bills and notes, mortgages, real property, corporate law, and so on. His attention was centered not on legal theory, but on what happened when financial credits were involved. William O. Douglas had abandoned the conventional course on corporate law and was writing on business units, and including the law of corporations, partnerships, bankruptcy, receivership, and so forth, all rolled into one course which gave the students a picture of what happened in corporate enterprise. Walton Hamilton, an economist who had never been graduated from law school, was examining cases that related to the operation of a competitive market place in a free-enterprise society, using materials that might ordinarily come under a course on the antitrust laws, constitutional law, or administrative trade regulations. I was giving a course on the psychological basis for the law with that brilliant professor of psychology at Yale, Edwin Robinson. Out of this course came my two books *The Symbols of Government* and *The Folklore of Capitalism*. The conservatives charged that we were not operating a law school, but instead were denizens of a cave of the winds. Today even the Harvard Law School offers courses in psychiatry. I like to think, though I am probably overstating the case, that it all started at Yale.

In any event, since the days of Franklin Roosevelt, there has been a startling revolution in our attitudes toward law, legal procedures, and the sanctity of the Constitution of the United States. The old idea that the common law was a seamless web built case by case throughout the ages, all of which had been reconciled into legal principles by irrefutable logic, has all but disappeared. Legal procedure is no longer an abstract science: its delightful complications, its technical traps, and its abstract logic are no longer available to the skilled craftsmen of that dark science. The Constitution of the United States that in the early days stood as an unyielding obstacle to practical legislation attempting to relieve human needs and correct social injustices has gone and a different kind of Constitution has taken its place. The new Constitution stands as a vision of racial equality, civil rights, and human freedom. It is no longer available as a weapon against social reform of any kind.

The emergence of this new Constitution was the product of the first eight years of the administration of Franklin D. Roosevelt. There have been few ideological conflicts in our history bitterer than the struggle of the conservatives to save the old Constitution. But today the words and incantations that were so effective during the first days of the New Deal have lost their magic. The notion that special privileges were property rights, the impairment of which leads to socialism, which would change into communism and end in a dictatorship in which human freedom would be destroyed, is no longer held by our most reputed economists and lawyers. The word "bureaucracy," which used to strike terror in the minds of every God-fearing conservative, no longer makes them afraid except in connection with the purely theological economic ideal of balancing the budget. For example, take the debate in the United States Senate over President Lyndon Johnson's civil-rights program. For a while during that debate these formerly sacred ideas whirled about like snowflakes in a Western blizzard. But it was apparent that the Senators who were using these words realized that they were talking nonsense. The dream of the followers of Senator Goldwater that there is a conservative majority in the United States who want to return to the old Constitution is rapidly dissolving. To read the old debates carried on with such bitterness before Congress, before the Supreme Court of the United States, and in the columns of conservative newspapers serves no useful purpose other than to illustrate the fantastic unreality of those bygone times.

The instrument by which this change was accomplished was the Court-packing fight initiated by Roosevelt in 1937. It was a fight that Roosevelt lost in terms of his immediate objective, which was to pack the Supreme Court with men who followed his own social philosophy. But he came so close to achieving it that the bare majority of the Supreme Court which had stood so firmly against social change disappeared. Its ghost still haunts the marble building. Phrases from the former opinions of the Court still appear in lawyers' briefs, but men of common sense know that the old Constitution is only a ghost.

It is indeed fortunate that Roosevelt did not succeed in destroying the Supreme Court as a sacred institution by packing it with Justices who he was sure would support his legislative program. Had that been done the Court would not today be our most effective symbol of freedom and human rights. The answer to the question who won the Supreme Court fight of 1937 is this: The people of the United States won it.

Thus the law responded to the industrial revolution of the twentieth century, and after a comparatively short and bitter fight gave us a new attitude and outlook on everything from legal procedure to the Constitution of the United States.

Much of the credit for the establishment of this new Constitution must go to the new attitude toward the law contributed by the legal realists. As I have indicated, legal realism is not effective in giving to our judicial institutions the public respect required to symbolize the great ideal of a rule of law above men. But in a period when our judicial institutions were a frustrating force, the exposure by legal realists of the psychology that lies behind the façade of legal logic was a breath of fresh air. It performed the necessary function of destroying respect for the decisions that stood in the way of progress.

CHAPTER SEVEN

Saint Thomas Aquinas Still Lives

A new and more realistic attitude toward the purposes and aims of the Constitution on the part of the Supreme Court of the United States has had tremendous consequences on the social and political scene. Aside from constitutional questions, the Court has felt that its function is the administration of justice rather than the creation of a seamless web of abstract principles based on precedents. Prior to the Depression it was generally thought that the rules of procedure were the province of the legislative branch of government. For the Court to do any more than interpret the rules was judicial legislation. And the Court having once made an interpretation contrary to common sense, it could not be changed by anyone except by legislation. In this way a vast body of procedural theology was built up.

Today the Court has rule-making power, formerly a legislative function. The abstract procedural learning that was once such an important part of the study of the law has disappeared. Convenience and justice to litigants based on observation and experimentation are the guiding principles of judicial procedure today.

Centuries ago Saint Thomas Aquinas liberated the Catholic church from a kind of blind acceptance of ancient creeds and formulas that is similar to the formerly blind acceptance of such matters by the Supreme Court of the United States. He taught that there were certain things in connection with the church, which in his time occupied the entire area of individual, political, and economic activity, that could not be questioned without danger of hell-fire. But there was another area in which God permitted the experimental use of human reason. In the area of reason, absolute and rigid faith was not required. There ancient and respected authority was not infallible. In that field man could learn from experience and change his ideas and attitudes, not on the basis of pure faith, but through the process of rational thought.

That dichotomy pointed out so long ago by Thomas Aquinas has always persisted in man's thinking about his own conduct and his social organizations. Only in the physical sciences can men think and act without it.

The cement that binds social organizations together is reverence and faith in existing institutions. That faith in the United States is represented by the magic words "capitalism" and "free enterprise." These words have no exact meaning, but they are of immense social consequence. The faith that dignifies the Supreme Court is the belief that through logic and reason it may discover impartial principles of law that are independent of the whims, prejudices, or the economic philosophy of the justices.

The social necessities that made the Supreme Court adapt the Constitution to the needs of the twentieth century conflicted with the old image of the Court as the protector of property rights rather than human rights. The 1954 decision on public-school segregation would certainly not have been handed down by the Supreme Court prior to the Depression. The Court made a bold attempt to distinguish the old cases from the new, which seemed, to me at least, to be logical. Nevertheless, the feeling remained that something new had happened. For the Supreme Court to change its attitude toward the constitutionality of racial discrimination was denounced as judicial legislation. Judicial legislation, as every God-fearing man knows, inevitably leads to a dictatorship by the Supreme Court, invades the province of Congress, throws the Court into politics, and makes the law the whim of every new majority of the Justices.

Hence, today the Supreme Court is being attacked for judicial heresy in violating an old theology. Those who defend the Court assert that it is the function of the Supreme Court to establish principles of justice and to consider carefully the social consequences of its decisions. Those who attack the Court say that it is legislating on legal and political problems, that it is destroying states' rights by refusing to approve the abuse by states of individual rights. The Court is thus allowing its decisions on important and controversial matters to be influenced by its observations of the social consequences of those decisions. Such controversial decisions are based upon the citations of cases and the distinctions between old authorities and new, so that the appearance of continuity with the past is preserved. But the reasoning of the Court's opinions on constitutional law, for example, seems new and different from that which guided the interpretation of the Constitution prior to the Depression.

This new reasoning and the different use of precedents to support results that the Court would have rejected a quarter of a century ago has had the same liberating effect on the Supreme Court of the United States that Thomas Aquinas had on the Catholic church of the Middle Ages.

The Court has been charged with the sin of judicial legislation by such diverse sources as many of the distinguished members of the Harvard and Columbia law-school faculties, the Southern segregationists, the John Birch Society, and the last Republican candidate for President of the United States; and finally, in the reapportionment case, by a minority of the Court itself. Indeed, in the Eighty-eighth Congress there was an attempt made to deprive the Supreme Court of jurisdiction in the field of protecting the rights of the voter from the rotten-borough system, with all its evils of minority control, which had grown up in the United States in the last half-century.

It is fortunate that all these attacks have failed. So far as the professors are concerned, their learning is too abstruse to be felt outside of bar associations and academic halls. The controversial decisions of the Supreme Court have made law-school courses in constitutional law and the doctrine of separation of powers more difficult to teach. A number of books on the theory of jurisprudence will have to be thrown away and new ones written. Give the professors time and they will discover new theological principles, which will still keep the Court separate from Congress. The important and refreshing fact is that the vast mass of voters respect the Court for what it has done in establishing new and necessary canons of interpretation for the United States Constitution in a new age.

The areas in which the Court has made the greatest contribution toward the ideal of justice, and for which it has been most bitterly attacked, are three. In the first area—administration of criminal law—the Court has insisted on fairness to the underdog. It has ruled, for example, that every person charged with a criminal offense is entitled to the assistance of a lawyer at his trial, and that if he is indigent, the state must furnish the attorney. It has decided that confessions secured by the police after arrest must be carefully scrutinized. It has reached out its hand to protect the right of accused persons to a fair trial even though it is more than likely that many of them are guilty of the offenses charged. In doing so the Court is blamed by police chiefs for being somehow or other the cause of crime in our cities. But every competent sociologist and psychologist knows this is nonsense. What the Court has done in this field is to dramatize before the nation the ideal of a fair trial. This is of more importance in society than the escape of an inconsequential number of indigent and mentally disturbed criminals who spend their lives getting in and out of penitentiaries regardless of what the Court does. When the history of our time is written there will not be a line in it about the responsibility of the Supreme Court of the United States for the increase of crime, even if the problem of crime is given a whole chapter.

The second area where the Supreme Court is accused of exceeding its theological jurisdiction is the field of civil liberties and civil rights, particularly with respect to Negroes. Had the Court failed to act on this crucial social problem, a quarter of a century might well have elapsed during which time the evil would have grown worse and worse. Without the Court's leadership and authority, expressed by a unanimous Court in its 1954 decision in the school segregation cases, the 1964 civil-rights act could not possibly have been passed.

The third great decision made by the Court, which may rescue this country from fifty years of political control by minorities, was in the decision compelling reapportionment of voting districts so that our cities could have adequate representation in their state legislatures as compared with backward rural communities. Justice

Felix Frankfurter saw in the majority opinion a precedent that would throw the Court into politics. It was better, he thought, for the safety and sanctity of the great tribunal to endure a rotten-borough system, such as England endured at the beginning of the nineteenth century, than to permit the affirmative use of the Constitution to give the city voter equal rights with the farmer.

Only a person obsessed with the theology of the past could have asked for such needless patience from an electorate deprived of its full voice. It was the desegregation decision, however, in which Mr. Justice Frankfurter concurred, that made the Court temporarily a political football. The reapportionment decision was accepted with far less protest, because the emotions of the minority group who opposed it were not stirred to the fever heat created by the desegregation decision.

The theological battle still continues on a lower level. An occasional state legislature resolves to impeach Chief Justice Earl Warren. A minority of unreconstructed conservatives did what they could in the last election to throw the Court into politics. On a higher level, law-school professors are flooding law reviews with articles defining the exact line between judicial decision and judicial legislation, with reasoning so profound that nobody can understand it but themselves. But the Court has emerged triumphant, having made the greatest contribution in our judicial history since John Marshall in 1803 first established the power of the Supreme Court to declare acts of Congress unconstitutional in *Marbury* v. *Madison,* a decision that was judicial legislation under the standards of those who now attack the Court. The new Court began by liberating Congress and state legislatures from the former judicial ban on experimental social legislation. It finally achieved the distinction of making the Constitution an affirmative instrument in the advancement of human rights and political progress.

CHAPTER EIGHT

Why the Full Employment Act of 1946 Became a Dead Letter

A student of the growth and change of social ideas in the United States will be interested in inquiring into why the startling revolution in our ideas and attitudes toward the common law and the Constitution was not accompanied by acceptance of a realistic attitude toward economic organization. Why is it that the American people, realizing the almost limitless productive capacity of the new age, fully aware of the fact that automation is creating structural unemployment and hereditary poverty, are unable to devise a respectable formula for the distribution of goods in the new age except in time of war? How is it that a new legal constitution can emerge in a short period of time and become a positive force completely supplanting the frustrating effects of the old pre-Depression Constitution and at the same time our economic ideas, inherited from the days of Andrew Jackson, prevent us, for example, from cleaning up the Potomac River basin?

The ideas of both law and economics are religious in character. They are inherited from the past. But there are two types of religious ideas. The first consists of the fundamental, unchangeable truths that must be accepted on faith. These truths cannot be debated. In the days of the ancient Catholic church, those who refused to accept them were heretics. Today the attackers range from unsound thinkers who are the dupes of demagogues to wicked and malicious Communists who are striving to change our system of government. A nation that fails to follow fundamental economic truths is on the road to hell. Such are the ideas and attitudes that lie behind the so-called science of economics.

The second type of religious idea may be described as a moral attitude. It lies in the ideas that support our reverence for the common law and the Constitution. Such ideas are subject to change in changing times. Behind them is the vague ideal of justice, which is far from rigid. Justice is always subject to rational re-examination and analysis.

There are three ways of thinking about the relationship between a citizen and his government. The first is the ideal of a rule of law above men. The second is based on faith in fundamental economic principles. That way of thought makes us believe in a capitalist system as an automatically operating set of principles functioning somewhere in the sky and the following of which will bring forth peace and prosperity. Even a minor violation of this faith is an economic sin, punishment for which will be visited on future generations. This way of thinking may be described as the domino theory of government. If a set of dominoes is set upright, each close to the next, and you push over the first domino, all the rest of them will fall in rapid succession. This notion is at the root of theoretical economic thinking. Such a faith, exemplified and celebrated by the sacred writings of an economic priesthood, seems to be a psychological necessity for the perpetuation of stability in government institutions. When that faith does not depart too far from reality, it clothes our social organizations with dignity and prestige, and persuades the less fortunate among our citizens to accept their lot with resignation and equanimity. It preserves the social hierarchy by preventing individuals from being contumacious toward holy men. But in periods of rapid economic change, such as the Reformation, the French Revolution, the Russian Revolution, and the present era, the conflict between that faith and the necessity for change brings consequences ranging from our own feeling that we are living in economic sin to revolutions and dictatorships in less-fortunate countries.

The third way of thinking about the relationship between a citizen and his government is that of the government planner, who had a brief day in the sun during the Depression. The planner cannot understand why, if private industry is unable to distribute the goods our industrial plant is capable of producing, government should not step in and fill the gap. Why can we not be as practical in meeting our needs and expanding our production in a cold war as we are in a hot war?

This way of thinking enjoyed a brief acceptance at the close of the First World War, when many responsible people thought the government should plan the coming adjustment from a wartime to a peacetime economy, but it was soon abandoned.

During the Second World War our economy was managed by government to an extent unheard of during the First World War. At the end of the war most economists predicted a painful adjustment as the result of shifting from a wartime to a peacetime economy. In 1946 an act, commonly called the Full Employment Act, was passed by Congress. The act starts out with the following declaration of policy:

The Congress declares that it is the continuing policy and responsibility of the Federal Government to use all practicable means consistent with its needs and obligations and other essential considerations of national policy, with the assistance and cooperation of industry, agriculture, labor, and State and local governments, to coordinate and utilize all its plans, functions, and resources for the purpose of creating and maintaining, in a manner calculated to foster and promote free competitive enterprise and the general welfare, conditions under which there will be afforded useful employment opportunities, including self-employment, for those able, willing, and seeking to work, and to promote maximum employment, production, and purchasing power. (15 United States Code Annotated, § 1021)

This is the most revolutionary statement of the function of the federal government in our history. Nothing done or said during the Roosevelt administration, not even the measures considered most radical, approached this statement in its broad conception of the responsibility of the federal government for national planning. It is astonishing, therefore, that such a startling declaration of principle could have been passed with so little comment and so little dissent that the average layman and many lawyers have never heard of it.

The other sections of the act require the President to transmit to Congress an economic report setting forth the levels of employment, production, and purchasing power actually obtaining in the United

States, with a comparison of what levels are needed to carry out the policy of the act. It further requires that the President prepare and submit to Congress a program to carry out the policy of the act, together with his recommendations for legislation. Finally, the act provides for a council of economic advisers to inform the President.

The fundamental theory behind the act is that if Congress by appropriate *ad hoc* legislation sees to it that there is sufficient purchasing power in our economy to run our industrial plant at full capacity and that purchasing power is expanded to meet the increasing capacity of the twentieth-century industrial revolution, there will be jobs enough for all. The act might be called an act to balance our economic budget; that is, our national productive capacity should be balanced against the purchasing power needed to make it run at full capacity. The policy decreed by the act runs directly contrary to our traditional principle of balancing the fiscal budget.

Today in France, Germany, and Sweden this notion of national planning is accepted as a matter of course. But in the United States the Full Employment Act of 1946 is all but forgotten. The only thing still alive about it is the President's Council of Economic Advisers, which continues to function in a peculiarly ineffective way. When the policy of the act is called to the attention of sound thinkers, it is always pointed out that such a policy would lead to bureaucracy, inflation, interference with business, and the loss of business confidence.

One of the organizations that today attempts to regulate our economy is the Federal Reserve Board, which claims an independent power to frustrate even the President of the United States. Board members are obsessed with the fear that European central banks and governments, by exercising their rights to buy gold from the United States Treasury, will exhaust our supply. To avoid this catastrophe the Board is constantly raising interest rates in the United States and thus curbing our money supply and restricting our production. Their object is to end the accumulation of dollar obligations payable in gold in the hands of central banks in Europe. Lying behind this is the feeling that the richest nation in the world is unable to obtain credit from the poorer nations of Europe. After eight years of this kind of control by the Federal Reserve Board, the Secretary of the Treasury became so alarmed about the flight of gold that he made a special trip to Germany with his hat in his hand begging for relief to bolster up what he told the Germans was an unsound American dollar.

The current management of the Federal Reserve has been erratic and restrictive because it is based on the balancing of the budget. It ignores the policy of the Full Employment Act of 1946, which was designed to balance the budget, to avoid inflation by not creating more purchasing power than our productive plant can fill and to avoid deflation by seeing that the purchasing power is not insufficient to run our productive plant at full capacity. The reason the Full Employment Act has been on the shelf is because of fear of government planning, and the basis for that fear lies in the fact that government planning is not considered from the practical standpoint of what it will do, but is still regarded as a humanitarian measure designed to bring about the dreaded welfare state. Humanitarians are dangerous people; they have no proper philosophy of government; their proposals cannot be given any weight by God-fearing, sound-thinking men.

With this observation I am curiously enough in agreement. It is true that revolutions are ordinarily begun by humanitarians seeking to relieve the lot of the poor. But there is no sanctity, no stability in humanitarian thinking. It has never yet been possible, in church or state, to found a permanent institution based on purely humanitarian ideas. It is impossible to clothe such ideas with psychologically authentic ritual or ceremony. This is the reason why in every revolution where social institutions are suddenly overthrown and new ones substituted the result has been the loss of individual freedom and the establishment of dictatorship. Humanitarian thinking was what gave socialism its appeal to the intellectual. But the day of humanitarians in power was short.

An orderly adjustment of society to a period of rapid social change must be slow. It always begins with fear and anxiety on the part of the conservatives, as is evidenced by the bitterness during the Roosevelt era. It takes time for conservative faiths, which are frustrating forces, to disappear. A period of doubt and uncertainty, which accompanies a dawning realization that the old principles are no longer effective, is inevitable. Old religions never die. They simply dissolve in an orderly society. Their passing is always accompanied by the kind of anxiety that made, for example, intelligent people believe in the 1950's that a small Communist group was capable of overthrowing the government of the United States. Sooner or later we are going to accept the philosophy of the Full Employment Act as a fundamental principle of economics, a principle, moreover, that can be put into practice by free enterprise without embracing either dictatorship or socialism.

CHAPTER NINE

The Change from Fundamental Principles to Practical Expediency in International Affairs from the First World War to the Present Cold War

The slow but revolutionary change from old ideas to new is illustrated by observing a difference between the First World War and the Second.

The First World War was fought to preserve the fundamental principle that the world must be made safe for democracy. At the end of that war the accepted doctrine of right-thinking Americans was that Germany, the enemy of democracy, must not be permitted to rise again. And so the Allies insisted on German reparations as a matter of principle, completely blind to the fact that it was impossible for the Germans to pay them. As a further adherence to the same principle, an embargo was placed on Germany. To get the goods that she sorely needed for her economic rehabilitation, Germany was forced to adopt a policy of the greatest monetary inflation that the world has ever known. It was this inflation that bankrupted the entire German conservative middle class. The disappearance of that class left Germany exposed to the revolutionary forces of its industrial adventurers and intolerant mobs. The Weimar Republic received no Western support. Western policy was to keep it as impotent as possible. Reparations from Germany were enforced beyond the limit of German capability. As President Calvin Coolidge expressed it, with the routine economic wisdom of the time: "They hired the money, didn't they?"

There was nothing complicated about the German situation that a man of common sense unblinded by faith in principle could not have understood. Had we been able to see the situation as it was, the last thing we would have done would have been to bankrupt the German middle class in the interests of peace and security. But our faith in principle was too strong, and we did not waver in it until Adolf Hitler was firmly established in power. Instead, we resolutely refused to make the concessions to the Weimar Republic that were necessary to re-establish a government in Germany that the German voter could support with pride and confidence.

Once Hitler's rule became an established fact, the Western powers looked at his performance with terrified acquiescence, thus building up his political strength and destroying the effectiveness of his opponent. American as well as British industrialists eagerly accepted his invitation to join international cartels, in defiance of American antitrust laws. And with these economic ties with Hitler's cartels came a reluctant but growing respect for Hitler himself in American and British industry. General Motors bought the Opel Automobile Company, and somewhat shamefacedly ended, as was then required, all its business correspondence in Germany with the slogan "Heil Hitler."

The growing business tolerance of Hitler is illustrated by a conversation I heard at a private dinner attended by some of our most prominent industrialists. They were shocked by Hitler's treatment of the Jews. But they argued that there was nothing anyone could do about it. And they further argued that it would pass with the civilizing process of Germany's industrial expansion. This was after Hitler's remarkable series of political victories made him the dominant economic force in Europe. One of these business leaders had read a book entitled *The Lost Fruits of Waterloo*. The book, he said, proved that if Napoleon had won at Waterloo, Europe would have become a great free-trade area, nationalism, which was the chief cause of war, would have disappeared, and the Western world would have been on the highroad to peace and industrial prosperity. He admitted that it was distressing that economic progress should come at the cost of violating every moral principle. But one must be realistic.

These ideas were not publicly proclaimed by either American or British business leaders. The moral indignation of the public would have been too strong. But they were sufficiently widely held to form a background of respect in the business community for the surrender at Munich. It required Hitler's conquest of France to disclose to these businessmen the complete unreality of their so-called *realistic* thinking. Realistic thinking that conflicts with moral principles always leads to the wrong conclusion. Such realistic thinking is not realistic at all.

The Second World War, unlike the First, was not so much a war of principles as it was a war of survival. It was not clothed with illusions or slogans. This, of course, did not remain true. There was a period after peace broke out when we went off chasing rainbows in all directions. The old League of Nations, repudiated in 1920, was revived in the United Nations as a solution to all international problems. This was the constructive feature of a brief daydream. On the preventive side we had faith in the theory that if some properly constituted court would declare, after a judicial trial and clothed in the panoply of due process, that aggressive war was a crime then that basic principle of international law would be enshrined and established for all time to come. Surely, if Russia was made a member of that court as well as a member of the United Nations, a unity of principle would be created governing all the civilized powers in the world. And so the international Nuremberg tribunal was set up. Its minor objective was, of course, to punish men guilty of mass murder. Only in that minor respect were the Nuremberg trials successful in creating a precedent for the future. Trials for mass murder are still going on in Germany in which the defense of obedience to military orders is outlawed.

But the principal objective of Nuremberg, the outlawing of aggressive war, was a symbol that prevented us from seeing Russia as she really was. Before that iridescent soap bubble had burst, we made mistakes with respect to Russia, such as the partition of Germany, which did us more harm than all the machinations of the international Communist party could possibly accomplish.

With Russia as our most powerful ally, marching with us, her face set like a flint Zionward, the principal objective of an influential group became the same as that after the First World War. Germany must at all costs be prevented from again becoming a threat to world peace. From this arose the plan of Secretary Henry Morgenthau to prevent Germany's industrial recovery by making it a purely agricultural nation. Under this plan, such things happened as that an important bridge over the Rhine was rebuilt with two lanes only. It was considered dangerous to permit German traffic to flow freely.

Then there was the problem of creating a sense of moral guilt among the German people. Following the Nuremberg trials, American judges and lawyers were exported to Germany to sit on so-called denazification tribunals. More than a million Germans were indicted. The offenses over which these tribunals had jurisdiction were classified as: major offenders, minor offenders, and followers. The penalties ranged from imprisonment to limiting the offender to manual labor in gaining his livelihood. I had a cousin who had marched in Nazi parades. She had been a schoolteacher. She was neither more nor less stupid and bigoted than many American women I have known. But she was forbidden to teach school any more.

Trials before these tribunals were conducted without any pretense of what in American jurisprudence we call due process. Secret evidence from faceless accusers was freely admitted. My contact with such trials came when I was called to Germany to represent Baron Freiherr von Weizsaecker, who had been Hitler's Secretary of State for Foreign Affairs and later ambassador to Rome. Part of the evidence against Weizsaecker had been the testimony of another German State Department official. Counsel for the defense had discovered that this witness had been threatened with having his denazification clearance taken away if he did not testify as directed. But this had made no difference; the evidence had been admitted, and Weizsaecker had been condemned to a long period of imprisonment.

Actually, Weizsaecker had been one of those who risked his life in the plotting against Hitler. When I was appointed his attorney, along with Warren E. Magee of the District of Columbia Bar, in 1950, to persuade John McCloy, who was then High Commissioner, to release him, we were able to get letters on Weizsaecker's behalf from the Vatican for the period when he was ambassador to Rome; from Lord Halifax, with whom he had been in touch during the war; and from the leading bishop in Norway, who had also been in secret communication with him during the period of German occupation. McCloy, a man of unusual ability and common sense, promptly released Weizsaecker from prison.

But this period of retaliation against Germany proved to be a short one. Because the Second World War was not a war to establish a fundamental principle, there was room for change in our theology in the interests of decency and common sense. We soon abandoned ideas of preventing German economic recovery and assumed the responsibility, new in the world's history, of putting industrial Germany back on her feet. In the light of Russia's repudiation of her treaties and agreements, we soon recognized that the United Nations, while it had its function as a forum for international debate and communication, offered no neat and final solution of the problems of international affairs.

With this dream exploded, the principal results of the brief period of devotion to the great principle of world order after the war were that we found ourselves committed to the support of Berlin with the Russians in control of all land communications between West Germany and that beleaguered city; we were filled with fear and distrust of the security of our institutions at home; and we began to believe that an insignificant group of crackpots, known as the Communist party, had the actual power to overthrow the government and create a Communist state.

On this tide of distrust and fear, Senator Joseph McCarthy rose to such power that the President of the United States felt compelled to follow his command with respect to the hiring and discharge of government personnel. President Harry Truman set up a system of tribunals patterned after the denazification proceedings in Germany. Government officials were convicted, without any evidence against them that a rational court would accept, of an offense akin to treason known as a reasonable doubt with respect to their loyalty.

The spectacle the United States presented to the civilized world during this era was a shameful one. Emissaries of Senator McCarthy roamed over Europe at government expense terrorizing the Foreign Service. The Supreme Court of the United States in a number of cases affirmed lower-court convictions for contempt of the un-

American Activities committees of Congress. The committees conceded that the principal purpose of their hearings was exposure. A minority of four Justices held that a hearing for the purpose of exposure was not a proper activity of Congress. The majority did not disagree but nevertheless held that courts could not inquire into the motives of a congressional committee even when those motives were apparent on the face of the proceeding.

This distressing era did at last end. Protected still by a bare majority of the Supreme Court, the inquisitions of the un-American activities committees of Congress still go on, but they no longer make headlines, and there is hope that some day in the future the American public will feel safe enough to stop these disgraceful proceedings.

Today we have become realistic about our leadership of world affairs. We no longer feel that our principal danger is the overthrow of our government by the subversive ideas of the Soviet-inspired American Communist party. In the 1964 presidential campaign the charge that negotiations and accommodations with the Soviets were a violation of our duty to support a capitalistic ideology at all costs and without compromise no longer had the appeal to the public that it had in the close election four years before. This may well be the beginning of the end of the Cold War. If it is, our relations with the Communist powers will no longer be devoted to the exemplification of the fundamental principles of capitalism versus Communism, but, rather, to the voice of plain reason and wholesome expediency.

CHAPTER TEN

The Fundamental Economic Principles
That Were the Basis for Political Action during
the Administration of President Eisenhower

The election of Dwight D. Eisenhower to the Presidency meant the return of conservatives to power. The atmosphere was similar to that when Harding was elected. Adlai Stevenson's brilliant speeches on the economic issues in his two campaigns for the Presidency fell on deaf ears. As in the time of Harding, what the voters wanted was a return to "normalcy." Stevenson was trying to get the voters to think when they did not want to think. They wanted to be secure in their fundamental economic preconceptions.

I would like to attempt a brief summary of what a conservative public in the United States believed to be the fundamental economic principles that would insure us stability during the administration of President Eisenhower.

The conservative majority believed that somewhere in the bright and not-too-distant heavens there is ticking away a machine capable of regulating the economy and producing prosperity for all. The machine is made up of closely meshed gears. These were forged long ago out of the basic principles of our forefathers. The machine is capable of working perfectly under the right conditions. But this means that we must let it alone and not tinker with the delicate mechanism. Unfortunately, there were a number of groups in our society who insisted on tampering with it. These groups may be classified and described as follows:

1. The Communists. J. Edgar Hoover offered the best study of this group in his book *Masters of Deceit*. It was their purpose to

persuade American citizens to change their form of government and give up the American way of life. If they did this by open debate, the citizens would soon discover the hollowness of their views. So they did not work in this way. Instead, they infiltrated colleges, the press, and many other groups, not revealing the fact that they were Communists. They worked by occult means and indirect suggestion; they got their students and their comrades dissatisfied with the American way of life. With minds thus softened, their adherents were ready to vote to change our system of government, and may actually do so one fine morning before our sound thinkers can wake up and say "Joe McCarthy." To avoid this danger, the House Un-American Activities Committee was bending every effort during the Eisenhower administration.

2. The unsound thinkers. Unlike the Communists, these people were men of good will. They had no desire to change our system of government. But they were too easily persuaded by the blandishments of demagoguery. They believed in all sorts of alien notions, such as planning and the regulation of industry, that sound thinkers instantly recognize as economic sin. The sound thinker is one who believes that government should do nothing about anything. The plans of the unsound thinkers to do something are humanitarian and superficial. They inevitably creep toward socialism and then to the welfare state. I am not entirely clear whether advocacy of humanitarian measures leads to the welfare state or whether advocacy of the welfare state leads back to unsound humanitarian measures, but to the conservatives it is bad enough either way. The plans of the unsound thinkers well deserve the epithet commonly attached to them: "pie in the sky." What this phrase means may be illustrated by the following: Suppose A wants to clean up the Potomac River basin and promises to do so if elected. This means that he is willing to mortgage the future of his grandchildren and waste the taxpayers' dollars on a nonrevenue-producing project that will be a continuing financial burden. When, therefore, he promises the voters this, he is promising "pie in the sky."

3. The bureaucrats. These men were really incredible individuals. They had three main objectives. Their first was to waste all of the taxpayers' money they possibly could. The second was to perpetuate their wasteful organization and increase it as quickly

as possible. The third was to interfere with business and cause businessmen to lose confidence. How and why these bureaucrats sink to such low estate is a mystery. There must be some poison gas distilled in government offices. For the plain and simple fact is that the moment an individual is employed by the government he becomes a bureaucrat, contumacious to all holy men, and someone geared to run this country down the road to hell.

This rigidity of economic thinking was confined to the two greatest industrial powers, the United States and Russia. Elsewhere in industrial countries it had long since been forgotten. Sweden, for example, was a nation poor in resources compared to the United States. But it had no unemployment and one of the highest standards of living in the world. In the light of our economic theology we were utterly unable to understand this phenomenon. And so we passed it off with the observation that Sweden was a victim of creeping socialism. She was living in economic sin. Why she hadn't yet gone to the economic hell of inflation and finally embraced Communism conservative writers were unable to understand. They remained steadfast in their faith in an old economic order, convinced that we should continue on the path of economic virtue rather than solve our unemployment problems by national planning as Sweden had. During this period Gunnar Myrdhal, a leading Swedish economist who has spent much of his time studying the social institutions of the United States, stated in an interview that the reason for the lagging and stagnant economic growth in the United States as compared to the faster growth of European industrial nations was our illiterate economists. A prominent official, replying to this kind of attack, noted that the suicide rate in Sweden was much higher than it was in the United States.

I remember a conversation I had with a friend from Vienna. He greatly admired the beauty of the Potomac River and asked if he could be taken to one of our bathing beaches. "We have no bathing beaches," I explained. "The Potomac is an open sewer. If you are on a boat on the Potomac and the boat catches fire, you have an even chance if you stay on the boat or swim to shore. Your choice depends entirely upon whether you prefer a sudden death to a lingering one." "But we swim in the Danube," he said. "Why on earth don't you clean up the Potomac?" "We can't afford the cost," I replied. "I don't understand," he said. "We can afford the cost in Vienna, and you have a much richer country than ours." "You don't understand basic economic principles," I answered. "The reason you have a poor country and we have a rich one is that we at least try to balance our national budget, though we hardly ever succeed, because a bunch of greedy bureaucrats is constantly wasting the taxpayers' money. The reason you have a poor country is that you spend your money on things like public bathing beaches, which are not revenue-producing. You are mortgaging your grandchildren's future and don't even realize it."

The rigidity of economic thinking in Russia stems from adherence to the nineteenth-century economics of Karl Marx. Year after year crops fail and the Russian people go hungry. But any deviation from Marxist collectivism is economic sin. And so Russian planners must go on making the same mistakes over and over again, world without end, amen.

Sound economic opinion in the United States prior to the First World War believed that the greatest burden of national debt the United States could bear was one hundred million dollars. More than that would mean national bankruptcy. (The sound thinkers were never very precise about what national bankruptcy meant. Their opposite numbers in the old church priesthood were able to be much more descriptive about the horrors of hell.) Then came the war. The national debt rose to twenty-five billion dollars. During the war the idea of national planning raised its head. When the war ended there were members of the National Resources Planning Board who thought that some sort of national planning would serve a good purpose in adjusting our economy to peacetime. But Woodrow Wilson, apostle of the free-enterprise system as he was, would have none of it. So the automatic operation of this system took over. After a short recession came the great stockmarket boom of the 1920's. Agriculture settled into a depression from which it never recovered. But in spite of this the nation followed the sound economic principles of the nineteenth century. Under the brave leadership of Harding and his successor, Calvin Coolidge, in the ten years that followed the First World War we balanced our budget and in addition paid off nine billion dollars of the national debt.

Surely such sound economic policy should pay off. And for a time it did. The stock market boomed. Merger followed merger, showering profit on a gullible public. But in 1929 something went wrong. The great stock-market crash deprived everyone of the fruits of their foresight. The Great Depression settled down on us, not to be broken until the Second World War forced on us a program of astronomical spending.

But the rigidity of our economic philosophy still continued. Roosevelt in his first campaign ran on a platform of balancing the national budget. He criticized Hoover for being an extravagant spender of the taxpayers' money. He attacked the Reconstruction Finance Corporation which Hoover had set up to relieve financial distress. The RFC never lost a dime of the taxpayers' money. It took over shaky business loans that the commercial banks would not touch. Nevertheless, it made tremendous profits. But of what avail are tremendous profits for a government corporation that is engaged in economic sin?

Roosevelt was elected. The extraordinary thing about that remarkable man was that, conservative as his economic philosophy was, he still believed in doing something about current problems. The New Dealers with whom he surrounded himself differed violently and almost came to blows about what should be done. But they were a unit in believing that something ought to be done by the federal government.

The first attempt was the National Industrial Recovery Act. On paper nothing more foolish was ever proposed. The central idea of the NRA was that the nation could get rich by restricting production. Apart from its weak economic basis, the NRA was unique in United States history in that it envisaged a nationwide plan for the economy. Never before in time of peace had such an idea obtained legislative sanction. But the NRA was soon killed by the Supreme Court, and we returned to our historic economic tradition. Thus the notion of an automatically working economy on a balanced budget persisted throughout the long period of economic stagnation that preceded the Second World War.

The necessities of that war forced us to adopt a planned economy while the war was going on. This did not bother anyone, because planning during the course of a war does not lead to socialism in the way that it does in peace. But at the end of the war, in 1946, there was a growing fear that the economy would not adjust itself to the sudden cessation of war production. Consumer purchasing power would not be sufficient to absorb the vast new productive capacity created by the war. And so the Full Employment Act of 1946 was passed.

Contrary to these fears, the economy did adapt itself to the change from war to peace, and by the time Dwight D. Eisenhower was inaugurated, everybody, soothed by the tranquilizing influence of that benign figure, had ceased to worry about economic affairs. In the years following 1953, our only economic worry was inflation, which could be prevented only by stopping government spending. Eisenhower's great popularity was in part owing to the fact that he represented in the public mind the ideal of thrift and a balanced fiscal budget.

The result of the conservative effort under Eisenhower has been succinctly expressed by Edwin L. Dale, Jr., Financial Editor of the New York *Times,* as follows:

After five years of trying, the regime had produced (or found itself with), in fiscal 1959, the biggest budget deficit in peacetime history and the first really serious wave of "inflationary psychology" in modern times.

The only answer seemed to be more conservative than ever. Squeeze the budget—Russian challenge and depressing slums and dirty streams to the contrary notwithstanding. Stretch out the national debt at every opportunity—at the risk of even more uncertainty in the bond markets. Keep money tight and interest rates high—even with nearly five million people out of work in the winter of 1958–59. Keep trying to return functions to the states to relieve federal finance—even with the State of Michigan so tightly pinched for money that it had to appeal to large corporate taxpayers to pay in advance.

And given their view of the world and the dollar, the conservatives were right. The only cure for the disease was a stronger dose of the familiar medicine. (*Conservatives in Power,* by Edwin L. Dale, Jr., Doubleday, 1960, pp. 209–210.)

But even Mr. Dale, in spite of the accuracy of his observation, still believes that our only salvation lies in avoiding economic sin and following sound economic faith. He concludes by saying:

This book is the story of why the objectives are far more difficult to achieve than was realized in 1952, but the story does not warrant the conclusion that they cannot ever be achieved, at least in great part. Indeed, they probably *were* achieved in part, and with a better knowledge of the realities they may be even more closely approached in the future. We shall all be the losers if conservative objectives become discredited because we now know some of the obstacles to conservative performance. (P. 214.)

The nation's industrial plant during the Eisenhower administration was running at seventy-five per cent of capacity. We lost in goods and services, development of water resources, construction of schools, hospitals, and recreation areas, and all those things that make life pleasant, the sum of $550 billion from 1953 to 1960 (measured in uniform 1963 dollars). All this real wealth we might have had. But in the economic thinking of our time we have lost nothing.

Our principal fear is still inflation. We can conceive of only one way to avoid inflation, and that is to see that our productive wealth does not expand too rapidly. So we adopt monetary measures and raise interest rates to keep production down. In the meantime jobs are not increasing fast enough to take care of the new labor force caused by our explosive population increase. To remedy this we talk about retraining the unemployed for new jobs that require new skills. But by the time these men are trained, automation has abolished more jobs. We are developing a vast amount of unemployment, for which we have invented a new name: "structural unemployment." Statisticians tell us that by 1970 there will be two and a half million teen-agers without jobs or any chance of getting any. But in the last election there were millions of people who voted for a conservative who ascribed the increase in crime to the failure of the President to set a moral example.

To a man from Mars the indulgence by intelligent people in this kind of thinking would seem absurd. But to a historian examining the records of the commercial revolution prior to the Reformation and the industrial revolution of the nineteenth and twentieth centuries these ideas always accompany the influx of new productive wealth into an established order that has no acceptable formula by which that new wealth can be distributed. For example, prior to the Reformation the discovery of gold in America was ushering in an age of commerce in which credit played an important part. Usury was a sin according to the Catholic church, which had, however, come to tolerate it as a sort of necessary evil. The conflict between moral principle and toleration of the great banking house of the Fugger family made the church seem a hotbed of hypocrisy. When Luther started the Reformation, one of his targets for denunciation was the Fugger banking institution. Yet banking and credit were to become the dynamic force of the new commercial age.

In the same way, England's first answer to the problem created by the increase of productive wealth in the nineteenth century was to restrict the supply of food by the Corn Laws. Agricultural labor was starving. Under the Speenhamland Law of 1796 farm families were given a dole called "rates," the amount of which depended on the size of the family. In order to pay that dole the price of grain had to be kept up by a protective tariff. And in order to give food to the poor it was necessary to cut down the amount of food in England. The same psychology was apparent in the United States at the beginning of the Depression. The NRA was devoted to the theory that we could become rich by restricting production. The NRA quickly disappeared, but the idea still persists in our agricultural program.

In addition, we are worried about the stability of our dollar. Again, the conservative answer is to restrict imports and handicap investment of American capital abroad. This recommendation is made at the very time when the trade balance of the United States has never been better. As reported in the New York *Times* of Monday, February 15, 1965, it shows a surplus that has increased by almost $2 billion since 1958 until, in 1964, it reached the level of $6.5 billion to $7 billion. France's economy, on the other hand, has the largest trade deficit in Europe. The trade equilibrium in France is supplied by American investments there. Foreign businessmen are worried about the economic consequences in Europe of curtailing the flow of American dollars abroad. Yet De Gaulle wants to stop that flow of dollars and go back to an impossible gold standard.

In the days of the NRA, restriction of production was used as a cure for deflation. Today our monetary theory insists that restriction of production is the only proper remedy to prevent inflation. The psychological reason for this is that the respectable and well-established sector of any society is instinctively afraid of the social changes that may come about if unorthodox ways are used to distribute the new wealth that a major industrial revolution creates. That fear was intensified in the eighteenth century by the spectacle of the French Revolution. Today our own fears are intensified by the spectacle of the Soviets. We say to ourselves, "If a system of planned production has destroyed individual freedom in Russia, any form of government planning is bound to lead to socialism here."

Such fears repeated in similar times in the past cannot be reasoned away. The only solution is to grow out of them gradually. That growing process is always a painful one. John F. Kennedy, who knew as a politician that he could not win the election if he were precise in his economic program, had to state the economic issue vaguely by telling the voters that it was time for the nation to get going somewhere. After his election, he talked in his speech at Yale about economic myths. Finally, he endorsed the unorthodox notion that he could balance the fiscal budget by cutting taxes.

Neither President Kennedy nor his economic advisers ever endorsed the idea of avoiding inflation and insuring full production through the implementation of the Full Employment Act of 1946. The greatest apostle of this economic idea was Leon Keyserling, former economic adviser to President Truman, whose economic pamphlets drew a wide audience. He pointed out that the tax cut proposed by Kennedy did not meet the real problem of providing enough consumer purchasing power to promote the full growth of our expanding productive plant. Nevertheless, Kennedy's tax cut did have the psychological effect of getting the public and the business community to accept the idea that you could reduce taxes and increase national income at the same time.

President Johnson, who succeeded in getting the tax bill passed, made a further advance in the growth of realistic ideas concerning our economy when he started his war on poverty. It was accepted by the business community. This fact represents a revolutionary change in the former conservative belief that poverty is due to lack of initiative on the part of the poor. And it is significant that at the same time that Johnson advanced this revolutionary idea of state responsibility for poverty he gained credit with the American voter by personally turning out lights at the White House as a symbol of our faith in the economic traditions of a balanced fiscal budget.

CHAPTER ELEVEN

The Power of Private Credit Organizations to Provide Consumer Purchasing Power, Which Started with the Wildcat Banks at the Time of Andrew Jackson, Has Not Since the Depression Been Sufficient to Absorb the Productive Capacity of the Twentieth-Century Revolution

The religious economic faiths, the fear of inflation, the insistence on balancing the fiscal budget, the anxiety about the soundness of the dollar, all were established in the public mind as fundamental truths in the early days of this republic. The economic planner of those times was Alexander Hamilton, who conceived the idea of regulating the economy of the nation through a Bank of the United States, which would determine the amount of money and credit necessary to produce an expanding industrial economy.

The hard-money group consisted of the farmers. These agrarians had little use for money on their farms. They were obsessed by the fear of depreciated currency. They thought that the idea of endowing a central bank with power to depreciate the currency was like John Law and his Mississippi Bubble. Law's famous project in French Louisiana failed not for any defect of its own, but because of speculative and political intrigues. The image of the failure of the Mississippi Bubble was familiar to everyone. It was constantly used in debate as an argument against expansion of the currency. Hamilton had studied John Law. He thought that Law was right in his realization that to expand the economy of France

98

a credit institution was needed. But Law's execution of the scheme was disastrous. After giving the Mississippi Bubble a monopoly on all state credit he failed to provide it with curbs or safeguards. The privately held stock in the Bubble soared to fantastic heights and then collapsed. Hamilton's plan was to expand and control credit in the United States through the Bank of the United States, fashioned after the Bank of England.

Thomas Jefferson hated banks. His ideal was a rural economy where no one had money and therefore could preserve those simple virtues ordinarily ascribed to tillers of the soil. He spoke for the hard-money agrarians when he pointed out that the Bank of the United States was an institution that would eventually destroy democracy and private capitalism. He said:

Can it be thought that the Constitution intended that, for a shade or two of convenience, more or less, Congress should be authorized to break down the most ancient and fundamental laws of the several states, such as those against mortmain, the laws of alienage, the rules of descent, the acts of distribution, the laws of escheat and forfeiture, the laws of monopoly? Nothing but a necessity invincible by any other means can justify such a prostration of laws which constitute the pillars of our whole system of jurisprudence. (*Banks and Politics in America,* by Bray Hammond, Princeton, 1957, p. 117.)

Andrew Jackson hated banks with equal fervor and finally succeeded in destroying the Bank of the United States as an enemy of the maintenance of a sound and undepreciated currency. Yet, curiously enough, in pursuing that ideal and destroying the bank, Jackson was supported by private bankers who were issuing notes with no regulation or control. The last thing these private banks wanted was a Bank of the United States which would put a limit on their power to print paper money. If the Bank of the United States were destroyed as a regulating force, these banks would be able to print all the money they wanted. Strange to say, it was that unlimited power to expand the currency that gave the United States a growing economy as compared to the stagnant English economy, the growth of which was limited by a conservative and timid Bank of England.

Thus the hard-money agrarian group created the softest currency this country has ever known, to the great economic benefit of the new nation. A great deal may be learned about monetary theory in operation by observing this process. Bray Hammond has described it in a brilliant book, *Banks and Politics in America,* and I am greatly in his debt for many of my ideas.

At the end of the Revolution there were twelve million dollars in specie (gold or silver currency) in the United States and only four million people. This meant that there was about three dollars a head, a sum utterly incapable of supporting an industrial economy. Virginia planters were getting on well enough with English credits for their tobacco. Small farmers were largely self-sufficient units. But Shays' Rebellion in 1786–87 showed that even the farmers were being destroyed by the hard-money system. Hammond points out that historians have misinterpreted Shays' Rebellion. They have looked at it through the spectacles of Thomas Jefferson and thought of it as an example of the independence of Americans and their distrust of central government.

Actually, Shays' Rebellion in no way represented Jefferson's notion. Instead, it was the result of a drastic shortage of currency. Even prosperous farmers could not lay their hands upon enough specie to pay the tax on whisky levied by the government. They saw their farms liable to be put up at public auction, not because they were insolvent, but because they had no specie to pay the tax. It was as simple as that. But such has been our rigid economic faith that I know of no historian aside from Hammond who has interpreted it correctly.

It was through the free and unlimited power of private banks to print money that the United States finally got enough currency and credit to carry on the commercial expansion that followed the Revolutionary War. This necessary commercial development has been condemned by some economic historians as the era of wildcat banking. It has been regarded by the same authorities as an inflationary economic evil. Yet, as Hammond demonstrates, this privately printed money was our economic salvation. Apart from a few conspicuous exceptions, the banks that issued the notes were not deserving of the name "wildcat banks." The paper money they printed depreciated only about ten per cent as compared to the paper money of today, which takes the form of installment credit and is depreciating at the rate of about eighteen per cent because of the high interest rates necessary in the issuance of such credit.

Anthony Biddle, who managed the Bank of the United States, was too conservative to meet the needs of his time, and Jackson finally succeeded in wrecking it in the interests of sound currency and to prevent inflation. The result of this destruction was the creation of a rapidly expanding currency made available by the private banks that took the place of the Bank of the United States. It was the devotion of Jackson to the cause of sound money that accomplished this extraordinary result—a consequence he certainly did not intend or anticipate.

Economic historians usually ascribe the growth of private banks in the Jackson era to farmers who wanted inflation. They regard the early history of banking as an example of the Populist movement that took place after the Civil War, and which culminated in William Jennings Bryan's free-silver campaign. Since farmers wanted easy money in Bryan's day, it must be a part of their nature to want easy money. That myth has become part of our economic faith, and so history was written to conform to it.

As Hammond says, in the early days of the republic the farmers were unalterably opposed to currency expansion. It was the business interests in New York who felt repressed by the conservative fiscal policies of the Bank of the United States and who exerted the real pressure in support of Jackson's efforts to destroy the bank.

Today we stand with respect to the inadequacy of our consumer purchasing power in much the same situation as we were in after the Revolution. We have achieved something like Hamilton's dream in our Federal Reserve System. But the Federal Reserve today is acting in the same way that Biddle did with his Bank of the United States. Its principal fear, as mentioned previously, is inflation and its principal policy has been to raise interest rates and thus prevent the rapid industrial expansion that is supposed to lead to inflation.

Today private corporations, like the old wildcat banks, are busily engaged in "printing" the paper money without which there would be no effective consumer purchasing power to absorb the production of houses, automobiles, and so on through a long list of necessities and luxuries the distribution of which makes our economy go as well as it does. With credit cards, installment loans, government-financed housing, revolving credit at department stores, and other forms of credit, no one has to pay for anything in hard cash any more. Unfortunately for the farmers, the sole exception is food. No credit device has yet evolved that enables consumers to pay their grocery bills in anything other than cash. So surplus farm products are stored in warehouses while the automobile industry sells cars on credit to people who theoretically cannot afford them. It is interesting to note that John Steinbeck in his novel *The Grapes of Wrath* attempted to portray a family living in utter poverty. They did not have enough to eat, but they were able to travel across the continent during the Depression in an automobile —a product that in 1910 was the principal symbol of wealth and affluence. That people have been able to have cars has been accomplished by the private printing of money by automobile finance companies.

That type of money is increasing by leaps and bounds. The cost of service of the private debt has increased from fourteen per cent of national income in 1951 to twenty-one per cent today. Yet even this vast outpouring of private credit, which has grown from one hundred and four billion in 1929 to five hundred and eighty-five billion today, has not been sufficient to provide enough consumer purchasing power to keep our industrial plant working at full capacity. The period when it was able to do so ended with the Great Depression.

It is interesting to look back to the prosperity of 1928 and examine what conservative businessmen thought could be achieved by expanding private credit. In 1928, Garet Garrett, a wealthy newspaper owner and a conservative economist, wrote expressing the growing faith in the promise of business. He said:

It has made wealth available to an aggregate extent, hitherto unimaginable in the world. . . . In production it has brought about a marvelous economy of human effort. . . . For the distribution of goods it has perfected a web of exchange, so elaborate that the breaking of one strand is a disastrous one and yet so trustworthy that we take its conveniences every day for granted and never worry. . . . In the field of finance and credit it has evolved a mechanism of the highest dynamic intensity known. . . . In the Great War, American business amazed the world. John Law's

Mississippi Bubble dream of three centuries ago was a phantasy of escape from the boredom of toil. The bubble itself has been captured. That is the story of American business. The big problem was that American business despaired at overproduction. But the escape would come when business is no longer a feudal-minded thing . . . and perceives itself in the light of a subordinate human function, justified by service. (*The Economic Mind in American Civilization,* Joseph Dorfman, Volume IV, p. 84.)

This was written before the Great Depression, when the whole system of private credit collapsed. Today the printing of paper money by private organizations is infinitely greater than it was in 1928. Yet no one except perhaps the *Wall Street Journal* fears a similar collapse. Large areas of private credit, such as banks and housing, are covered by guarantees. Social security is a brake against absolute destitution. And, most important of all, the attitude that formerly prevented the government from doing anything in case of disaster because such government intervention would be socialistic has disappeared. Today we are confident that if some unexpected circumstances made it necessary, the government would take active and affirmative measures to restore consumer purchasing power. It will not be inhibited by the idea existing during the Depression that such measures are radical and unsound.

But even this vast expansion of private credit is not enough to make our productive wealth operate at full capacity as it did from the time of Andrew Jackson to 1928. The reason for this lies in the character of the industrial revolution of the twentieth century. That revolution has increased our capacity to produce so rapidly that the private sector of our economy cannot absorb it. There is no intellectual difficulty today in expanding currency and credit for any project the future income of which can be translated into dollars. The credit for such projects can be guaranteed by the government. Thus we can print money under the Federal Housing Administration and give it to contractors and builders to construct vast housing projects. Either the rents or the future purchase installments will pay for them. The cost does not appear anywhere in the fiscal budget.

But we cannot build schools and hospitals, preserve our water supply, improve recreational areas, or train doctors, because such programs are not self-liquidating in money terms. A trained doctor, for example, is not an asset, because his benefit to society cannot be expressed in monetary terms. Hence his training at public expense is an economic sin and a burden on the taxpayers and leads hell-bent to inflation.

Yet the social needs that cannot be met except by public spending are so pressing that the government never can balance its budget. Social legislation like medicare and federal aid to public projects meets thunderous opposition. Projects that are a direct claim on the federal treasury are considered more inflationary regardless of their future benefits to society than those, like housing, where financing is guaranteed by the federal government.

The contribution that the hard-money theorists made toward the creation of a soft currency by their destruction of the Bank of the United States is an interesting example of conservative monetary theory in action. The conservatives at the time of the Constitutional Convention wanted to restrict credit in order to avoid inflation, following the same general image that the Federal Reserve today uses as the basis for imposing high interest rates. James Madison wrote in *The Federalist:*

> The extension of the prohibition to bills of credit, must give pleasure to every citizen, in proportion to his love of justice, and his knowledge of the true springs of public prosperity. The loss which America has sustained since the peace from the pestilent effects of paper money on the necessary confidence between man and man, on the necessary confidence in the public councils, on the industry and morals of the people, and on the character of republican government, constitutes an enormous debt against the states chargeable with this unadvised measure, which must long remain unsatisfied; or rather an accumulation of guilt, which can be expiated no otherwise than by a voluntary sacrifice on the altar of justice, of the power which has been the instrument of it. (Hammond, *Banks and Politics in America,* p. 103.)

Curiously enough, this constitutional prohibition had little effect on the issue of bank notes. Bank notes, argued the learned men of the time (as they do today with respect to installment credit), were not money. They were merely IOU's which were only transferred from hand to hand. Nothing in the Constitution prohibited such private transactions. And so Madison's admonition was evaded.

Yet the feeling that we were living in economic sin still persisted and resulted in the most amazing legislative paradoxes. The theory was that the bank notes were redeemable in specie. But the need for specie in foreign trade was so great that the notes rapidly depreciated. This was because the colonies were constantly importing more than they exported. At the same time the need for an expanding currency was such that private banks seemed to have no limit on the notes they could circulate. This situation afforded to the private banks an opportunity to reap where they had not sowed, which is certainly an immoral way of making money. Therefore, to keep the banks honest, laws were passed requiring any bank that refused to redeem its notes in specie to forfeit its charter.

It was not easy to present a note for redemption at the issuing bank. This was because the banks circulated their notes in places as remote from the home office as possible. To carry a note from New York to Boston required a long and uncomfortable journey. For that reason it was unprofitable to present notes to an issuing bank unless they had been collected in substantial sums. But to present notes for redemption in large amounts was most disquieting and appeared to undermine the entire currency system. The law proved adequate to meet this situation. As Hammond wrote:

Individual creditors who sued to recover on unredeemed notes as on any unpaid debt seldom if ever gained anything. Stephen Girard's bank was sued in 1814 for refusing to redeem its notes during general suspension, but the plaintiffs seem to have sought to harass Mr. Girard rather than obtain payment—the amounts were small, one claimant, an umbrellamaker, suing for $25—and to have been discouraged by the firmness of his defense. Isaac Bronson, president of the Bank of Bridgeport, Connecticut, and a prominent capitalist in his day, sued in 1815, also during general suspension, for payment of notes of New York banks that he held. He seems to have got no satisfaction, but he got some prolix and extravagant abuse in the New York press for a course that was "unjust, impolitic, and odious." It was said in the New York *National Advocate,* 1 November 1815, that "any attempt at present or during the approaching winter to curtail discounts with a view to the payment of specie is fraught with misery and ruin to every class of society who depend upon their enterprise and industry for their prosperity in life."

In Windsor County, Vermont, in 1808 an indictment was sought against a man who held notes of the Vermont State Bank and demanded specie for them. It alleged that Jireh Durkee, of Boston, "being an evil-disposed person and not minding to get his living by truth and honest labor but contriving how he might injuriously obtain . . . money to support his idle and profligate way of life and diminish and destroy the resources of the state of Vermont and rendering it difficult and impossible for the good citizens thereof to obtain money," had presented $9,000 of the bank's notes at the Woodstock office and obliged the bank to pay them. The effect of such action, which would enable Durkee "to realize a filthy gain," said the complaint, was to prevent the bank from making loans to "good citizens." (Hammond, *Banks and Politics in America*, p. 179.)

Thus traditional moral problems were neatly resolved, and at the same time economic needs were adroitly met. This is the way that law, unlike economics, keeps up to date. But it is sometimes necessary for the law to move in mysterious ways its wonders to perform.

There was also a constitutional difficulty in the way of compelling banks to redeem their notes in specie. States and, by necessary implication, corporations chartered by the states were not authorized to print money. They did so only on the theory that it had been previously held that bank notes were not money. But if this were true, what right had a state to penalize the issuance of notes? Therefore, it became necessary for courts to hold that bank notes were money after all, which they promptly did.

A most amazing example of the effect of the economic morality of the time is found in an act passed in Virginia prohibiting the issuance of bank notes of less than five dollars in value. This would be about the equivalent of a hundred dollars today. There was such desperate need for small change that notes that would be used for that purpose never had to be redeemed. They stayed in circulation until they were worn out. Certainly it seemed most immoral for a private party to reap an unjust reward in this way. Therefore, the Virginia legislature passed an act abolishing all notes that could be used for change. Thus economic morality was vindicated though the citizens of Virginia were deprived of their small change.

One of the few men of his time who had a realistic conception of the needs of the American economy was Alexander Hamilton. Unlike Jefferson, who would have kept the United States a rural agricultural economy, Hamilton was interested in rapid industrial development. To accomplish that, a vast expansion of the currency was immediately needed. Soldiers were engaging in riots because they were unpaid, but no one seriously considered issuing currency for such a purpose. It would have smacked of the welfare state. There was, therefore, only one proper way to expand the currency. That was for the federal government to guarantee the depreciated bonds the states had issued to carry on the Revolution. Hamilton was successful in loading the impoverished union with thirty million dollars of debt. He went around saying that a public debt was a public blessing.

This was economic immorality of the worst order, and it was so considered by the best minds of the time. Nevertheless, it worked. The money went into the hands of industrially minded entrepreneurs, and the United States got its start in the development of manufacturing.

No political figure with ideas similar to Hamilton's appeared on the American scene until Harry Hopkins, with his proposal to spend us out of the Great Depression. It is indeed strange that Hamilton should today be the patron saint of the hard-money Republican party while hard-money Jefferson should be the patron saint of the free-spending Democratic party.

The struggle between Andrew Jackson and the Bank of the United States is another amazing illustration of the identity of our present economic thinking with that of the early days of the republic. Above all, Jackson was a hard-money statesman. He hated and distrusted banks of any kind or character. When Jackson finally decided to break the Bank of the United States, he withdrew all its government deposits and placed them in private banks, commonly known as Jackson's pet banks. There was at the time a surplus in the U.S. Treasury amounting to about thirty million dollars. This Jackson determined to apportion among the states. There was another factor that complicated the currency situation. Jackson, being a hard-money man, insisted that public lands be paid for in specie. For this reason the greater part of the nation's specie was out west. When the surplus was distributed, the states drew on Jackson's pet banks for their shares. The pet banks were, of course, unable to pay. The restriction of credit due to removal of deposits from the Bank of the United States caused a severe depression. In the meantime, the specie supply was carried up the rivers and down the rivers, and to and from the West and East— a truly ludicrous spectacle.

And what became of the government surplus? It was never distributed. It simply disappeared into thin air, dissolved by the financial calamity that shook the country. The collapse of private credit due to the calling of its notes by the Bank of the United States caused bankruptcies and the consequent falling off of federal revenue. Jackson himself was angry and amazed. He could not understand what had happened, any more than the budget-balancing and hard-money experts can understand what is happening in our economy today.

In spite of Alexander Hamilton, the main current of American economic thinking has remained adamantly opposed to spending as a way of achieving prosperity—except, of course, in time of war, when economists are shoved aside in the face of stern necessity.

We are now faced with a world situation in which only two nations, the United States and Russia, have any semblance of a logical and systematic philosophy of government. No one can quite tell what system industrial Europe is following. Economists who examine it to see what makes it tick are baffled and describe it as a mixed economy—a phrase that leaves much to be desired with respect to clarity.

Of the two great powers that attempt to follow a logical economic philosophy, Russia adheres to the revolutionary ideal of a welfare state designed to fill the needs of its people through direct action by a central government. But Russia is incapable of producing enough goods to meet the needs of its people. The United States, for reasons buried deep in its traditions, regards humanitarian ideas and the welfare state as the most extreme living example of economic sin, but its system since 1953 has been unable to generate the purchasing power to distribute its vast productive capacity to the people who desperately need the goods.

CHAPTER TWELVE

The Rise and Fall of the Blue Eagle

Since the passage of the Sherman Anti-Trust Act in 1890 the American business economy has been based upon the ideal of free competitive enterprise. Prior to the Depression we departed from that ideal in practice, but we never accepted the cartel system of Europe as a legitimate principle of government.

The story of the rise and fall of the National Industrial Recovery Act is the story of our first and only attempt to set up a European cartel system giving private business concerns the right to fix prices and restrict production, an attempt that ended in failure and the reinstatement of the antitrust laws as a cornerstone of our business structure.

Prior to the Depression, during the 1920's, the antitrust laws had been put upon the shelf. As we pointed out earlier, a system of absentee ownership of local enterprise in the West and the South by the industrial East had robbed the West and the South, particularly the agricultural communities, of their purchasing power. For a time this lost purchasing power had been replaced by the stock-market boom, in which everyone participated and during which brokers' offices were opened in the smaller cities. With the crash of 1929 that purchasing power disappeared.

It was natural, according to the economic creed of that time, for the public to believe that the cause of the Depression was not the disappearance of purchasing power, but, rather, the falling prices that were causing nationwide bankruptcies. In every depression the public has felt the same at the outset. Communities have no money because they cannot get their former prices for their goods. Inevitably, the belief arose that economic salvation depended upon restoring prices to their former level. This, of course, could not be done without restricting production. And so the nation's business, with few dissents, organized itself under the National Recovery Administration.

The symbol of the NRA was the Blue Eagle. Parades were formed under the auspices of that benevolent bird. Every shopkeeper prominently displayed it in his window. Those who did not were ostracized. The nation had determined to pull itself out of the Depression and get rich again by the simple device of raising prices and restricting production. Never before had the country exhibited so much unified enthusiasm for such an alien ideal.

Perhaps this was fortunate. The very fact that the ideal of fixed prices and restricted production was so foreign to our traditional economic faith made this adventure a short-lived one. The businessmen who supported it devoutly believed that strong labor unions were inflationary and a dangerous threat to maximum production under monopoly prices. Section 7(a) of the NRA was designed to compel industrial leaders to recognize and bargain with strong labor unions. It was the insistence of the government on observance of the principle of Section 7(a) that wrecked the NRA. Try as he would, General Hugh Johnson, NRA administrator, could not get industry to accept this principle. NRA officials worked in a fever of activity, and the lights in their offices burned all night, but few codes providing for the rights of union labor were accepted by industry.

Meantime, disappointed industry leaders began to retain learned counsel, who expressed grave doubt as to the constitutionality of the National Industrial Recovery Act. NRA officials shared these doubts and were afraid to go into court to impose on industry the codes that industry refused to accept voluntarily. Enforcement was rapidly going to pieces. Finally, the issue could be avoided no longer. The case of *A.L.A. Schechter Poultry Corporation* v. *United States,* 295 U. S. 495 commonly known as the "Sick Chicken" case, reached the Supreme Court. The decision came down in May, 1935. A unanimous Court, composed of both liberal and conservative justices, decided that the NRA was unconstitutional. The decision was based on the ground that the act, which permitted committees chosen from industry to fix prices and restrict production, was an unconstitutional delegation of legislative powers by Congress to private parties. As Justice Benjamin Cardozo said in his concurring opinion, it was "delegation running riot."

The doctrine of unconstitutional delegation of power has never been applied by the Supreme Court of the United States since the Schechter case. Many cases have been brought before the Court in reliance upon the principle of the Schechter decision; arguments based on the Schechter case have been made over and over again. But so far as I have been able to ascertain, the Supreme Court has ignored them. It has not attempted to distinguish the Schechter case. That decision stands on the books as an anomaly rather than a valid precedent. But the decision was fortunate in that it freed our economy from an obsolete idea completely alien to both our economic and our legal traditions.

The initial popularity of the NRA among businessmen was based on the theory that management of our economy could safely be left to the heads of our great corporations. James Burnham, in a book entitled *The Managerial Revolution,* published in 1941, which became a best seller in business circles, later tried to revive the NRA. He thought that in the control of production and distribution by managers of big business, acting in concert, lay the economic hope of the future. The difference between Burnham's idea and the NRA was that Burnham saw no necessity for any government curb on management by the American business elite. Burnham argued that American businessmen had matured since the robber barons, who operated in violation of the principle of the antitrust laws in the latter part of the nineteenth century. Private ownership, Burnham said, had disappeared. The trained business managers who were responsible for the activities of great nationwide business corporations were the elite who were destined to plan and conduct our economy and to make it a rational system instead of a disorderly competitive system. This was in effect the philosophy of the European cartels with which United States business leaders had been so zealously co-operating in the days before the Depression. Fortunately, this ideal, logical as it appeared to be, was so foreign to our competitive economic faith that it could not survive. It had already failed in practical operation when the Supreme Court of the United States struck it down. Because of its practical failure, President Roosevelt, I believe, was greatly relieved when the Supreme Court put it out of its misery.

But there is one result accomplished by the passage of the NRA that was a totally unexpected side benefit. The freedom and independence in growth of our present labor unions have their origin in the attempted enforcement of Section 7(a) of the NRA. This section, the application of which to NRA codes was so violently opposed by our industrial leaders and which was one of the rocks on which the practical administration of the NRA was wrecked, has now become a part of our economic and legal traditions. It is the authority on which our present labor law is based and to which the National Labor Relations Board owes its present power. Section 7(a) reads as follows:

Every code of fair competition, agreement, and license approved, prescribed, or issued under this title shall contain the following conditions: (1) That employees shall have the right to organize and bargain collectively through representatives of their own choosing, and shall be free from the interference, restraint, or coercion of employers of labor, or their agents, in the designation of such representatives or in self-organization or in other concerted activities for the purpose of collective bargaining or other mutual aid or protection; (2) that no employee and no one seeking employment shall be required as a condition of employment to join any company union or to refrain from joining, organizing, or assisting a labor organization of his own choosing; and (3) that employers shall comply with the maximum hours of labor, minimum rates of pay, and other conditions of employment, approved or prescribed by the President. (Vol. 48, United States Statutes at Large, p. 198.)

Today the principle of this section of the discarded and discredited NRA has been embodied in the Taft-Hartley Act. The opposition has withered away. Thus, the NRA, which started out as a grand design to make the nation prosperous by raising prices and restricting production, has become the origin of great reform in labor relations.

CHAPTER THIRTEEN

"An Idiot in a Powder Mill"

In March, 1938, shortly after the death of the NRA, I was appointed by President Roosevelt to serve as the head of the Antitrust Division of the Department of Justice. I eagerly accepted. The enforcement of the Sherman Act at that time seemed to me to be the most important objective of our national government.

When I took office, years of disuse of the Sherman Act, culminating in its repudiation by NRA, had made violation of the antitrust laws common, almost respectable. I will never forget the amazement of the Wisconsin Alumni Research Foundation, an organization whose profits were used to support the University of Wisconsin, when the Justice Department charged it with using a vitamin patent to raise prices and restrict manufacture of important food products. It never occurred to the high-minded management of this foundation that it was doing anything wrong. The indictment was considered an attack on education itself.

I believed that my principal function was to convince American businessmen that the Sherman Act represented something more than a pious platitude; second, that its enforcement was an important economic policy. But there was very little support among economists for the latter notion.

Roosevelt was a great innovator. When the NRA failed in practice, he was bold enough to try something else. When I was appointed, he had put the monopoly problem at the top of his list. The staff of lawyers employed by the Antitrust Division was doubled, and then doubled again. Young lawyers of great talent—Hugh B. Cox, Edward Levi (now Provost of the University of Chicago), Fowler Hamilton (later head of the A.I.D.), Joseph Borkin (an economist), Leo F. Tierney, and others—became my assistants. I established branch offices in the principal cities of the United States. The economists on my staff studied the concentration of economic power in various industries, including building, oil, housing, medical care, and the press.

This change of policy on the part of the administration, which had previously favored restricted production and administered prices, was considered by the business community to be an outrage. One of the first of my prosecutions was against the principal oil companies for an illegal conspiracy to fix prices. Arthur Krock, of the New York *Times,* a favorite of the administration, and the press from coast to coast thundered their indignation. They charged, not without some justice, that the oil companies had been following the lead of the government and were now being indicted for their co-operation in the days of the NRA.

Two other indictments followed, and were met with equal indignation. One was the indictment of the American Medical Association for attempting to put all group health organizations out of business by refusing physicians attached to such organizations access to their local hospitals. The other was an indictment of the Associated Press, which would not permit new competitive newspapers to have the benefit of their essential wire service. The indictment was said to be an unconstitutional restriction on freedom of the press, an act of an unprincipled dictator. The Associated Press later gathered together and published two bound volumes of frenzied editorial denunciations of the Antitrust Division. These volumes are among my most treasured possessions.

As indictments of respectable people began to pour out from the Justice Department in unprecedented numbers, cries of outrage could be heard from coast to coast. I was pictured as a wild man whose sanity was in considerable doubt. One major newspaper referred to me as "an idiot in a powder mill." Letters of protest poured into the White House.

Among the prosecutions subject to violent editorial attack was the one against General Electric for a price-fixing conspiracy bra-

zenly and openly conducted, without the protective concealment
employed in the recent electrical-machinery price-fixing conspiracy
so prominently reported in the press. The prosecution was then regarded as an attack on big business, and General Electric had substantial editorial support. In the recent case, the conservative press
was unanimous in denouncing General Electric for failure to obey
the antitrust laws. Thus, the pendulum has swung during the short
period of twenty-five years, and the antitrust laws have regained
their place as part of our conservative economic faith.

Though antitrust prosecutions during my term of office had little
conservative support, there was one advantage that no longer exists.
Business leaders during the lull in enforcement of the 1920's and
the practical repudiation of the antitrust laws during NRA had
felt no necessity for concealment of their illegal activities. For example, in the files of the Standard Oil Company of New Jersey we
found memorandums signed by corporate officers with respect to
arrangements made after war had started in Europe (though before the attack on Pearl Harbor) showing agreement between
Standard Oil and I. G. Farben to suppress the production of artificial rubber in the United States in exchange for German agreement not to compete in petroleum products. It was common to run
across a letter confirming some illegal arrangement with the injunction at the bottom "Destroy this letter after you have read it,"
but which had nevertheless been preserved in the corporate files.
Business leaders before 1938 felt secure from antitrust prosecution.
Today that security no longer exists. Price-fixing schemes no longer
have the support of editorial opinion. It is now an exceedingly
difficult task, therefore, to uncover evidence of a conspiracy to violate the antitrust laws.

By and large, the antitrust prosecutions conducted by the Department of Justice when I was there were successful (with some exceptions). There was only one conspicuous failure, and that was
in a field where I thought the precedents were all in my favor: the
field of labor-union activity. It was my belief that the Norris–La
Guardia Act exempted labor from the antitrust laws so long as the
union was pursuing what was called, in the language of the act, its
"legitimate activities." I believed that the legitimate activities of a
labor union were confined to wages, conditions of labor, and fringe

benefits. To pursue these objectives, labor, I thought, could exercise the monopoly power of its unions. But when a labor union utilized its collective power to destroy another union, or to prevent the introduction of modern labor-saving devices, or to require the employer to pay for useless and unnecessary labor, I believed that the exemption had been exceeded and that the union was operating in violation of the Sherman Act.

My first labor prosecution was against the United Brotherhood of Carpenters and Joiners of America. Anheuser-Busch had had a collective-bargaining agreement with the International Association of Machinists under the terms of which that union was entitled to install machinery in the plants the company was building. The Carpenters union demanded that it be given the right to install the machinery. Because Anheuser-Busch adhered to its agreement with the machinists, the Carpenters union struck, thereby tying up the entire Anheuser-Busch project. I indicted individual officers of the Carpenters union and its president, William L. Hutcheson (who was later convicted of conspiracy in restraint of trade). My theory was that the destruction of one union by another was not a legitimate labor activity and, therefore, the union could not rely on its statutory exemption from the antitrust laws. The Supreme Court of the United States ruled to the contrary, though admitting that precedent was on my side, and held that the "legislative policy" expressed in the Norris–La Guardia Act required the Court to overrule former, decided cases. Thus the validity of the so-called jurisdictional strike was firmly established in *United States* v. *Hutcheson,* 312 U. S. 219 (1941).

I still believed that there were labor activities that exceeded labor's exemption from the Sherman Act. In New Orleans, a local union of truck drivers had obtained an agreement sanctioned by the National Labor Relations Board to carry on the trucking activities of certain employers. The rival Teamsters union demanded the right to conduct these activities, and when the employers relied upon the contract with the local union the Teamsters refused to transport shipments to any project which employed members of the union which the National Labor Relations Board had approved as the proper bargaining agent. I thought this was different from the jurisdictional strike in the previous case. Here the strike was against a contract approved by the National Labor Relations Board, which the employers had to carry out or be subject to penalty. This time the Supreme Court of the United States affirmed the dismissal of the indictment without an opinion, citing only the Hutcheson case. I do not understand the basis of that decision and, since the Supreme Court did not take the trouble to explain it, in all probability I never will.

A third attempt to limit the exemption of labor from the antitrust laws was an indictment of the International Hod Carriers Union in Chicago. The Hod Carriers union struck against construction projects that used ready-mixed concrete. The machinery that mixed the concrete was made by union labor. I thought that this was different from the Hutcheson case because it was a strike against efficient building methods to the irreparable damage of the consumer. Again the Supreme Court of the United States dismissed the indictment without opinion, citing the Hutcheson case.

I gave up the antitrust laws as a method of curbing labor abuses and brought a case against Local 807 of the Teamsters union in New York under the antiracketeering act. Members of Local 807 would wait at the tunnels from New Jersey for trucks from out of the state carrying products into New York. They would then demand that they be employed. If the owners of the trucks did not comply, violence was used, and men were brutally beaten. This, I thought, plainly came within the definition of racketeering that was condemned by the antiracketeering act. This time the Supreme Court of the United States favored me with an opinion, although it decided the case against me. Justice James F. Byrnes, writing for the majority, said that when members of Local 807 demanded unnecessary employment and pay at the point of a gun the relationship of employer and employee was firmly established, and the antiracketeering act did not apply. The decision puzzled me then and, after mature reflection, it still puzzles me (*United States* v. *Local 807, Etc.,* 315 U. S. 521 (1942)).

The keystone of the arch that supports labor abuses is a case decided by the Supreme Court long after I left the Antitrust Division in 1943—the case of *Guss* v. *Utah Labor Relations Board,* 353 U. S. 1 (1957). There a complaint had been made by the employers to the National Labor Relations Board against an illegitimate strike. The Board declined to act on the ground that though inter-state commerce was involved, it was not sufficiently important to justify the Board's taking action. Whereupon the employers appealed to the state labor board, which enjoined the union from striking. The Supreme Court of the United States reversed this decision on the ground that it was the intention of Congress to occupy the entire field of interstate labor relations and for that reason the state board had no jurisdiction.

Under this line of authority a few unions that occupy bottleneck positions, so that they can tie up the entire operations of a plant, have achieved extraordinary power. The Teamsters union under the benevolent dictatorship of James Hoffa is the most conspicuous example. The Teamsters union has the power (not the right) to direct its members not to handle at their destination goods shipped by any manufacturer whose conduct is unacceptable to the union. The near-monopoly control of the Teamsters over truck transportation is such that this power can put a manufacturer out of business. This is ordinarily called "hot-cargoing goods in transit." It is an unfair labor practice. However, the National Labor Relations Board has neither the time nor the personnel to handle the constant cases that arise with small businessmen. Under the Supreme Court decisions the state authorities have no jurisdiction. That leaves the small manufacturer the remedy of suing the union for damages. But before such a suit can wind its weary way through court the manufacturer will be gone. As a result, the Teamsters union has become the fastest-growing and most powerful union in the United States; it is able to take advantage of its strategic position as the sole highway by which the employer can get his goods to consumers. Our national industrial unions, such as the Automobile Workers and the Steelworkers, are unable to exercise such a power because they do not control the manufacturer's access to his market. Their only weapon is a direct strike against the manufacturer himself. Therefore, if the Teamsters choose to organize any branch of manufacturing, using the hot-cargo as their tool, they can make it difficult indeed for the employer to stick to his former union.

Today there is still no effective curb against the abuse by unions of their privileges, though some of the practices described have been declared unfair under the Taft-Hartley Act. But apart from the field of labor, the antitrust laws have been a tremendously effective force in keeping industry free. Without these laws the Jimmy Hoffas of industry would wield even more power than the Teamsters have been able to exercise in the field of labor.

CHAPTER FOURTEEN

The Sherman Act as a Charter of Economic Freedom

During the period from 1938 to 1943, when I was head of the Antitrust Division, I wrote a book entitled *The Bottlenecks of Business.* In that book it was irrefutably proved that in enforcing the antitrust laws there could be found the complete solution of all of the ills of the Great Depression. I no longer believe that this is true. Our economy is far more complicated than that. However, the antitrust laws have been a most effective brake against the cartelization of industry in the United States, which would inevitably have happened had Roosevelt not revived the Sherman Act and breathed the breath of life into it in 1938. The history of how it happened that the ideal of the Sherman Act became a dominant and enduring part of our industrial structure is an interesting one. And the real father of the Sherman Act is not Senator John Sherman, but Theodore Roosevelt, who took it off the shelf after ten years of innocuous desuetude as part of his campaign to assert the authority of government over business.

Ever since the Civil War there has been a continuous conflict between two opposing ideals in American economic thinking. The first of them says that business management, if relieved from the rigors of cutthroat competition, will be fair and benevolent. The age of competition is over, the theory continues, and great corporations with the power to dominate prices benefit the economy. In the field of big business, this philosophy justifies giant mergers. In the field of small business, it leads to the passage of fair-trade laws and similar forms of legalized price-fixing.

J. P. Morgan is the traditional hero of this philosophy. He organized United States Steel, our first billion-dollar enterprise, to make investments secure, and to eliminate cutthroat competition in steel. Andrew Carnegie, who was doing pretty well as an aggressive competitor, was paid twice what he thought his business was worth to go along. Morgan made the steel business safer for the investor but tough on the consumer, and it has been so ever since.

The opposing economic ideal says that industrial progress can best be obtained in a free market, where prices are fixed by competition and where success depends on efficiency rather than market control. Under this theory it becomes the government's function not to control or regulate, but only to maintain freedom in the market place by prosecuting combinations whenever they become large enough to fix prices. Henry Ford represents this ideal. By producing cars at cut prices on a nationwide scale, he helped wreck many of the existing automobile companies. But at the same time he revolutionized the industry.

This second ideal is also represented by a remarkable piece of legislation called the Sherman Anti-Trust Act, passed by Congress on July 2, 1890, which states that "Every contract, combination in the form of trust or otherwise, or conspiracy, in restraint of trade or commerce among the several States, or with foreign nations, is hereby declared to be illegal." The act goes on to authorize the federal government to proceed against trusts that violate the act, and empowers federal district courts with jurisdiction over such violations.

If I may be permitted to say so, as one who has had some experience with enforcing it, this law is historically unique. Prior to the Second World War, no other nation had any legislation like it. It is different from any other criminal statute because it makes it a crime to violate a vaguely stated economic policy—and a policy, what is more, on which public attitudes often change. The average American citizen—and, indeed, the average court which administers the Sherman Act—would like to believe simultaneously in both of the conflicting economic ideals described above. For that reason, the Supreme Court swings back and forth in Sherman Act cases, in more important ones splitting five to four. The history of the Sherman Act is the history of the conflicts and compromises between these two economic ideals.

But the dominant ideal in our economic thinking has been the ideal of the Sherman Act. The business pressures against its actual enforcement are great, but support of the *principle* of the act is so unanimous that no one ever suggests its repeal. Big business, labor, farmers—each economic group wants the Sherman Act strictly enforced, against everyone but itself.

In meeting these pressures the Sherman Act has shown extraordinary elasticity. It may bend at times, but it always bounces back. Thus it is like a constitutional provision rather than an ordinary statute, and its history tells much about our national attempt to create an economy that will be at the same time both disciplined and free.

How was this ideal born in the first place? The most improbable feature of the Sherman Act is that this apparently anti-big-business measure was introduced by a senator who was a high-tariff advocate and an extreme conservative, and was passed with only one dissenting vote by a big-business Republican Congress.

The initial pressure for it came from agriculture, which since the Civil War had been reduced to a fairly steady depression. Railroad monopolies were charging farmers all the traffic would bear, and sometimes a little more. Rates were rigged to favor big railroad customers and ruin small ones. As farm income fell, prices that farmers had to pay rose steadily. Monopolies kept them high. If the pressure from the agricultural states was strong, so was the rebellion against other aspects of the dog-eat-dog business ethics of the times. The necessity of some restraint on such practices came at last to be recognized even by business itself.

Big business during the latter half of the nineteenth century had come to regard competition as an unmitigated evil which could be alleviated only by combination. At first the combinations took the form of "pools" or agreements—regional rather than national—to restrain trade, to control prices, to restrict output and divide markets. But businessmen soon learned that agreements between members of an industry were too weak. Only the surrender of business independence by the units could make domination of the market certain.

Pools gave way to trusts, the first of which, established by Standard Oil in 1879, became a model for subsequent business combinations. Each party to the trust surrendered his stock-voting power to trustees, receiving trust certificates in return. Thus the nine trustees of the Standard Oil Trust, without the investment of a dollar, obtained absolute power over the nation's oil industry. The pattern set by Standard Oil was so widely followed that the name "trust" became a byword for any large industrial combination even after the trust device had been abandoned.

Prior to the Sherman Act the federal government had no power to prevent predatory business activities. Therefore, the states themselves began an ineffective attack on the trusts in state courts. In 1887 Louisiana prosecuted the Cotton Oil Trust; in 1889 California prosecuted the Sugar Trust; in 1890 Nebraska prosecuted the Whiskey Trust. The attorney general of Ohio sought to repeal the charter of the Standard Oil Company of Ohio.

In 1892 the supreme court of Ohio ordered the local oil company to sever its connections with the Standard Oil Trust. The order was never effectively enforced. But these state attacks on it made the device so risky that corporate organizations looked for some other form of combination that could not be prosecuted under state law. New Jersey provided the model, by amending its incorporation statute to permit one corporation to own the stock of another. From then on it was easy.

Corporations A, B, and C would give fifty-one per cent of their stock to holding company X. Holding company X would in turn give fifty-one per cent of its stock to holding company Y. Thus holding company Y, with only about twenty-five-per-cent interest in the operating companies, controlled them completely. Y would transfer enough stock to Z, at which point Z needed only twelve and a half per cent to control the industry. And so on until fantastic pyramids were built up. No state could attack these pyramids because they were legal in the state of incorporation. Only Congress could interfere with this process.

In July, 1888, John Sherman, Senator from Ohio, introduced the resolution that led to the passage of the Sherman Act. He had been

Secretary of the Treasury under President Rutherford B. Hayes and was known as an expert in finance and taxation. He was big-business-minded and an ardent advocate of high tariffs. In this important respect, he was opposed to the very interests that were demanding antimonopoly legislation. In the farm belt the tariff was called the mother of monopoly. Sherman could have no part in such radical doctrine. His resolution reconciled that contradiction very neatly. It asked the Finance Committee to report on a bill that would

tend to preserve freedom of trade and production, the natural competition of increasing production, the lowering of prices by such competition, and the full benefit designed by and hitherto conferred by the policy of the government to protect and encourage American industries by levying duties on imported goods.

In other words, Sherman contended that the increased production by local industry protected by tariffs would more than offset the increased prices due to the tariffs, if domestic competition was free and unrestrained.

The Sherman Act as it reads today was passed in the Senate fifty-two yeas to one nay, and signed by President Benjamin Harrison on July 2, 1890. No votes were cast against it in the House.

The act is unexampled in economic legislation. In effect it says: "We want competition in the United States and we will leave it to the federal judiciary to determine, case by case, just what action constitutes a restraint on competition." That this law could be passed by a conservative Republican Congress whose most influential leaders were closely associated with big business is remarkable in the extreme. Many writers have argued that the act was a hypocritical piece of legislation, designed as a political sop to the farm belt, and that no one expected it to be of any consequence. Even Senator Nelson W. Aldrich, who was known as J. P. Morgan's floor broker in the Senate, voted for it.

Such facts are sometimes cited to support the view that the original passage of the bill was only an attempt to placate Western senators in exchange for votes on higher tariffs. But this interpretation has been completely refuted by Hans B. Thorelli in his book *The Federal Antitrust Policy,* the most complete and objective analysis of the history of American monopoly policy. Thorelli concludes that a majority of congressmen were sincere and that the Sherman Act represented for men of both parties the symbol and the image of what they sincerely desired the American economy to become.

By that I do not mean that the Republican supporters of the act would have welcomed the breakup of great American combinations into smaller units. At the same time, they would have instinctively rejected the system of domestic and international cartels that had been growing up in Germany and spreading to France from 1870 on, which would surely have become the American pattern if the Sherman Act had not been passed.

The Sherman Act fitted in with the American economic and legal philosophy that was religiously held in 1890 and which is still our dominant philosophy today. In 1890 Americans distrusted any form of governmental regulation. It was the tradition of the American common law that the relation between business and government should be based on some broad common-law principle that would acquire definite meaning only through a series of court decisions. The Sherman Act followed that tradition. Our faith in the common law was such that Congress believed that the courts could give a better and more practical meaning to the principles of the act than Congress could possibly do by further definition or regulation.

The Sherman Act was definitely on the shelf during the administrations of Presidents Harrison, Cleveland, and McKinley. Cleveland's attorney general not only instituted no proceedings, but dropped the prosecution of the notorious Cash Register Trust, even though he had won a victory in the lower court. Under Cleveland the principal impact of the Sherman Act was against labor in breaking the Pullman strike. McKinley was equally indifferent to the act. During his four and one half years only three suits were brought.

The first Sherman Act decision by the Supreme Court was in the case of *United States* v. *E. C. Knight Co.* It amounted to a virtual repeal of the act. The Supreme Court held that the Sugar Trust, in acquiring a monopoly over sugar manufacturing, affected interstate commerce only indirectly and, therefore, did not violate the act. As Justice John Marshall Harlan pointed out in his dissent:

"While the opinion of the Court in this case does not declare the Act of 1890 to be unconstitutional, it defeats the main object for which it was passed." The Knight case thus emasculated the Sherman Act. As a result of that decision the government became powerless to prevent the formation of a monopoly through the device of a holding company.

Yet within the short space of eight years, through the daring and ingenuity of Theodore Roosevelt, the Sherman Act was transformed again from a meaningless and ineffective formula into a sharp weapon. Theodore Roosevelt was one of the few politicians of his time who had seriously studied the antitrust problem. He had his first experience with monopoly power as a New York State assemblyman during the investigation of Jay Gould. He campaigned for re-election on the antimonopoly issue in 1882. In 1899, as governor, he wrote: "I have been in a great quandary over trusts. I do not know what attitude to take. I do not intend to play a demagogue. On the other hand, I do intend, so far as in me lies, to see that the rich man is held to the same accountability as the poor man, and when the rich man is rich enough *to buy unscrupulous advice from very able lawyers, this is not always easy."* (Italics added.)

It was the empire-building ambition of J. P. Morgan that gave Roosevelt his chance. During the last year of the McKinley administration the Northern Securities Company had been formed as a compromise between E. H. Harriman and Morgan in their fight to control the Northern Pacific Railroad. The holding-company device was used to combine under one management two of the nation's largest competing railroads, the Northern Pacific and the Great Northern. Had the scheme succeeded, it could have led to the domination of all American railroads by this group. It could have created a pattern for the cartelization of all American industry.

Roosevelt, as one of the first acts of his administration, determined to attack this respected citadel of corporate power. This enterprise was very different from that of using the act to attack mere dishonesty in business, and Roosevelt must have realized that the legal odds were much against him. A careful lawyer would have advised him that the Knight case exempted J. P. Morgan's ambitious plans. The decision in the Knight case stood for the principle that the acquisition of monopoly control was immune from attack because, though it affected prices "indirectly," it was not a conspiracy to fix them "directly."

The issue as Roosevelt saw it went far beyond the merger of the two railroads involved in Northern Securities. The issue was nothing less than effective national sovereignty. The federal government had been relegated to such minor roles as distributing the mail and collecting tariff duties. Big business was the real sovereign in infinitely more important areas. In the Northern Securities case, Roosevelt was to obtain for the federal government a Magna Charta limiting the power of the business princes.

Roosevelt gambled that the Supreme Court, with new faces in it since the Knight case, would repudiate or at least alter that decision. He directed Attorney General Philander C. Knox to draw up a case against the Northern Securities Company. It was to be a head-on attack on the philosophy of the Knight case decision. Fully aware of the tremendous pressures that would be exerted against him, he directed Knox to prepare the prosecution in complete secrecy. Not even his close friend and adviser Elihu Root, the Secretary of War, was told.

When Knox finally released to the press his intention to prosecute Northern Securities, there was consternation and panic in the financial world. Root, a Wall Street lawyer, was dismayed and resentful. Morgan and his like-minded friend Senator Chauncey Depew, of New York, descended upon the White House like the emissaries of some independent sovereignty whose rights were being invaded. But by that time the prosecution was a *fait accompli*.

On this case all of Roosevelt's antitrust program depended. It came before the Supreme Court in March, 1904. By that time, Roosevelt had appointed Oliver Wendell Holmes to the Court, believing that Holmes's reputation as a liberal was an indication that he would vote against the tremendous extension of monopoly power. In this hope he was to be bitterly disappointed. Had Holmes been able to win over to his side Justice David Brewer, as he thought he had, the legitimacy of monopoly would have been established, perhaps for all time, in this country as it was in Europe.

The Court, which was bitterly divided, five to four, ruled for the government. The majority held that the Sherman Act was intended to prevent giant combinations formed under any device and that such exercise of congressional power over industry was not unconstitutional.

Holmes, who wrote one of the two principal dissents, made the statement, believed by many at that time, that the Sherman Act was not intended to prevent combinations in restraint of trade. He said: "It was the ferocious extreme of competition with others, not the cessation of competition among the partners, that was the evil feared."

Holmes had faith in the benevolence and efficiency of the rich. He believed that the Constitution should protect them in their efforts to create industrial empires. But the ideal of a dynamic competitive economy and government-maintained freedom of industrial opportunity, I believe, was beyond him. He would have sincerely approved of the system of domestic and international cartels that dominated industry and caused it to stagnate in Europe before the First World War. Holmes did not believe in the antitrust laws. In 1910, he wrote Frederick Pollock, "I don't disguise my belief that the Sherman Act is a humbug based on economic ignorance and incompetence."

Roosevelt, though a rich man himself, was one of the few men of his time to realize the destiny of America as a land of economic freedom. He had the ability to infuse the public with his point of view. Senator Sherman initiated the antitrust act, but it was Teddy Roosevelt who gave it vigor and meaning, made the policy of the Sherman Act an economic religion and its violation an economic sin, and, finally, made it emotionally impossible for American business to co-operate in the European cartel system.

To appraise the effect of the Sherman Act on American business institutions correctly we must view it apart from particular prosecutions, or particular periods of enforcement or nonenforcement. Theodore Roosevelt's achievement was to enshrine the ideal of the act as part of our national folklore. And its influence has continued in a far more potent way than perhaps any other statute on the books. The image of the Sherman Act has not prevented tremendous concentrations of economic power, but it has prevented such concentrations from obtaining legitimate status.

Only once since its passage has the principle of the act been repudiated. That was in production codes of the National Recovery

Administration during the New Deal. They were designed to raise prices and restrict production, after the European model. The theory was that this would protect investments and rescue business from insolvency.

But the competitive tradition represented by the Sherman Act was too strong for the NRA. The act over the years, even when it was unenforced, had built up an abiding faith that the elimination of competition in business was morally and economically wrong. Then the Supreme Court threw out the NRA, and Franklin Roosevelt turned back to the antitrust laws as a major instrument of economic policy.

The enforcement program of the Antitrust Division of the Justice Department on a nationwide scale between 1938 and the outbreak of the Second World War survived all attacks. This was because American businessmen did not want to repudiate the principle of the Sherman Act, however much they disliked particular prosecutions. It showed that the Henry Ford tradition was still dominant.

It is difficult now to appraise the economic effect of the revival of the Sherman Act at that time. Opinions differ, and my own is, of course, biased. But this at least can be said: American business learned that the Sherman Act was something more than a false front to our business structure. The public gained an idea of the purpose of the act, the act itself gained renewed vitality, and American business approved this revival.

There are two principal evils of concentrated economic power in a democracy. The first is the power of concentrated industry to charge administered prices rather than prices based on competitive demand. As a result, resources are not efficiently allocated; production is restricted and consumer wants go unfulfilled; and there is no incentive to reduce costs and to make innovations. A second evil is the tendency of such empires to swallow up local businesses and drain away local capital. Prior to the Depression this condition had advanced so far that our concentrated industrial groups had helped destroy their own markets by siphoning off the dollars that could have been a source of local purchasing power.

It is idle to say that periodic enforcement of the antitrust laws has solved these problems, but the laws themselves have given us an image of what our economy should be. In a cartel economy no one could question the legitimacy of the recent rises in steel—or any other—prices. In an antitrust-minded economy it seems a legitimate and natural thing for the President or a congressional committee to call the companies to account.

Some indication of what American industry might have become without the curb of the Sherman Act is to be found in the Senate hearings on labor so widely publicized. Then, a liberal majority on the Supreme Court of the United States refused to accept the argument that labor coercion should be limited to legitimate labor objectives. They gave the unions a broad and sweeping exemption from any application of the Sherman Act. No doubt the liberal majority that bestowed the exemption felt, as Holmes felt about business in the Northern Securities case, that labor leadership if not curbed by the Sherman Act would nevertheless be benevolent. But what has actually happened in the labor movement is the picture of what would have happened in American industry had Teddy Roosevelt lost his fight in the Northern Securities case fifty-six years ago.

CHAPTER FIFTEEN

My Career in Government

My first experience in government service was in the summer of 1933. Jerome Frank, a partner in a large New York firm, had left an affluent law practice to accept the appointment as general counsel for the Agricultural Adjustment Administration. Some time in June he asked me to join his legal staff for the summer.

The great question facing the country was what to do about the huge surpluses of staple crops. They were not doing anybody any good. There seemed no way to get them to the hungry and unemployed without ruining the character of the recipients and breaking down the capitalistic system. The confusion of ideas was incredible. There was no consensus on anything—except that everyone agreed that something had to be done. The wise men of agriculture, the big farmers, the packers, and the wholesalers wanted to dump the surplus abroad. Secretary of Agriculture Henry Wallace said the only way out, and it probably was at that time, was to restrict agricultural production and at the same time offer some leeway for the regulation of prices by marketing agreements among the processors. And so the Agricultural Adjustment Act was signed on May 12, 1933.

When I arrived in Washington I found the Department of Agriculture in a perfect bedlam. There were no parades such as were taking place to protest the Blue Eagle, Secretary Wallace was not as picturesque a character as Hugh Johnson, and the tumult and shouting were far greater at the NRA, but still

there was certainly enough uproar at Agriculture to satisfy anyone who liked noise and confusion. Everything that was being
done was unconventional and unheard of, and, therefore, unconstitutional. The Supreme Court of the United States hung over the
entire administration like an ominous dark cloud. The department
swarmed with unconventional-minded economists who wrote long
memorandums to prove that what was being done was economically
sound. They were denounced by more conventional economists,
mostly outside the government, but many of whom were entrenched in high government places. Arguments and debates went
on into the small hours of the morning.

The great task confronting the legal staff was determining
whether the Constitution was elastic enough to allow the measures
being taken by the government to relieve distress, or whether these
measures were violating the sanctity of such magic phrases as
"proper delegation of powers" by the federal government and "due
process of law." We said the Constitution was that elastic; the
leaders of the American bar were unanimous that it was not.

Unfortunately for the public image of Wallace (the term "image"
was not in use at that time, because everybody still believed in
principles), crops such as cotton had already been planted and a
lot of little pigs had already been born. There was nothing to do
but plow up the cotton and kill the little pigs. The slaughter of
the little pigs offended the humanitarian citizens who believed in
being kind to animals. It also seemed to waste good food. Plowing
up cotton seemed a waste, too. It was sound policy, and not waste,
to prevent farmers from using their land for future crops. This
had to be done in order to give them higher prices and a better
income. But destroying existing commodities for the same purpose
was a waste.

Economic measures cannot be taken unless they are consistent
with the mythology of the times. So I have always been convinced
that there was no alternative to Wallace's agricultural program.
Of course, a man from another planet, not obsessed with the economic hobgoblins that limited the government in every direction
during the Depression, might have thought it more sensible to
distribute surplus food to people who did not have enough to
eat. But in the climate of opinion then existing, such a solution

was impossible. As the student of history must recognize, in every industrial revolution the impact of new wealth on old institutions and old methods of distribution is most disquieting. To distribute that new wealth requires a revolution in people's attitudes as to what the needy deserve and what they do not deserve. Therefore, the first result of every industrial revolution is a movement to get rid of the obnoxious new wealth, which is causing all the ideological troubles, by restricting production. Even today we do not think of our failure to use our full industrial capacity as an economic loss.

I felt differently about the NRA. The businessmen would inevitably bounce back. There was no reason to help them by restricting industrial production. This was not true of farmers. The farmers had lost their competitive place in our society. The businessman had not. I was happy when the NRA was declared unconstitutional by the Supreme Court of the United States. But I was unhappy when the Court declared the Agricultural Adjustment Administration program unconstitutional.

Before that event I was working day and night, along with I don't know how many other attorneys. There were so many of us that nobody had a room to himself, you were lucky if you could find a desk, and there was scarcely a place to sit down. All of us were writing memorandums on delegation of powers and due process of law, which were kept in reserve to throw at the first court to whom the question of constitutionality was presented.

The first case to run the gantlet was against a peach-packing firm in California that had refused to limit its production. Abe Fortas and I were sent to assist James Lawrence Fly, then with the Department of Justice and later chairman of the Federal Communications Commission, in trying the case. We were in the midst of preparation of our brief when Jerome Frank called from Washington and said the case must be dismissed. It had been decided that this was not the time, and the peach-packing case was not the kind of case, to bring up the issue. The department was afraid to risk a decision that might seriously handicap the entire Agricultural Adjustment program. We solved the dilemma by waiving the fine. At that point the peach packers agreed that they would accept an injunction against further violations of the act. The judge handed down a decision to the effect that the Agricultural Adjustment Act was constitutional, and no one appealed. The case is not to be found in the reports.

From then on, the policy of the Department of Agriculture, as well as of the NRA, was to avoid presenting constitutional issues to the courts. The Supreme Court's decision declaring the Agricultural Adjustment Act unconstitutional (*United States* v. *Butler,* 297 U. S. 1) was postponed until 1936, a long enough time for the agricultural program to get well under way. New acts to replace the AAA were passed. Roosevelt's famous Court-packing plan followed, during which time the personnel and thinking of the Court changed. Justice Owen J. Roberts, who had written the opinion condemning the Agricultural Adjustment Act, in *Wickard* v. *Filburn,* 317 U. S. 111 (1942), concurred in a decision sustaining an agricultural program that limited production, using legal terminology. Thus the agricultural program of planned scarcity got on its feet again, and is still with us.

My next summer vacation from Yale was spent in the Philippines. An economist from the University of Texas, Carl Rosenquist, and I were sent to the Philippines to advise Frank Murphy, who was then the governor general, with respect to a program to limit the production of sugar beyond an established quota. Unlike American businessmen, the Philippine sugar refiners were friendly and affable. They agreed with everything we said, they thought our opinions were both economically sound and constitutional, they signed everything put before them. And they entertained us lavishly at the refineries.

I was informed after I left that the Philippine sugar refiners paid little attention to carrying out their agreements. It was apparent that they considered them more a friendly gesture of politeness and welcome to the great representatives of the United States government than a binding commitment. But it was a welcome relief, nevertheless, to be associated with businessmen who took a practical view and refrained from bitter arguments about creeping socialism, inflation, and the probability of an eventual Communistic dictatorship.

From 1934 until 1937, I spent my summers in Washington as

a hearing examiner for the Securities and Exchange Commission under the leadership of William O. Douglas, who was making a study of the effects of the existing system of corporate reorganization. In those days a great corporation was not thought of as an organization. It was deemed to be an individual, with all the rights and privileges of an individual. Under this corporate personification, a bankrupt corporation had to be treated as if it were a private individual who had become insolvent. To treat a corporation as anything other than a person whose liberties were protected by due process was a radical notion at that time. Therefore, the small investor usually lost out in the political struggle for control of a bankrupt corporation. One of the important reforms of the New Deal was legislation that recognized that a vast corporate empire is an organization and not a fictitious individual. That change in viewpoint now permits us to protect the individual investor as he could not be protected under the old symbol.

In 1937, my year of sabbatical leave from Yale, I again served the government. Robert Jackson, who was then head of the Tax Division of the Department of Justice, asked me to come to Washington, promising me a chance to argue tax cases before the Supreme Court of the United States. I accepted, and during my spare time I finished my book *The Folklore of Capitalism*. To the surprise of both myself and Yale University Press, it became a best seller. Most New Dealers liked the book, and perhaps as a result of that I received a call from Attorney General Homer Cummings, made at the suggestion of Jackson, asking me to accept an appointment as head of the Antitrust Division of the Department of Justice. He said that the President had become convinced that the monopoly problem was the most important economic issue facing the nation.

Yale University, somewhat reluctantly, since I had just been away on sabbatical leave with half-pay, gave me another year's leave without pay. I assured them that I would be back at the end of the year. But when the year ended I was so engrossed in the fascinating problem of antitrust enforcement that I asked for another year. This was granted with even more reluctance. At the end of that year, I plaintively asked for another six months, on the theory that the country needed me, a contention which I know must have been received with some skepticism by the governing board at Yale. Indeed, my good friend George Day, who was treasurer at Yale, had taken an oath that he would not set foot in Washington until Roosevelt was out of office. I never received a reply to my request for an additional six months' leave. But one day when I was visiting the Antitrust regional office in San Francisco, reporters called me up and said they understood I had resigned from Yale; was it true? I asked them where they had got that information. They said it had just been announced by the university. I replied, "Then, of course, it's true." Thus the Yale Corporation inflicted an injury on the cause of legal education from which it has not yet recovered. But one can hardly blame them. They were so obsessed with the narrow idea that a Yale professor should spend a little time at Yale that they were blind to the broader consequences of what they were doing. I felt sad and dispirited at the news. I had lost my tenure at Yale, a place I loved, and at which I had spent seven of the happiest years of my life. The chances of ever getting back did not seem to be particularly bright.

In my book *The Folklore of Capitalism* I had written a chapter entitled "The Effect of the Antitrust Laws in Encouraging Large Combinations." In that chapter I observed that the symbol of the antitrust laws had in actual practice been a barrier to effective regulation of large business corporations. Every time such regulation was proposed it would be argued that the antitrust laws provided for a competitive society that did not need regulation. And then, simply because the laws were not enforced during the 1920's, big business had it both ways. I said in that chapter: "And so the antitrust laws, instead of breaking up great organizations, served only to make them respectable and well thought of by providing them with the clothes of rugged individualism."

I wondered just how in my new job I was going to explain my present enthusiasm for the antitrust laws in the light of what I had written just a year before. My answer, of course, was to be that in writing the book I was merely an observer of what the antitrust laws had been during the period of great mergers in the 1920's. It would all be different once I was in office. But this was not the end of my anticipated troubles from the Senate committee that was to scrutinize my possible value to the government. One of the influential members of the committee was the famous liberal Senator William E. Borah, of Idaho. With respect to him I had written the following:

The antitrust laws remained as a most important symbol. Whenever anyone demanded practical regulation, they formed an effective moral obstacle, since all the liberals would answer with a demand that the antitrust laws be enforced. Men like Senator Borah founded political careers on the continuance of such crusades, which were entirely futile but enormously picturesque, and which paid big dividends in terms of personal prestige. And, of course, people like Borah were sincere in thinking that the moral answer was also the practical answer. Thus, by virtue of the very crusade against them, the great corporations grew bigger and bigger, and more and more respectable. (P. 217.)

How was I to explain this to the Senator? My only hope was that he was too busy and important a man to read such trivia as *The Folklore of Capitalism*. It was, therefore, with considerable trepidation that I noticed when I took my seat before the committee that Senator Borah had conspicuously displayed in his hand a copy of *The Folklore of Capitalism*.

He questioned me closely. Then he started to read the paragraph quoted above. He read the first sentence and asked me to explain what I meant. Then he skipped the two sentences in which his name appeared and read the concluding sentence of the paragraph. He knew I was worried, and his eyes twinkled. But to my relief, he voted for my confirmation, and thereafter we became friends.

At my first conference with President Roosevelt, there were present Robert Jackson, then Solicitor General of the United States, Attorney General Homer Cummings, Donald Richberg, who had been head of the NRA after General Johnson, Benjamin Cohen, and myself. It was evident that the President intended to make a real attack on the monopoly problem. Only Richberg dissented. It was planned that the President would read over the radio a special message on the problem. Cohen and I wrote drafts over and over again until we got one that was simple and comprehensible and short. I was with the President when he delivered it. Just before time to go on the air, he took the last draft and changed it in a way that gave it his own individual touch. He was a genius at this sort of thing. I do not think he ever took anything written by anyone else and delivered it just as it was written.

Antitrust enforcement as a national program was not received enthusiastically by most of the New Deal economists. There was a belief among liberals at that time that the age of competition had gone and the age of planning had come. The Agricultural Adjustment Administration, for example, in whose formulation the brilliant talents of Rexford Tugwell had been so conspicuously useful, was the antithesis of the competitive ideal. It is not unnatural, therefore, that in his book *The Democratic Roosevelt* (Doubleday, 1957), Tugwell should dismiss Roosevelt's antimonopoly program as follows:

. . . In the more than a score of years since the armistice of 1917, there had been no change; the liberal mind was still fixed on smallness, on independence, on self-government.

This, it will be understood, came out of the same package of principles as the dominating ideas of the Second New Deal. It was consistent with domestic free enterprise, atomization, competition, and, wherever it existed, the breaking up of monopoly. Trust busting was appropriately having a belated revival, *but it is hard to believe that it was regarded by Franklin, the experienced statesman and executive, as the principle that ought to dominate future organization.* [Emphasis supplied.] (P. 563.)

Greatly as I admire Tugwell, I think he missed the significance of the antitrust ideal in our economy. Enforcement of the antitrust laws goes up and down, but so does the course of any other economic program, including Tugwell's own. The advantage of the antitrust laws is that they are sufficiently vague so they cannot and do not prevent any inevitable industrial development. But without a program of antitrust enforcement, the vast industrial empires become governments of their own. Once that happens, something like the static cartel system that existed in Europe prior to the Second World War is bound to arise.

I have elsewhere in this book talked of the need for government planning in the sense that it becomes the duty of the government in its role of providing credit in both the public and the private sectors to create enough effective demand to run our industrial plant at full capacity. But I see nothing inconsistent in the notion of balancing the economic budget by creating enough effective demand through congressional programs for developing the resources of this nation and the carrying out of those programs by competitive private enterprise. The competitive ideal, represented for the first time since the beginning of the Depression by Roosevelt's antimonopoly crusade in 1938, is essential to keep our markets free and our industrial development efficient. There should be no antithesis between the planned development of resources and the competitive fulfillment and implementation of those plans by private industry. To my mind, one of the most important acts of President Roosevelt was his monopoly message of 1938, made after the years of burial of that ideal under the avalanche of codes in industry and marketing agreements in agriculture. Franklin D. Roosevelt proved to be a far more effective trust buster than Theodore Roosevelt. The latter did not treat the antitrust laws as a practical instrument; his contribution was to establish the ideal in American economic thinking. Franklin Roosevelt was responsible for the first sustained program of antitrust enforcement on a nationwide scale that this country had ever had. He realized that the only alternative to enforcement of antitrust laws is regulation by government. He had tried regulation by businessmen in co-operation with the government under the NRA. The NRA's failure, I think, convinced him that antitrust enforcement must be a vital part of the nation's economic future.

It was shortly after Roosevelt's monopoly message of 1938 that Senator Joseph O'Mahoney, of Wyoming, introduced the resolution, and saw it passed, that created the Temporary National Economic Committee, which is now forgotten but which made a tremendous splurge at the time. The program of the committee was entitled "Investigation and Concentration of Economic Power." The idea behind this ambitious project was that there was a reservoir of economic facts as yet undisclosed by research and study that, if studied long and hard enough, would produce an answer on which both conservatives and liberals would agree. It was thought that when the economic facts were publicly disclosed, legislators would stop throwing symbols at each other, and stop scaring each other with the hobgoblins abounding in the lexicon of theoretical economics.

The committee was composed of Senators, members of the House of Representatives, and officials of the principal government agencies that had some special interest. Leon Henderson, who was subsequently on the War Production Board and later head of the Office of Price Administration, was chairman, with the impressive title of Economic Coordinator. The members appointed from the government were for the most part liberal New Dealers, with the exception of Wayne C. Taylor, Under Secretary of Commerce, and Garland S. Ferguson and Ewin L. Davis, who represented the Federal Trade Commission. The members from Congress, with the exception of Senator O'Mahoney, were extremely conservative.

I was opposed to spending any money on such a study; I wanted it all for the enforcement of the antitrust laws. But the myth that understanding of major economic problems can be promoted by study was too strong for me. Everybody else was enthusiastic. And so the committee went to work on its report, which finally came out three years later. During its life the Temporary National Economic Committee produced 58 volumes of hearings and monographs, which might be of value if only somebody would read them. But I doubt if such a pious hope will ever be realized. The recommendations of the committee were harmless, and no one ever paid any attention to them.

The Antitrust Division, owing to the brilliant work of my assistant Hugh Cox, Fowler Hamilton, Joseph Borkin, and others, presented a chamber of horrors of current business practices. It was easy to collect specimens for such a chamber because prior to the Depression big business had considered the antitrust laws obsolete and their files were full of spectacular material.

Our first production before the TNEC was the investigation of the Hartford Empire Company. A small group of people in Hartford, Connecticut, had control of patents on machinery for making glass containers. They used that control to determine who would go into the glass business and who would not. The patents were of doubtful validity. Nevertheless, their superior resources and the expense of litigation against them were sufficient to keep independent business out of the field.

Where their own patents were not sufficient they combined with others. Corning Glass Company was making "specialty" glassware—kitchen dishes that would resist heat. Corning and the Hartford Empire got together and divided the field between them, giving

Corning a monopoly position in specialty ware and Hartford Empire a monopoly in glass containers. Both had the power to stop everyone else from making glassware.

But this was not all. Owens-Illinois Glass Company also owned patents, connected with the manufacture of bottles. It was the largest glass company in the world. Hartford Empire Company and Owens-Illinois Glass Company got together and agreed that Hartford should decide who should make glass containers, including bottles, and who should not make them. In return, Owens-Illinois got half the profits from Hartford Empire. The final result was that the three companies produced seventy-eight per cent of all the milk bottles in the United States. The other twenty-two per cent were manufactured by seven other companies, but they were so scattered and so restricted by the Hartford Empire Company that they offered no competition.

The cold-blooded murder of small business represented by this combination is illustrated by the testimony of a small company, the Amsler-Morton Company, that had been manufacturing glass machinery since 1915. In 1934 they were told to stop manufacturing. Hartford Empire brought an infringement against a customer of Amsler-Morton named Swindell.

I quote from the testimony of the treasurer of Amsler-Morton.

Q. Can you tell me how much the Swindell litigation cost your company?
A. Well, it was tremendous for a small concern.
Q. How much was it?
A. It amounted to close to $50,000 and that doesn't take into consideration the expense of our organization. . . .
Q. I would like to ask you this: You told us, I believe, that you have sold only one lehr [an annealing oven used in making glassware] so far this year?
A. That is correct.
Q. That you sold no lehrs last year. What would you say the value of the glass-manufacturing machinery business is now? That is, your business.
A. I will give you a comparison. In '28 we were doing $800,000 worth of business and last year we had $18,000 worth of business in the glass industry—quite a drop.

This pattern of the elimination of competition, the destruction of small business, the fixing of arbitrary noncompetitive prices was in 1938 repeated throughout American industry. It was destroying the purchasing power in small towns and communities. It was making the West and the South colonies of the industrial East.

I recall an amusing incident. We showed that a large New England company seemed in complete control of prices in its field. We had the president of a smaller company on the stand. He testified that the reason he always followed the prices published by the larger company whenever the larger company raised them was that he had great admiration and respect for the superior economic wisdom and experience of the officials of the dominating concern. He was just a country boy and not a marketing expert. He knew that the prices of the large company were not fixed until after long economic study of what a proper competitive price should be, considering all the cost factors, and so on, which he reeled off in some detail. After the hearing, I approached him and said, "Mr. Blank, I will not ask you this question on the stand and I will keep your reply strictly confidential. What would happen to you if you didn't follow the prices of the dominating company?" After

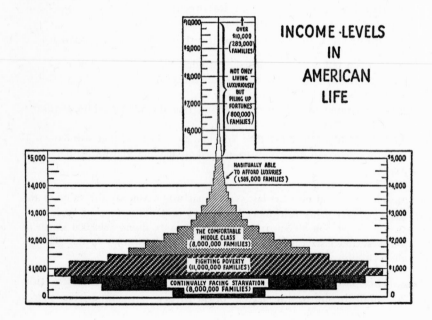

INCOME ·LEVELS
IN
AMERICAN
LIFE

OVER $10,000 (283,000 FAMILIES)

NOT ONLY LIVING LUXURIOUSLY BUT PILING UP FORTUNES (800,000 FAMILIES)

HABITUALLY ABLE TO AFFORD LUXURIES (1,585,000 FAMILIES)

THE COMFORTABLE MIDDLE CLASS (8,000,000 FAMILIES)

FIGHTING POVERTY (11,000,000 FAMILIES)

CONTINUALLY FACING STARVATION (8,000,000 FAMILIES)

deep thought, he said, "That is something, Mr. Arnold, which I never hope to learn from actual experience."

The problem of centralization of economic power was graphically illustrated by the chart, on the opposite page, made by Theodore J. Kreps, an economic adviser to the committee. The answer to the problem was to recognize the need for more consumer purchasing power. But any such solution would have been regarded as inflationary. The Temporary National Economic Committee never did come to grips with the realities of the economic problem before it. Nobody in those days had any idea of the extent to which the scientific industrial revolution was simultaneously going to increase production and abolish the need for unskilled labor. There was no way to convince any sound thinker that Harry Hopkins was the Alexander Hamilton of his time instead of a wild spender who would wreck the capitalist system if he could. We did not learn the real nature of our economic difficulties until the tremendous spending of the Second World War pulled us out of our static economy and made us the richest nation the world had ever known.

With respect to uncovering specific current abuses of the power of big-business empires the committee's staff did a thorough and excellent job. But in spite of the startling cases heard before the TNEC, nobody paid any attention to the study. The press did not carry the stories. The conservative members of the committee took refuge in the slogan that big business was not to be judged by the conduct of a few predatory companies—an attitude that recalls a conversation between my partner Paul Porter and a big-business official when Paul was head of the Office of Price Administration. The businessman said, "Mr. Porter, I'm afraid you are forgetting that ninety per cent of American businessmen are honest." "You've got that wrong," said Paul. "The correct statement is one hundred per cent of American businessmen are honest ninety per cent of the time."

When it became increasingly apparent that the Temporary National Economic Committee was simply piling up books and records that nobody was going to read, I lost interest and resorted to nationwide prosecutions for violation of the antitrust laws. The division had more than doubled its staff, and regional offices had been set up in the principal cities of the United States. More prosecutions for violation of the antitrust laws were brought during my short administration of the division than during the fifty preceding years.

As to the effect of this attempt to enforce the antitrust laws, there is, of course, a wide difference of opinion. But the economists who think it had little effect are those who specialize in economic doctrine rather than in economic ideals or symbols. When war broke out in 1939, there were many who thought that antitrust prosecution had lost its significance. There were severe pressures put on the Antitrust Division to cease its activities because it was interfering with the country's attempt to be an arsenal of democracy. For example, Rexford Tugwell, in *The Democratic Roosevelt,* comes to the following conclusion in connection with the conflict between the Sherman Act and the kind of business efficiency required during the war:

[Arnold's] activities naturally met head on the expansion of industry for war purposes which involved consolidation, co-ordination, central management, and monopoly—all the qualities anathema to the liberal progressives. Before long, trust busting was quietly put away for the duration of the crisis. But quite some stir had been made by the Arnold activities before they had to be smothered.

I do not share Tugwell's view. My belief is that the function of the Antitrust Division was just as important during the war as it was prior to the war. There is nothing in the principle of the Sherman Act that interferes in any way with business efficiency or co-ordination of effort. Nor does the existence of war require management by private monopoly, as Tugwell seems to infer. The vast government spending for war production went to turn the wheels of private enterprise. This created a great opportunity for conspiratorial agreements between businessmen with respect to prices, bidding, consolidations, and mergers. That this did not happen I attribute to the effect of the antitrust laws. In that connection I wish to pay tribute to John Lord O'Brian, who acted as general counsel of the War Production Board. He submitted to the Antitrust Division the plans and agreements necessary to carry on our war preparation. He was in control, and his would have been the final decision. But he never wavered in his purpose to prevent unnecessary combinations and restraints of trade from being excused on account of the war effort.

During the defense effort, Senator Harry S. Truman, through his Special Committee Investigating the National Defense Program, offered the Antitrust Division a public forum before which the Department of Justice could present its antitrust cases. At the time, the division was investigating the Standard Oil Company of New Jersey. We discovered that that great company had entered into an arrangement with German cartels. The agreement was that Standard Oil of New Jersey would not develop artificial rubber processes in exchange for the German agreement not to compete in the United States in petroleum products. When confronted with this evidence, Standard Oil of New Jersey promptly pleaded *nolo contendere* and accepted the imposition of a fine. But this did not get across to the public, as a trial would have, the dangerous nature of combinations with German industrialists. It was apparent from the evidence the Antitrust Division had that Standard Oil of New Jersey was contemplating renewing the cartel agreement with Germany after hostilities ceased. Senator Truman asked us to present this evidence before his committee.

Edward Levi, later dean of the University of Chicago Law School and now the provost of the University, was in charge of the hearings. He was assisted by the imaginative and indefatigable Joseph Borkin. He prepared the hearings and wrote the statement I subsequently gave before the committee. I was informed that a high government official attempted to dissuade Truman from holding the hearings because they might cause a loss of confidence in big business and thus disturb the war effort. Truman refused.

The effect of the statement prepared by Levi was electric—so much so that other Standard Oil companies advertised in the newspapers that they were in no way connected with Standard Oil of New Jersey.

I think that, unlike Tugwell, I give more importance to symbols than to precise programs. And I think that during the defense effort and even during the war the symbol of the antitrust ideal was kept alive by the Department of Justice. After the war this ideal spread to Germany. It resulted in the decartelization of German industry by the American High Commission. Today, in the

Common Market and in the coal and steel communities in Europe antitrust laws tougher in their terminology than those of the United States have been formulated. What will happen to them in actual enforcement must await the future. But in any event cartels have ceased to be legitimate in Germany. And throughout the Common Market a new competitive ideal or symbol has been created where none existed before. It is having its struggles today, but the easy acceptance of the noncompetitive idea that existed before the war is gone. This, I think, will be of immeasurable consequence to the future economic pattern of Europe.

I would like to end this chapter with a word about Franklin D. Roosevelt. I was not close to the throne; I hardly ever saw him. I recall only one evening my wife and I spent with him at a dinner; there were six people present. But this single small personal dinner is an example of his gift of making everyone feel as if they knew him intimately. He would reach out into the lower echelons of the government and by some touch give them a sense of personal acquaintanceship. He had the same touch in his fireside chats, when all the people were invited into his home. And he had an instinct for the expression of the ideals that at different times during his administration had the greatest therapeutic value for a distressed nation. The NRA, which I thought was economic nonsense at the time, I now recognize to have been an instrument that gave the American people hope and courage. When it ceased to do that, Roosevelt turned to other means. The most dangerous President that America could have had during the time of the Depression would have been a man who thought he understood and honestly tried to follow any form of consistent economic doctrine, whether liberal or conservative. And though Roosevelt was often attacked for not following any consistent economic doctrine, it was this quality, coupled with his ability to inspire the American public and his courage in taking decisive action, that made him one of the great political leaders of all time.

CHAPTER SIXTEEN

Why Government Service Is a
Dubious Career

The most exciting period of my career was when I was assistant attorney general under Franklin Roosevelt in charge of the enforcement of the antitrust laws. This is an experience, however, not likely to be repeated for one in a similar government post. In the ordinary course of events an administration would have been intimidated by the outcry in the press against such prosecutions as those of the American Medical Association and the Associated Press. Any President who did not share the qualities of Franklin Roosevelt would have nipped them in the bud. There were, of course, other exciting experiences for the advisers of Presidents Kennedy and Johnson. But in the long years of the Eisenhower administration such a position as I held under Roosevelt would have been dull indeed, or if not dull, it would have been dangerous.

Thus, Robert A. Bicks, who for a time was the acting head of the Department of Justice Antitrust Division under Eisenhower, showed courage and imagination in attacking respectable nationwide conspiracies in restraint of trade. It was he who initiated the prosecutions of General Electric, Westinghouse, and other large electrical concerns for a price-fixing conspiracy. He obtained indisputable proof of secret meetings and a secret code to determine which company would be the next successful bidder on a new contract. But Bicks was never made an assistant attorney general. His appointment and confirmation might have offended large interests. When Eisenhower reluctantly did finally nominate him, no fight was made for his confirmation and he was never confirmed by the

Senate. Therein lies one danger that awaits a young man who deliberately chooses a government career.

It is not easy to correct this situation. It has behind it the traditional distrust of a strong central government, which goes back to the times of Thomas Jefferson and Andrew Jackson. It is apparently psychologically necessary for the American voter to distrust the government servant and call him a bureaucrat. Indeed, under government service there is something akin to a policy of segregation in hotel and restaurant accommodations. When a government lawyer travels to try a case in a distant city his travel allowance restricts him to second-rate hotels and cheap restaurants. I had a travel allowance of fifteen dollars a day, and I traveled approximately half the time. When it became necessary, as it often did, to rent a conference room in a hotel, it had to be done at my expense. Otherwise, the conference would have to take place in the hotel suite of opposing counsel. But to avoid expense in this way was exceedingly dangerous; if some columnist learned about it, you would find yourself denounced because you had accepted favors from the other side. Even the minor matter of accepting social invitations to lunch had its risks.

There was, too, always the remote possibility that a government servant prominent enough to be mentioned in the news might be convicted of conflict of interest for no good reason at all. At the end of President Truman's first full term the slogan "cleaning up the mess in Washington" had, and still has, a strong appeal to the average voter. Political campaigns are conducted under this battle cry. When a new administration comes in, it must find a sufficient number of victims to justify its campaign promises.

The strange case of Lamar Caudle is an example. He prosecuted and convicted a well-known person for tax evasion. He resisted all the pressures put on him to drop the prosecution. One day he learned that a certain oil interest of trivial value had been transferred to him by the defendant he was investigating. He immediately wrote an indignant letter and repudiated the gift. Nevertheless, he found himself prosecuted and convicted and sent to prison, his entire career ruined, and his family impoverished.

What was his crime? He could not be prosecuted for bribery, because he had not accepted any gift from the defendant, and he had not declared himself unwilling to prosecute the case against the defendant. The offense chosen as the vehicle for his persecution is one that, so far as I know, is confined to government officials. It consists of conspiring with oneself to deprive the government of one's services. I had the opportunity to examine the evidence in this case and could find nothing to justify a conviction even for that curious crime. The only thing that Caudle had done that in any way favored the defendant was to agree that the defendant should be released from prison because his continued confinement constituted a grave danger to his health. The evidence that this was true seemed, to me at least, quite conclusive, and it is common in a case not a *cause célèbre* for a defendant to be released when confinement endangers his life. But no editorial commentator on the case of Lamar Caudle appeared to understand the strange nature of Caudle's offense and the outrage of his conviction except Drew Pearson. The average editor, like the average voter, is convinced that Washington's bureaucracy is a mess and that an accused bureaucrat must be guilty.

Admittedly, the case of Lamar Caudle is a most unusual one. But I happen to know of another one: the prosecution of Herbert Bergson; another assistant attorney general who headed the Antitrust Division, on the charge that he violated the conflict of interest laws by representing a client after he left the government who had a problem with the Antitrust Division. Bergson had served under Truman; he was prosecuted during Eisenhower's presidency. Bergson was more fortunate than Caudle. The government's case against him was so weak that the judge directed a verdict of not guilty from the bench. The government lawyers must have realized the frivolous nature of the evidence against Bergson. So the injury they inflicted on him—the headlines across the front pages of newspapers saying that he had been indicted—must have been intentional. This in all conscience was injury enough. Moreover, responsible commentators generally failed to analyze the case, and Bergson did not get the benefit of a public exoneration.

The rule against conflicts of interest as applied to government service has become a strange and fearsome thing. Businessmen may be prosecuted for acting in conflict with the interests of their corporations, but there—unlike the case of a government servant—

an atmosphere of common sense has been permitted to seep in. Such businessmen cannot be convicted of conspiring with themselves to deprive the corporation of their services. They may be sued in what is called a "stockholders derivative proceeding," and their illegal profits recovered for the benefit of the corporation. But conflicts of interest that fall short of embezzlement cannot be prosecuted as crimes on the part of businessmen.

Furthermore, a corporate executive must have caused actual damage to his corporation by his self-dealing before a stockholders derivative suit can be successfully prosecuted against him. But in the case of a government official, the fact that no damage has been occasioned by the conflict of interest is no defense. Damage to the public will be conclusively presumed. If the confused rules of ethics represented by the phrase "conflicts of interest" were enforced by criminal proceedings in the business world, they would as disastrously impair the efficiency of corporate operations as they now impair the efficiency of government.

The government of the United States needs younger executives in its Cabinet. It needs creative minds. You can find them in industry or in the law. But these younger men cannot accept government employment. To do so they must give up their directorships, their stock options, their future capital, in order to avoid the taint of conflict of interest. Charles E. Wilson and C. Douglas Dillon, wealthy in their own right before they are chosen, can divest themselves of their various stock interests. A younger man cannot do it. Does anyone think that Charles E. Wilson, president of General Motors Corporation, would feel any differently about there being an identity of interest between General Motors and the public whether or not he kept a stock interest in General Motors? Certainly not. Everything that makes the man tick prompted him to declare that "what was good for General Motors was good for the country." If the government wishes to appoint a great industrialist, his divestiture from all stock interest in his corporation will not change his point of view.

If we wish an efficient industrialist, who has not grown old in the service of corporate enterprise, to accept government responsibility we must adopt the same tolerance toward conflict of interest that the business community now adopts. If in the days of Daniel Webster, John Marshall, and Alexander Hamilton, we did not need this moralistic conception of the purity and virginity required for government service, it is time that we got rid of it today.

Another serious handicap to government efficiency is our system of civil service. It was originally instituted to prevent some modern Andrew Jackson from changing the entire personnel of the government on the principle that to the victor belongs the spoils. It has survived as a symbol of the government's fairness to its employees. Actually, however, the civil service affords practically no protection in the tenure of government service. The head of a department, if he is conscientious, can always get rid of an employee by the process of a reorganization that abolishes his job. If he is not conscientious, he can file a list of charges against an employee, listen to the employee's defense in an absent-minded way, and then fire him. The employee can appeal to the courts if he wants to spend his money uselessly. Of course, there are decisions that assert that if the employee can furnish evidence that his discharge was owing to bias rather than the merits of the charges, he may obtain reinstatement. But the chances of the court finding in favor of the employee on the merits are about one in a hundred. I have undertaken cases of discharged employees where I was convinced that the evidence of bias was clear and convincing. I lost them all.

On the other side of the ledger, civil service puts a handicap on the official's judgment in selecting his staff. On one occasion I hired a man who I thought was exceptionally competent, but he was turned down by the Civil Service Commission because he was a year short of having a college degree. On another occasion I asked for a raise in salary for a number of my best trial attorneys. The commission refused to grant it on the ground that the men recommended for a raise did not have sufficient executive responsibility to justify a reclassification of their jobs. I appeared before the commission and explained that executive responsibility was not an important qualification in classifying positions of lawyers. The most important work in the Antitrust Division is the necessary trial work. The executive job of assigning the cases and keeping track of their progress and assigning the personnel can be done by almost any intelligent man, but good trial lawyers are rare. In the opinion of the Civil Service Commission the man who assigns lawyers to cases was entitled to a higher salary than the man who tried the cases. I tried to point out to the Commission that in any large New York law firm there was a managing junior who distributed the work burden among the senior trial lawyers of the firm. A leader of the American Bar, like John W. Davis, tried the cases. He was too busy to do the assignment work of the managing junior partner. Indeed, I offered to take the Commissioners to Lexington, Kentucky, to observe the trial of the tobacco cases so they could understand the rare qualifications of the men who were conducting that trial. This made no impression whatever upon the commission.

Nevertheless, there are ways by which adroit government officials may circumvent such foolishness and make the rules of civil service a minor annoyance only. I reorganized the Antitrust Division and had a chart drawn showing the executive responsibilities I had decided to confer upon the men whose jobs were being reclassified. At the top of the chart was a little square box labeled "Assistant Attorney General." A line connected this box with a series of smaller boxes, which were occupied by the men whose salaries would be raised. Each of these boxes was connected by neatly drawn lines with a whole lot of other little boxes, and there were other boxes below these. By this device the men whose jobs I was seeking to reclassify appeared to have such staggering executive responsibility that a grave doubt arose whether they could ever find time to visit their wives and families. As a result, the raises were approved by the Civil Service Commission.

If corporate management had to go through this process of subjecting the personnel and salaries of its staff to some higher authority, even the ordinary citizen unversed in the mysteries of corporate operation would be able to detect that it was nonsense. But any kind of restriction on government management would be regarded by the same citizen as a necessary and wholesome restriction in the interests of preventing government executives from ruining their own departments by the free exercise of their feeble personal judgments.

Thus the civil service has acquired an impregnable position in the mind of the public as a symbol of respectability and decorum in the conduct of government affairs. Anyone who doubts it is apt to be charged with being contumacious toward holy men.

Another reason why a young man should hesitate before embarking upon a permanent career of government service is the salary scale. The beginning salaries are fully competitive with private industry. But they are completely frozen at the top at a scale that has no relevance to the importance of the duties involved. But I am inclined to believe that the salary scale is far less significant than the other factors I have mentioned. The teaching profession does not fail to attract good talent at salaries that are no larger than the government pays to its highest grades. Working for the public interest in an atmosphere of dignity and prestige has great appeal. The fortunate money-makers in the law or industry owe their success to talents not particularly desirable in public service. The government servant may not be able to live in the luxury of a successful businessman, but he will live as well as his friends. That is enough in the teaching profession, and I am convinced it should be enough in the government. The best government service cannot be obtained by hiring men who are chiefly interested in monetary rewards. An atmosphere of respect and dignity, in which the government servant can hold up his head, must be restored, or, rather, created.

Of course, the government service today works as well as it works. There is no lack of applicants for government jobs. The millstone around the neck of efficiency in government operation is psychological. It consists in the segregated and inferior status in which government career men must live. It is owing to this factor that the ablest men in government accept jobs in private industry as soon as they have acquired the skill and experience that make them useful in other fields. Those who remain are for the most part the persons who cannot get such jobs. So the public, which regards government service as bureaucracy and government career men as mere bureaucrats, has by that very attitude created the kind of bureaucacy that would not otherwise exist. The bureaucrats who grow old in the service and head the important sections gradually become copies of the kind of person the public insists on thinking they are. They invent rules and procedures for their own protection. Once adopted, these procedures become as inflexible as military regulations. Anyone who attempts to change them in the interest of speed or efficiency meets with resolute and fanatical resistance. The purpose of these procedures is to relieve the bureaucrats from the anxiety and risk of following their own judgment. What is precedent and authority in law becomes red tape in bureaucracy. It never achieves the esteem of legal precedent because it does not have that atmosphere of reason and common sense which gives the law its peculiar dignity.

The assistant Cabinet officers and the commissioners who compose government administrative tribunals are, for the most part, men who have enjoyed previously successful careers. They have not been selected by civil service; they are happy to work for the government because in the higher echelons of government service an atmosphere of dignity and prestige exists. But, as Judge Henry Friendly recently pointed out, these assistant Cabinet officers and commissioners find themselves the prey of their bureaucratic staffs. They are bound hand and foot by the procedures that were firmly entrenched before their appointment.

It is as impossible to move one of these departments in a new or different direction as it is to change the direction of a glacier. Even the language the appointed head of a department must use in order to communicate with his staff has a strange and alien sound. Policies must first be formulated, then they must be implemented. Committee is piled on committee. Memorandums are piled on memorandums and sent on their mysterious way down what are usually called "administrative channels." Queer terms spin like snowflakes in a Wyoming blizzard, until all sense of direction is lost.

Thus the only way to initiate a new policy is to start a new department, with new personnel, one that has not been solidified in the freezer of older government offices. In such new departments there will be excitement and enthusiasm and flexibility. The Alliance for Progress and the "war against poverty" are conspicuous examples. It would have been impossible to initiate these difficult enterprises, requiring as they do the constant use of expert individual judgment, in any of the older departments of the government. Certainly there is plenty of personnel in the older departments. But the inexorable working of Parkinson's Law has made these individuals so busy with their memorandums and committees that they have no possible time for any new ideas.

This phenomenon is not even dimly understood by most students of government. No doubt they have read about Parkinson's Law, but they think Parkinson is joking when, as a matter of fact, he is observing the realities in bureaucratic government operation. The editors of the *Wall Street Journal* violently protest the increase of bureaucracy in Washington caused by the organization of new departments. They do so even though they are heartily in favor of the new projects. Looking at the government through the spectacles of traditional theories, they fail to comprehend that the new plans cannot possibly be "implemented" by any existing divisions of government. They have failed to study that essential supplement to Parkinson's Law commonly known as Arnold's Corollary, the principle of which is as follows: No new government activity can possibly be effectively carried out by any established government organization.

Thus government bureaucracy expands to meet the necessities of changing times by adding the new and keeping the old. And it is unfortunately inevitable that Parkinson's Law will begin to operate on the new organizations, so that any future change can only be met by adding another new organization.

The roots that support this vast and expanding government bureaucracy are distrust and lack of respect for the strong central government that has become an absolute necessity because of the twentieth-century industrial revolution. The effect of this attitude can be seen in all sorts of minor ways. President Johnson has undoubtedly improved his political position by going around turning off lights in the White House and by depriving Cabinet officers of the prestige of being driven about in Cadillacs. Floodlights are still permitted to shine on the Lincoln Memorial, but Lincoln is a dead hero who has no budget to balance. The President of the United States is turning out all the lights within his own jurisdiction as an example of thrift and budget balancing.

A further symbol of lack of respect for the government can be found in the housing for our expanding bureaucracy—the ugliest buildings that were ever built in any capital of the world. Artistic decoration of these stark, boxlike structures is absolutely prohibited. Washington is gradually changing from a beautiful capital to an ugly one. Thus we attest our distrust of and lack of respect for strong central government, a faith we adhere to with greater intensity than does any other nation in the world.

CHAPTER SEVENTEEN

A Brief Career on the Federal Bench

In March, 1943, President Roosevelt informed me that he was appointing me a judge of the United States Court of Appeals for the District of Columbia. This was completely unexpected. The last thing that I had ever anticipated was a federal judgeship. I accepted with great pleasure. It solved all my own problems. Since I had lost my connections with Yale, I had thought that sooner or later I would have to see what I could do to find a position with a New York law firm where my antitrust experience might be of some value. I had made some inquiries and had an attractive prospect. The emoluments of a federal judge are low compared with those of a successful city practitioner; nevertheless, they are adequate. In addition, a federal judgeship is the only position in the government where one can get one's full salary until death. Neither sickness nor incompetence nor failing mental powers can ever deprive a federal judge of complete financial security. This feature alone is worth hundreds of thousands of dollars. And so when I accepted the judgeship I confidently expected to spend the rest of my life in a position of great dignity, with long vacations in the summer, in an atmosphere where the wicked cease from troubling and the weary are at rest.

There was some comment in the press that the President might have been better advised to have given the position to some member of the District of Columbia bar rather than to a carpetbagger whose only claim was service in the New Deal. But the Senate

Judiciary Committee did not take these comments seriously, and I was confirmed. This was, no doubt, because appointments to the federal bench in the District of Columbia are considered to be within the area of Presidential patronage.

A federal judgeship in any sovereign state is a part of the patronage of the Senators from that state. This is an unfortunate situation, because it makes a political plum out of an appointment to the federal bench. The result is that a lawyer unfitted by experience or temperament for the office may be, and occasionally is, elevated to the federal bench if his Senators are sufficiently obligated to him that they will accept no alternative. In addition, no one can be appointed outside the District of Columbia over the opposition of a Senator. For example, when his term as governor of Virginia expired, J. Lindsay Almond, Jr., was appointed by President Kennedy to the federal bench in Virginia. He richly deserved this judgeship. In my view, he was responsible for the acceptance by Virginians of the integration of their schools. He had taken a courageous course in the battle over civil rights and in doing so had incurred the enmity of Virginia's Senator Harry Byrd. Byrd opposed the appointment, and its confirmation was impossible. Kennedy subsequently appointed Almond to the United States Court of Customs and Patent Appeals, a position considered to be within Presidential patronage, and, in spite of Senator Byrd's lack of support, he was confirmed.

The power of Senators to veto judicial appointments of the President is one that is bound to cause trouble in obtaining judges in the Deep South who will follow the Supreme Court's decisions with respect to the civil rights of Negroes. I should point out that some judges in the South, for example, Judge Skelly Wright, have acted with great courage and wisdom. It is not likely, however, that the power of a Senator to veto the appointment of a federal judge will be given up. It is one of the unwritten perquisites of senatorial office, and one the Senate values highly. Senators will support a brother Senator from another state and refuse to confirm a Presidential appointment of a judge who is obnoxious to the Senator from the state in which the judge is expected to serve.

After my confirmation, President Roosevelt wrote me a congratulatory letter. It contained a typographical error which the President had corrected in his own handwriting. I think this was intentional. Most of the letters that the President signs are necessarily written by someone else, but, by leaving the typographical error in the letter and correcting it, Roosevelt let me know that, whether or not he had written the letter, he had at least read it. It was by such methods that he gave to his subordinates the feeling that he was personally interested in them and that his letters were not a mere formality.

In spite of my intentions to spend the rest of my life on the federal bench, I resigned three years later to go into the practice of law. In England and Canada a judge would not be permitted to do this. The British believe that the acceptance of the high office of judge means that one has renounced forever the more materialistic aims of a private practitioner. With this idea I am in complete accord. It does seem to me that it detracts from the dignity of the bench to permit a judge to resign and resume his practice.

The British idea has never taken hold in the United States for the very practical reason that judges of our state courts are elected. Occasionally, though not often, a sitting judge loses an election. In such a case there is nothing else for him to do except resume the practice of law. Hence the American people have become used to the idea that a former judge may resume practicing at any time he chooses.

After I resigned from the bench, the first case I argued was against George Wharton Pepper in the United States District Court in Philadelphia. Pepper was one of the greatest advocates that I have known. He was the lawyer who persuaded the Supreme Court that the Agricultural Adjustment Act was unconstitutional. When our argument was finished he asked me to lunch with him. His first question was, "Why did you ever resign from the Court of Appeals?" I hesitated, not knowing what to say. He said, "Let me help you out—I think I know. Some years ago I was offered an appointment to the bench—it wobbled me. I was almost ready to accept. But I finally decided that I would rather make my living talking to a bunch of damn fools than listening to a bunch of damn fools." This meant, in simpler language, that it was more fun to argue a case than to have the responsibility of deciding it.

I think it was my preference for partisan argument, rather than for impartial decision, that made me dissatisfied with a career on the appellate court. Furthermore, I was beginning to doubt whether a person of my temperament could ever be an ornament to the bench. I was impatient with legal precedents that seemed to me to reach an unjust result. I felt restricted by the fact that a judge has no business writing or speaking on controversial subjects. A judge can talk about human liberties, the rule of law above men, and similar abstractions. All of them seemed to me dull subjects. To sum it up, a person who is temperamentally an advocate, as I am, is not apt to make a good judge. I could cite many examples of good advocates with whom I was acquainted who made bad judges, but since this is classified information, I must refrain.

With many regrets and misgivings, I took advantage of the opportunity allowed to a judge in the United States, and resigned from the bench to resume the practice of law.

CHAPTER EIGHTEEN

The Puzzling Problem of Obscenity in American Law

When I assumed the position on the bench, the practical problems that obsessed me as head of the Antitrust Division disappeared into the dim haze of the past. I was free to philosophize and to adumbrate. And in order to support my conclusion in the last chapter that an advocate cannot make a dignified judge, I reprint an opinion I wrote (151 F. 2d 49) on a subject that at the time fascinated me: what is and what is not obscene.

United States Court of Appeals

DISTRICT OF COLUMBIA

No. 8899

ESQUIRE, INCORPORATED, APPELLANT,

v.

FRANK C. WALKER, as Postmaster General of the United States,
APPELLEE.

Appeal from the District Court of the United States for the District of Columbia

Argued April 20, 1945   Decided June 4, 1945

Before MILLER, EDGERTON and ARNOLD, Associate Justices.

ARNOLD, *Associate Justice:* Esquire is a well known magazine of general circulation. It contains stories, articles, literary and dramatic reviews.

Its contributors include distinguished authors, clergymen, and professors in our best educational institutions.

The Postmaster General revoked the second-class mailing privileges of this magazine, not on the ground of obscenity but because he thought its dominant purpose was to publish writings and pictures described in his order as being "in that obscure and treacherous borderland zone where the average person hesitates to find them technically obscene, but still may see ample proof that they are morally improper and not for the public welfare and the public good".[1] The revocation order would cost Esquire about $500,000 a year and put it in such a disadvantageous competitive position that it probably could not continue as a current magazine of general circulation.

The theory of the ruling depriving Esquire of second-class mailing privileges, while at the same time permitting it to be mailed at higher rates, is stated by the Postmaster General as follows: "A publication to enjoy *these unique mail privileges* [emphasis added] . . . is bound to do more than refrain from disseminating material which is obscene or bordering on the obscene. It is under a positive duty to contribute to the public good and the public welfare."

No doubt such a duty exists. But it does not follow that an admin-

---

[1] The applicable sections of the Postal Law relating to second-class mail read, 39 U. S. C. §§ 224, 226 (1940):

"§ 224. Second-class matter. Mailable matter of the second class shall embrace all newspapers and other periodical publications which are issued at stated intervals, and as frequently as four times a year and are within the conditions named in sections 225 and 226 of this title."

"§ 226. Same; conditions admitting publications to. Except as otherwise provided by law, the conditions upon which a publication shall be admitted to the second class are as follows: First. It must regularly be issued at stated intervals, as frequently as four times a year, and bear a date of issue, and be numbered consecutively. Second. It must be issued from a known office of publication. Third. It must be formed of printed paper sheets, without board, cloth, leather, or other substantial binding, such as distinguish printed books for preservation from periodical publications: . . . Fourth. *It must be originated and published for the dissemination of information of a public character, or devoted to literature, the sciences, arts, or some special industry,* and having a legitimate list of subscribers. Nothing herein contained shall be so construed as to admit to the second-class rate regular publications designed primarily for advertising purposes, or for free circulation, or for circulation at nominal rates." (Italics added.)

The above italicized words of the fourth condition are those with which we are concerned on this appeal.

istrative official may be delegated the power first to determine what is good for the public to read and then to force compliance with his ideas by putting editors who do not follow them at a competitive disadvantage. It is inconceivable that Congress intended to delegate such power to an administrative official or that the exercise of such power, if delegated, could be held constitutional.[2] Congress established the second-class mailing privileges because it believed that periodicals which disseminated public information, literature, art or science deserved to be encouraged on account of their contribution as a class to the public good. But the American way of obtaining that kind of contribution is by giving competitive opportunity to men of different tastes and different ideas, not by compelling conformity to the taste or ideas of any government official. This basic idea has nowhere been more eloquently expressed than in the famous quotation from Mr. Justice Holmes, dissenting in *Abrams* v. *United States:*[3]

> "But when men have realized that time has upset many fighting faiths, they may come to believe even more than they believe the very foundations of their own conduct that the ultimate good desired is better reached by free trade in ideas,—that the best test of truth is the power of the thought to get itself accepted in the competition of the market; and that truth is the only ground upon which their wishes safely can be carried out. That, at any rate, is the theory of our Constitution."

What the Government appears to assert is that the power to charge Esquire an additional $500,000 a year for use of the mails, unless it conforms to the Postmaster General's notions of the public good, is not a power to censor because the magazine may be mailed at the higher rate. The key to an understanding of this extraordinary contention is

---

2 No case has been cited involving the precise facts before us here. However, the broad principles outlined in the following cases make this conclusion inescapable: *West Virginia State Board of Education* v. *Barnette*, 319 U. S. 624 (1943); *Hague* v. *C. I. O.*, 307 U. S. 496 (1939); *Lovell* v. *City of Griffin*, 303 U. S. 444 (1938); *Grosjean* v. *American Press Co.*, 297 U. S. 233 (1936); *Near* v. *Minnesota*, 283 U. S. 697 (1931); *Pike* v. *Walker*, 73 App. D. C. 289, 121 F. (2d) 37 (1941).

See also dissenting opinions of Mr. Justice Holmes and Mr. Justice Brandeis in *United States ex rel. Milwaukee S. D. Pub. Co.* v. *Burleson*, 255 U. S. 407 (1921). The majority in the *Burleson* case does not sustain the position taken by the Postmaster General since it held that the publications involved there were nonmailable.

3 250 U. S. 616, 630 (1919).

found in the Postmaster General's reference to second-class mailing rates as "unique privileges". He appears to think of his duty under the statute, not as administration of nondiscriminatory rates for a public service, but as analogous to the award of the Navy E for industrial contributions to the war. The Navy E is an award for exceptional merit. The second-class mailing rate is conceived by the Post Office to be an award for resisting the temptation to publish material which offends persons of refinement.

But mail service is not a special privilege.[4] It is a highway over which

---

[4] "Whatever may have been the voluntary nature of the postal system in the period of its establishment, it is now the main artery through which the business, social, and personal affairs of the people are conducted and upon which depends in a greater degree than upon any other activity of government the promotion of the general welfare. Not only this, but the postal system is a monopoly which the government enforces through penal statutes forbidding the carrying of letters by other means. It would be going a long way, therefore, to say that in the management of the Post Office the people have no definite rights reserved by the First and Fifth Amendments of the Constitution, * * *." *Pike* v. *Walker, supra* note 2, at p. 291.

Mr. Justice Brandeis dissenting in *United States ex rel. Milwaukee S. D. Pub. Co.* v. *Burleson, supra* note 2, at p. 430:

"Congress may not, through its postal police power, put limitations upon the freedom of the press which, if directly attempted, would be unconstitutional. This court also stated in Ex parte Jackson, that 'liberty of circulating is as essential to that freedom as liberty of publishing; indeed, without the circulation, the publication would be of little value.' It is argued that although a newspaper is barred from the second-class mail, liberty of circulation is not denied; because the first and third class mail and also other means of transportation are left open to a publisher. Constitutional rights should not be frittered away by arguments so technical and unsubstantial. 'The Constitution deals with substance, not shadows. Its inhibition was leveled at the thing, not the name.' Cummings v. Missouri, 4 Wall. 277, 325."

Mr. Justice Holmes, dissenting in the *Burleson* case, at p. 437:

"The United States may give up the Postoffice when it sees fit; but while it carries it on, the use of the mails is almost as much a part of free speech as the right to use our tongues; and it would take very strong language to convince me that Congress ever intended to give such a practically despotic power to any one man. * * *

"To refuse the second-class rate to a newspaper is to make its circulation impossible, and has all the effect of the order that I have supposed. I repeat. When I observe that the only powers expressly given to the Postmaster General to prevent the carriage of unlawful matter of the present kind are to all business must travel.[5] The rates charged on this highway must not discriminate between competing businesses of the same kind. If the Interstate Commerce Commission were delegated the power to give lower rates to such manufacturers as in its judgment were contributing to the public good the exercise of that power would be clearly unconstitutional. Such a situation would involve freedom of competitive enterprise. The case before us involves freedom of speech as well.

Little more need be said to decide this case. Nevertheless, since we hope that this is the last time that a government agency will attempt to compel the acceptance of its literary or moral standards relating to material admittedly not obscene, the voluminous record may serve as a useful reminder of the kind of mental confusion which always accompanies such censorship.

The first source of that confusion is, of course, the age old question when a scantily clad lady is art, and when she is highly improper. Some refined persons are hopeful that an answer to this vexing riddle may some day be found. Others are pessimistic. But whichever school eventually proves correct it is clear from the following cross-examination of one of the expert witnesses for the Post Office that the problem had not yet been solved when the record in this case went to press:

> Q. Now that you have heard Mr. O'Brien, could you tell me in your opinion whether that picture is decent or indecent? A. Well, taking the expression of the picture and who the person is and

stop and to return papers already existing and posted, when I notice that the conditions expressly attached to the second-class rate look only to wholly different matters, and when I consider the ease with which the power claimed by the Postmaster could be used to interfere with very sacred rights, I am of opinion that the refusal to allow the relator the rate to which it was entitled whenever its newspaper was carried, on the ground that the paper ought not to be carried at all, was unjustified by statute, and was a serious attack upon liberties that not even the war induced Congress to infringe."

5 Even if second-class mail service actually were a privilege which could be withheld in the Postmaster General's discretion we still do not think it could be used to purchase compliance with his literary standards. If a publication is not actually obscene the publisher's right of free speech is clearly involved. In our opinion the principle of *Terral* v. *Burke Construction Co.*, 257 U. S. 529 (1922), and *Western Union Telegraph Co.* v. *Kansas ex rel. Coleman*, 216 U. S. 1 (1910), which involves state imposition of unconstitutional demands on foreign corporations is broad enough to cover this situation. For a comprehensive review of cases supporting this principle see article by Robert L. Hale, 35 Columbia L. Rev. 321 (1935), entitled *Unconstitutional Conditions and Constitutional Rights.*

what her attitude in life is, I think it is decent. I think the purpose for which you do things in life has a great deal to do with it. It is the motive in those pictures which is harmful.

Q. Will you look at this Exhibit 133, and tell me if this picture is decent or indecent? A. I think I am being trapped, Your Honor.

Q. You found that out, haven't you? A. Yes. I knew I was going to be trapped when I came here and I know I shall be in every column tomorrow.

Q. You haven't been reading the newspapers, have you? A. I read Dr. Marshall's testimony yesterday.

Q. You did? A. Yes.

Q. Now, just where and how are you being trapped? A. I am trying to be made a prude. I am not a prude.

Q. Well, would you mind telling me if that picture is decent or indecent? A. If I had a daughter I shouldn't like to have her photograph in that costume. I have no daughter, I have only sons.

Q. Is that your criterion for decency, Madam? A. My criterion for decency is anything that is proper, in order, certainly not harmful to human dignity. This woman is evidently by the ocean. I see the ocean there. She has probably come in and out of the ocean and if she stays there all right for me, but I do not wish to see that picture displayed except where it belongs. I believe in suitability, suitability; I don't like the picture. It is not pleasing to me and to my eye because I don't believe in such poses.

Now, I am going to be raked, I know, over the coals by those people over there for being a prude. No, I am not a prude. I know I am not a prude; I am a dignified woman who believes in life being lived for a purpose.

Have you ever been to the headquarters of the National Education Society and seen the statue of Horace Mann: "Be not afraid to die unless you have won some victory for humanity". Do you think this sort of thing is winning a victory? I don't.

Q. Well, do you think it is decent or indecent? A. I think it is indecent. You force me to an answer. I say it is indecent for a picture, not for the beach. You asked me about the picture. Now, I don't know that young lady. On the beach I think it would be all right, but not as a picture to be published in a magazine.

Q. This picture, Exhibit 131, do you think it is decent or indecent? A. I object to it very much.

Q. Do you think it is decent or indecent? A. Do I have to answer, Your Honor?

Q. I wish you would, please. A. It is a matter of please?

Q. Yes. A. Then I refuse to answer. You have shown me enough. You know my state of mind.

Q. Now, why do you refuse to answer? A. Because I will be misinterpreted.

A second source of confusion in determining what kind of literature furthers public welfare is the dividing line between refined humor and low comedy. To illustrate the difficulty inherent in this problem we cite the following colloquy between counsel for the Post Office and counsel for Esquire. It is typical of hundreds of similar instances.

Mr. Bromley: I would like to know, Mr. Hassell, if you don't mind telling me now, just what it is in that article you don't like. I can't find it.

Mr. Hassell: I would be glad to read it to counsel.

Mr. Bromley: Thank you.

Mr. Hassell: Third column at the bottom of page 144. "He noticed how large the uniform made her behind look."

It may be that the above encourages the use of unscientific terms. Or it may be that it is in the public interest to omit all comment on the part of the lady referred to. Yet it is difficult to make such judgments with the feeling of certainty which one should have when the result of one's decision is to cost a publication $500,000 annually.

This same kind of uncertainty appears in a third problem which must be faced whenever this censorship is exercised. How far will this reform of periodical literature go if the Postmaster General is given a free hand? [6] For example, recently the New York Times (on Sunday, of all days!) carried the following quip by Mayor LaGuardia on the front page where few churchgoers could fail to see it:

"Sorry. Racing does no one any good. It has nothing to do with horses. It has as much bearing on improving the breed of horses as a bawdy house has on eugenics." [7]

Does this mean that the New York Times will lose its second-class mailing privileges if it does not stop that sort of thing?

[6] Over 25,000 publications now have second-class rates. Briefs amicus curiae filed in this case by the Reader's Digest Association, Inc., The Curtis Publishing Company, The American Newspaper Publishers Association, the American Civil Liberties Union, and The Authors' League of America, Inc., indicate that the above question has caused genuine anxiety in our most respectable publishing circles.

[7] New York Times, May 20, 1945.

The Postmaster General gives serious consideration to this aspect of the problem. His conclusion is that occasional indifference to the public welfare may be indulged by an editor provided that it is not so frequent as to be classed as a habit. His opinion puts it in this way:

> "When such writings or pictures occur in isolated instances their dangerous tendencies and malignant qualities may be considered of lesser importance.
>
> "When, however, they become a dominant and systematic feature they most certainly cannot be said to be for the public good, and a publication which uses them in that manner is not making the 'special contribution to the public welfare' which Congress intended by the Fourth condition."

The Postmaster General appears to think that the improper dominant motive which he suspects from reading Esquire is corroborated by its editor's statement. He quotes the editor as follows:

> "The editor of this publication admits that from its origin 'our humor and our articles and our fiction all stressed a man alone angle—you might call it a stag party type of treatment', and testified 'we called it the smoking room type of humor'."

Now it is well known that when men gather together without the companionship of women an unrefined atmosphere is apt to spread over the entire gathering like a fog. And so the Post Office argues that only an editor indifferent to the public welfare would permit an atmosphere of this kind to dominate his magazine.

Unfortunately this still leaves the dividing line between an occasional vulgar lapse and a vulgar dominant purpose in a good deal of obscurity. It also leaves unsettled the question who is finally to decide what the dominant purpose is. For example, when we turn to the record we find that the weight of the evidence is that the magazine as a whole is unobjectionable. Far more witnesses testified against the Postmaster General's conclusion, than for it. They included men of national distinction as writers, scientists and educators. They also included the vigilant New England Watch and Ward Society. The Postmaster General is supported only by five clergymen, a psychiatrist, a lady prominent in women's organizations, and an assistant superintendent of schools. In this situation, assuming the existence of the power to censor, may a court review the issue of dominant vulgarity on its merits?

The answer of the Government is an unqualified no. It contends with some reason that this court has no right to review the Postmaster General's notions of dominant vulgarity if they are supported by substantial evidence. It argues even more persuasively that no right minded man can brush aside as insubstantial the opinions of five clergymen (among whom is a bishop) on what is good for the public.

We think the Government is clearly right in its contention once the power claimed by the Post Office is assumed to exist. There is a practical reason, apart from respect for the testimony of clergymen, why the administrative imposition of literary and artistic standards cannot be reviewed by a court on its merits. Opinions on such matters differ so widely that if the evidence in the record before the Post Office were to be weighed each side would have to continue calling witnesses indefinitely in order not to be outweighed by the other. We have no doubt that thousands of reputable experts on the public good could have been obtained by each side in this case.[8] We know of no way a court can evaluate the comparative expert qualifications of persons who hold opinions on what the public should read. Once we admit the power claimed here we see no room for effective judicial review of its exercise. And so in practical effect it amounts to a power in the Postmaster General to impose the standards of any reputable minority group on the whole nation.

In addition, the record suggests that the power claimed here would be used by sincere and conscientious officials to bind modern periodical literature to the standards of a former generation. This is dramatically illustrated by the cross examination of H. L. Mencken, who appeared as a witness for Esquire. No one today would question either Mr. Mencken's eminence or his complete respectability. Yet counsel for the Post Office attempts to impeach his testimony because about twenty years ago an issue of the American Mercury was refused all mailing privileges. It would be difficult to find anyone today who could with reason object to this issue of the magazine. The attempt to impeach Mr. Mencken on this account reads as follows:

> Q. Mr. Mencken, you are the author of a story called "Hat-Rack", aren't you? A. I am not, sir.
> Q. You published it in your magazine? A. I did, sir.
> Q. That story had to deal with some sexual activity in a boxcar or freight car? A. Not specifically. It dealt with people who engaged in sexual activity, but there was no scene of sexual activity in the story.
> Q. Was "Hat-Rack" the name of the woman who did that? A. Nickname. Did you ask who wrote it?

---

[8] The printed record in this case apart from several hundred pounds of exhibits contained 1,986 pages.

Q. No, sir; I did not. A. I will tell you if you want to know. It was written by Herbert Asbury, the great grand-nephew of Bishop Asbury, the first American Methodist bishop.

Chairman Myers: For whom De Pauw University was originally named.

The witness: I didn't know that. There was a report that Asbury was the great-grandson of the Bishop, but the Bishop actually was a bachelor. He is a great-grandson of the Bishop's brother.

By Mr. Hassell:

Q. Mr. Mencken, was the issue of your magazine containing that story declared non-mailable by the Post Office Department? A. Yes, sir. I think you ought to let me explain what happened, if you care to.

Q. Yes, sir; go right ahead. A. The Post Office entered that case rather late. An effort was made in Boston to suppress the magazine as a measure of revenge by the Boston Watch and Ward Society, which we had been denouncing. They proceeded by threatening a newsdealer. The poor newsdealer had no stake in the thing and was willing to subside and withdraw the magazine, so I went to Boston and sold the magazine myself on Boston Common and insisted on the Watch and Ward Society arresting me.

I was arrested, tried and acquitted.

Meanwhile, subsequent to my arrest, and four or five weeks subsequent to the time the magazine had gone through the mails, the Post Office Department issued an order barring it from the mails. It was a purely imaginary order. There were no more to be mailed.

So I went to court on that and I had injunctions against the Post Office by two Federal judges, both of whom denounced the Post Office as obscene, indecent, unfair and ignominious.

I agreed with the verdict thoroughly and believe it was just to this minute.

The Post Office tried to hit me in the back when I was fighting with the filthy Comstocks in Boston. I fought the Comstocks and I fought the Post Office, and I put my magazine back in the mails and they have never molested me since.

Q. Didn't the Federal Court in New York refuse to issue an injunction as the case was moot? A. That is not precisely what happened. I had my injunction in the district courts of Boston and in New York, and the Post Office, pursuing its filthy course of trying to persecute me, appealed to the Circuit and the Circuit after two years decided that the case was completely moot because we were in point of fact through the mails. They decided I could not get relief because the Post Office barring me from the mails was completely dishonest—I wasn't an applicant to the mails.

The three examples cited above effectively illustrate the intellectual standards required for the kind of censorship exercised in this case.

We intend no criticism of counsel for the Post Office. They were faced with an impossible task. They undertook it with sincerity. But their very sincerity makes the record useful as a memorial to commemorate the utter confusion and lack of intelligible standards which can never be escaped when that task is attempted. We believe that the Post Office officials should experience a feeling of relief if they are limited to the more prosaic function of seeing to it that "neither snow nor rain nor heat nor gloom of night stays these couriers from the swift completion of their appointed rounds".

Reversed and Remanded.

The Supreme Court, in a less frivolous opinion, subsequently affirmed my decision in the *Esquire* case.

After my opinion was published, I got a letter from Henry L. Mencken as follows:

My dear Mr. Justice:

If it is not an indecorum I would like to thank you for your judicial certificate of decency. When my pastor heard of it he went on a roaring sacerdotal drunk and had to be knee-haltered. The Maryland Club, on the other hand, was so delighted that one of its members had a judicial certificate of decency that it hung out the Confederate flag and reduced the price of all 15¢ cigars to 25¢.

Yours in Christ,
H. L. Mencken

After my return to the practice of law I again had occasion to deal with the obscure and puzzling law of obscenity. This time I acted as attorney for *Playboy* magazine, a large part of the contents of which was designed to prove that women were mammals. At that time the Postmaster General had abandoned the position taken in the *Esquire* case that the second-class mailing privilege could be withdrawn from magazines not obscene in themselves on the ground that they might offend decent and God-fearing citizens. Unlike *Esquire, Playboy* was found to be actually obscene by the Postmaster General on account of its nude pictures and risqué jokes and articles. The issue of the magazine in question was banned from the mails on the ground of obscenity.

I learned of this at ten o'clock in the morning. Had the issue been kept out of the mails for ten days it would have meant a serious financial catastrophe for *Playboy,* which was then distributing close to a million copies. It was necessary, therefore, to get a temporary restraining order against the Postmaster General. The hearing was held before Judge Luther W. Youngdahl, a great judge but thoroughly puritanical in his thought and habits. In view of the unabashed nudity of the pictures in the magazine, we approached him with some anxiety. But Judge Youngdahl was not one who decided cases on his personal predilections. After argument, although I suspect he thoroughly disapproved of the magazine, he gave us our temporary restraining order. The ground on which that order was based was that the Postmaster General had not accorded *Playboy* magazine a hearing on the issue of obscenity. And so the magazine was distributed.

Whereupon, the Postmaster General lost interest in that particular issue and did not attempt to pursue the matter to a hearing. The next we heard from the Postmaster General was a telephone call one evening from Chicago, where the magazine was published, to the effect that another issue of the magazine had been barred from the mails and the hearing set for ten o'clock the next morning. We again sought a temporary restraining order on the ground that a hearing set on such short notice was not a hearing at all and did not conform to due process under the Constitution. At noon we obtained a temporary restraining order. The Postmaster General appealed, the temporary restraining order was affirmed about two o'clock by a special order of the United States Court of Appeals, and the magazine went out through the mails.

A temporary restraining order was, of course, not a final adjudication of the issues of the case. The hearing on the merits was postponed to a later date. When that date arrived, the Postmaster General appeared in court and asked that the case be dismissed. My law partner Paul Porter, who argued the case, at this point protested. He said that it was the second time that an issue of *Playboy* had been banned on grounds of obscenity by the Postmaster General without a judicial hearing, that we were entitled now to hear it on the merits. He characterized the action of the Postmaster General as a hit-and-run procedure, a method of constant harassment without ever giving *Playboy* a chance to prove that the magazine was not actually obscene. Nevertheless, the judge permitted the government to dismiss the case.

The final act in the *Playboy* comedy occurred when the Attorney General of the sovereign state of Vermont indicted a newsdealer who was selling this and other magazines. The brief I filed in that case sets forth my own ideas on the fascinating subject of obscenity in sufficient detail that it may be of interest to the reader of this book.

I

Under current standards which the Court should apply the publications involved in this case are not obscene.

We think it is a tribute to the civilized tolerance of Vermont prosecutors that this Court has never before been called on to define the standards of obscenity and to differentiate between risqué or daring literary material and obscene material. The decision of such an issue is fraught with such danger to free speech and creative literature that elsewhere it has often resulted in absurd censorship. It has put courts in the role of literary critics for which task they have no fitness. So grave is the danger to freedom of the press implicit in judicial definitions of obscenity that in the recent case of *Roth* v. *United States*, 354 U. S. 476, two members of the Supreme Court of the United States were of the opinion that no statute making obscenity a crime could be constitutional. Mr. Justice Douglas in his dissenting opinion declared (354 U. S. 476 at 511–512):

> "The standard of what offends 'the common conscience of the community' conflicts, in my judgment, with the command of the First Amendment that 'Congress shall make no law * * * abridging the freedom of speech, or of the press.' Certainly that standard would not be an acceptable one if religion, economics, politics or philosophy were involved. How does it become a constitutional standard when literature treating with sex is concerned?
>
> "Any test that turns on what is offensive to the community's standards is too loose, too capricious, too destructive of freedom of ex-

pression to be squared with the First Amendment. Under that test, juries can censor, suppress, and punish what they don't like, provided the matter relates to 'sexual impurity' or has a tendency 'to excite lustful thoughts.' This is community censorship in one of its worst forms. It creates a regime where in the battle between the literati and the Philistines, the Philistines are certain to win. If experience in this field teaches anything, it is that 'censorship of obcenity has almost always been both irrational and indiscriminate.' Lockhart & McClure, op. cit. supra, at 371. The test adopted here accentuates that trend."

Much can be said for the position taken by Justice Douglas. In theory at least speech or writing cannot be suppressed unless it would lead to acts which are harmful to society. Modern psychiatry teaches us that the reading of pornographic literature, even in its worst forms, does not lead to any form of dangerous activity. It does not cause juvenile delinquency. It does not tend to make its readers sexual offenders.[3] Psychiatrists generally agree with the statement of Dr. Benjamin Karpman, chief psychotherapist at St. Elizabeths Hospital in Washington, D. C.:

> "Contrary to popular misconception, people who read salacious literature are less likely to become sexual offenders than those who do not, for the reason that such reading often neutralizes what aberrant sexual interests they may have."

Nevertheless we do not think that this Court will or should go so far as to declare unconstitutional the portion of the obscenity statute involved in this case. Obscenity laws rest on a different constitutional basis than any other constitutional restriction on free speech. Other constitutional restrictions must rest on the tendency of the forbidden literature to result in harmful conduct and the probability of such harmful conduct must be great indeed.[4]

But an obscenity statute rests on a different basis. It is in its essence a moral declaration on the part of the legislature, a recognition of a taboo which is as old as history. Such laws are passed because most men are stimulated by erotica and at the same time they are ashamed of it. Society requires a public denunciation of this almost universal sin whether or not it leads to positive harmful conduct.

---

[3] The best judicial analysis of the alleged harm done to society by pornography is found in Judge Frank's exhaustive concurring opinion in the case of *United States* v. *Roth*, 237 F. 2d 796, 801 (2d Cir. 1956).

[4] *Dennis* v. *United States*, 341 U. S. 494, 502–511.

Thus from time immemorial laws making obscenity a crime have been a psychological requirement of a society which wants to be considered moral and virtuous.[5] Even in ancient Greece, a society not distinguished for its puritanism, Plato in 378 B.C. urged that the *Odyssey* be expurgated for children's reading. In ancient Rome Ovid's book "The Art of Love", —a book which today freely circulates because it is a classic, caused the emperor Augustus to banish Ovid in 7 A.D. The fact that laws against obscenity do not have a rational or scientific basis, but rather symbolize a moral taboo, does not make them any the less necessary. They are important because men feel that without them the state would be lacking in moral standards.

But because obscenity statutes represent a moral taboo and not a rational process the field of pornography is full of curious contradictions. For example, distinguished artists are not prone to committing or assisting in the commission of ordinary crime. But the literature of obscenity contains some of our greatest names. Mark Twain, whose dialogue called "1601" is today widely but secretly circulated, wrote to a Cleveland librarian, "If there is a decent word findable in it it is because I overlooked it." [6] Great painters have lent their talents to producing erotic material so extreme that it had to be secretly circulated. Such names include Hogarth, Rowlandson, Aubrey Beardsley, Rubens, Rembrandt, Jan Steen, Michelangelo, Raphael, Tintoretto, Titian, Boucher and Rodin. In music Gilbert and Sullivan produced an obscene musical play called "The Sod's Opera". Yet Sullivan was the man who wrote "Onward Christian Soldiers". The list could be extended indefinitely. One of the most widely read pornographic articles was written by Benjamin Franklin; another star in this galaxy was Eugene Field.

There is a certain high comedy in the contradictions which roam throughout the area of pornography. At the same time that men insist on suppressing obscene literature and punishing those who write it they enthusiastically go on collecting it and preserving it in libraries of priceless value. The Catholic Church is a leader in the fight against obscenity. Yet it maintains in the Vatican library the most famous collection of erotica in the world, consisting of 25,000 volumes and 100,000 prints.[7] Ralph Ginzburg in his recent book states that among libraries the Vatican

---

[5] The historical discussion which follows is drawn from Ginzburg, *An Unhurried View of Erotica* (1958).

[6] Id. at 77.

[7] Id. at 103.

erotica "is probably most accessible to the nonprofessional bibliophile".[8] Erotic material was collected by that good churchman J. P. Morgan. Henry E. Huntington, the railway magnate, had the greatest collection in the West. Yale, Princeton and Harvard have collections of erotica.[9]

Access to this material is ordinarily made difficult. But this is not true of the Library of Congress which has the largest collection of erotica in the United States. Anyone over sixteen may see the books. In addition, the Union catalogue of the Library of Congress publicly lists existing erotica works giving information which could be used by any pornographic bookseller. Logically it might seem that the Library was contributing to the crime of obscenity but no sensible man would want to change its present practices. Thus the moral problem of obscenity is as full of inconsistencies and contradictions as was another moral crusade, i.e., the enforcement of prohibition where good citizens wanted liquor and prohibition at the same time.

One way by which legislatures have tried to reconcile some of those contradictions was to follow the widely held theory that erotic material is harmful to children. It is no doubt for this reason that the Vermont statute condemns material "which tends to the corruption of the morals of youth". But this test of criminal obscenity was struck down by the Supreme Court of the United States in the case of *Butler* v. *Michigan*, 352 U. S. 380, in which Mr. Justice Frankfurter speaking for a unanimous Court, said:

> "It is clear on the record that appellant was convicted because Michigan, by §343, made it an offense for him to make available for the general reading public (and he in fact sold to a police officer) a book that the trial judge found to have a potentially deleterious influence upon youth. The State insists that, by thus quarantining the general reading public against books not too rugged for grown men and women in order to shield juvenile innocence, it is exercising its power to promote the general welfare. Surely, this is to burn the house to roast the pig. Indeed, the Solicitor General of Michigan has, with characteristic candor, advised the Court that Michigan has a statute specifically designed to protect its children against obscene matter 'tending to the corruption of the morals of youth'. But the appellant was not convicted for violating this statute.
>
> "We have before us legislation not reasonably restricted to the

---

[8] Id. at 107.

[9] Id. at 103–105.

evil with which it is said to deal. The incidence of this enactment is to reduce the adult population of Michigan to reading only what is fit for children. It thereby arbitrarily curtails one of those liberties of the individual, now enshrined in the Due Process Clause of the Fourteenth Amendment, that history has attested as the indispensable conditions for the maintenance and progress of a free society. We are constrained to reverse this conviction." 352 U. S. 380, 382–384.

It is therefore clear that other ways must be found for preventing children from reading erotica than condemning its distribution and sale to the general public.

Assuming that a line has to be drawn between material so offensively obscene that it is a crime to distribute it and material which is merely suggestive of sex, the question before this Court is where and how to draw that line. Two considerations should, we think, be in the mind of the Court. First, the line should not be drawn in such a way as to interfere with the literary artist. Moral censorship as it has existed, for example, in Boston, which went so far as to condemn H. L. Mencken's *Mercury* Magazine while at the same time burlesque shows were running full blast at the old Howard Theatre, is indefensible. Yet such is the zeal of reformers that the banning of works of real merit is an inevitable consequence unless the definition of obscenity is strictly limited. Over the ages it has been proved that it is impossible for moral reformers to let good books alone. It is the responsibility of the courts to prevent zealots from curbing art in trying to cut down on the number of impure thoughts per capita among the general public.

Heretofore the most frequently applied test of obscenity was whether the material in question had a tendency to produce lustful thoughts. This test is tempered by giving allowance to the serious character or artistic merit of the work as a whole. This test has proved useless in the past. It puts courts in the role of literary critics, a task for which they are unfitted. It achieves fantastically inconsistent results.

Another evil of the commonly applied "lustful thoughts" test in judging obscenity is its tendency to create attitudes towards sex which are akin to fetishism. For example, in 1900, when women were required to bathe fully clothed and bare legs were a mark of indecency, youths were stimulated by the sight of an ankle or a calf. Certainly no one can call this a healthy reaction. In 1911, a book was widely sold named "Three Weeks" in which the obscene passages consisted only of pages of asterisks at appropriate places. The book was passed from hand to hand in every college. Certainly it is unhealthy to be stimulated by asterisks. Human beings can be trained like Pavlov's dog so that they are stimulated by sights and sounds completely unrelated to the things they desire. A strict standard of obscenity contributes to such unhealthy training.

Furthermore, the broader the definition of what is forbidden, the greater number of objects become obscene but stimulating fetishes—solely because they have been forbidden. The more tolerant standards of today as compared with those of 1900 have reduced the number of indecent works to a minimum and thus have reduced the amount of "obscenity" in our culture. Certainly we have today a healthier attitude toward sex in literature or art than the days when fig leaves had to be put on statues. Taking the pin-up girls away from American soldiers would not make their minds more pure. It would only mean that they would be aroused by some less healthy or attractive substitute.

The moral censor who tries to make all literature decent is like a man who wants everything up and nothing down. He may succeed in getting things higher and higher but some of them will always be down or else none of them will be up. For example, at the turn of the century the old Police Gazette had a nation-wide pornographic appeal. A dance called the Can-Can in which the chorus girls kicked up legs covered with black stockings was wicked and highly stimulating. Today a person with an appetite for pornography would not pay ten cents to see either the magazine or the dance. This is how censorship makes material sexually stimulating which would not have any stimulation at all if that censorship did not exist. And that is why anything but the most tolerant standards creates an unhealthy psychology.

If we are right in these observations a court in applying an obscenity statute should construe it to include only the most extreme forms of erotic material. If this attitude is not taken the result of the broad censorship will be to create an artificial erotic appeal in writing which without it would be considered as harmless.

Certainly the magazines before the Court in this case are harmless from any healthy standards. They contain pictures of very pretty and undraped women. They contain smoking room stories. But men have enjoyed this kind of material from the beginning of time. To condemn these magazines is to turn the clock back to the 19th Century when men could be stimulated by the sight of a woman's ankle. Two of the magazines, "Playboy" and "Rogue", have been granted second class mailing privileges by the Post Office Department. In the case of "Rogue" a hearing was given and the Judicial Officer of the Post Office Department, overruling the Department's Assistant General Counsel, affirmatively held that the magazine was not obscene.[10] We submit that the magazines before the Court are more or less alike and there is no reason why the ruling in the case of one should be any different than in the others.

II

If the Court construed the statute in such a way as to include the magazines in issue here within the statutory definition of obscenity, such a decision would violate the Federal Constitution.

The above proposition, we believe, can be established by the following recent cases in the Supreme Court of the United States:

> *Roth* v. *United States,* 354 U. S. 476, June 24, 1957;
> *Alberts* v. *California,* 354 U. S. 476, June 24, 1957;
> *One, Inc.* v. *Olesen,* 355 U. S. 371, Jan. 13, 1958;
> *Sunshine Book Co.* v. *Summerfield,* 355 U. S. 372, Jan. 13, 1958;
> *Times Film Corp.* v. *Chicago,* 355 U. S. 35, Nov. 12, 1957.

These cases represent a significant departure from former decisions. Taken together they constitute a complete review, from a constitutional point of view, of all former standards of obscenity in the light of the changing mores of our times. We recognize this is a bold statement. It is not based upon the written opinion in the *Roth* and *Alberts* cases but follows as a result of the three *per curiam* opinions cited above which follow the *Roth* and *Alberts* cases.

In the *Roth* case itself certiorari was granted limited to the question whether the federal obscenity statute on its face violated the freedom of speech guarantees of the First Amendment, whether it violated the Due Process Clause of the Fifth Amendment, and whether it violated the First, Ninth and Tenth Amendments by invading the powers granted to the states. Combined with the *Roth* case, which involved a federal offense, was *Alberts* v. *California,* which involved the constitutionality of a state statute under the Fourteenth Amendment.

In the majority opinion in *Roth* and *Alberts* seven Justices held that a statute making obscenity a crime did not, if properly applied, violate the Federal Constitution. The alleged obscene material in *Roth* and *Alberts* was not before the Court because of the limitation on certiorari. Nevertheless a bare majority did approve of an instruction in *Alberts*

---

[10] Departmental Decision, *In the Matter of Petition by Greenleaf Publishing Co.,* H. E. Docket No. 4/202 (attached to this brief as Appendix A).

which allowed the jury to convict where the material had a "substantial tendency to deprave or corrupt its readers by inciting lascivious thoughts or arousing lustful desires" (354 U. S. 476, 486) if "applying contemporary community standards, the *dominant* theme of the material taken as a whole appeals to prurient interest" (354 U. S. 476, 489). (Emphasis supplied.)

This test does not differ materially from former standards of obscenity which are all so loose that they require the Court not only to judge what would arouse prurient interests but also to be a literary critic. But, as the subsequent *per curiam* opinions show, the Court did not consider this to be a test to be used in determining whether an obscenity case should go to a jury. And the Chief Justice in his concurring opinion refused to approve the language of the instruction, limiting his decision to the validity of the statute on its face.

Mr. Justice Harlan, dissenting, held that as a matter of law the instruction approved by the majority in the *Roth* case violated the Federal Constitution. He said (354 U. S. 476, 506–507):

"I judge this case, then, in view of what I think is the attenuated federal interest in this field, in view of the very real danger of a deadening uniformity which can result from nation-wide federal censorship, and in view of the fact that the constitutionality of this conviction must be weighed against the First and not the Fourteenth Amendment. So viewed, I do not think that this conviction can be upheld. The petitioner was convicted under a statute which, under the judge's charge, makes it criminal to sell books which 'tend to stir sexual impulses and lead to sexually impure thoughts.' I cannot agree that any book which tends to stir sexual impulses and lead to sexually impure thoughts necessarily is 'utterly without redeeming social importance.' Not only did this charge fail to measure up to the standards which I understand the Court to approve, but as far as I can see, much of the great literature of the world could lead to conviction under such a view of the statute. Moreover, in no event do I think that the limited federal interest in this area can extend to mere 'thoughts'. The Federal Government has no business, whether under the postal or commerce power, to bar the sale of books because they might lead to any kind of 'thoughts.'

"It is no answer to say, as the Court does, that obscenity is not protected speech. The point is that this statute, as here construed, defines obscenity so widely that it encompasses matters which might very well be protected speech. *I do not think that the federal statute can be constitutionally construed to reach other than what the Government has termed as 'hard-core' pornography."* (Emphasis supplied.)

However, in the companion *Alberts* case which involved a state statute and state interests Justice Harlan held that the test laid down by the majority was not unconstitutional. He thought that a different and more liberal standard should be applied in restricting state condemnation of obscenity than in restricting the Federal Government. In a federal prosecution nothing short of "hard core" pornography would justify a criminal conviction.

Justice Harlan did not define "hard core" pornography but it is not difficult to understand what he meant. The Government had lodged with the Court a sealed carton for examination by the Court on the theory that a mere examination without analysis or description was enough to judge such material. In its brief [11] (pp. 34–39) the Government divided erotic material into three classes. The first class consisted of skillfully written books which had an apparently serious intention but which contained descriptions of sex conduct in four-letter words. There are not many such books, less than 2% of the items on which convictions were obtained under the Post Office statute.

The second class consisted of magazines which are publicly distributed. Such magazines hope to stay on the legally acceptable side of obscenity but at the same time compete with others in seeing how far they can go and still be available on the newsstands. These are the close cases. The Government cites nudist magazines with pictures of completely nude women as an example of a borderline case.

The third classification of obscenity made by the Government is not borderline at all. It is the largest category of all obscene material. Chaffee in a study he made estimates that this class constitutes easily 90% of all items seized by customs officials (Brief for the United States, p. 39).

An examination of the magazines in issue in this case makes it obvious that they can only come within the second class of erotica described by the Government's brief. Justice Harlan considered it unconstitutional to consider this second class of material as criminally obscene even though it had a tendency to incite prurient interests.

Justices Black and Douglas dissented on the ground that the Federal

---

[11] A copy of the Brief for the United States in the *Roth* case has been lodged with this Court.

Constitution prohibited making the distribution of any literature criminal however obscene it was. Mr. Justice Douglas said (354 U. S. 476, 509–510):

> "The test of obscenity the Court endorses today gives the censor free range over a vast domain. To allow the State to step in and punish mere speech or publication that the judge or the jury thinks has an *undesirable* impact on thoughts but that is not shown to be a part of unlawful action is drastically to curtail the First Amendment. As recently stated by two of our outstanding authorities on obscenity, 'The danger of influencing a change in the current moral standards of the community, or of shocking or offending readers, or of stimulating sex thoughts or desires apart from objective conduct, can never justify the losses to society that result from interference with literary freedom.' Lockhart & McClure, Literature, The Law of Obscenity and the Constitution, 38 Minn. L. Rev. 295, 387."

At the time the *Roth* case was decided the following appeared to be a constitutional standard approved by the Supreme Court to test whether material could be banned as obscene: If a book or article aroused prurient interests its distribution could constitutionally be a crime provided that the prurient portions were so frequent as to color the entire work. Under this test a prosecutor would have a fair chance, depending upon his luck in getting the right jury, to suppress a very large number of our current publications including some of our best selling books. However, this test was supported by a bare majority of five. Of the four who did not accept it, Chief Justice Warren thought that the issue was not before the Court in the *Roth-Alberts* cases; Justice Harlan thought that the test was unconstitutional if applied to federal statutes but not unconstitutional if applied to state laws; and Justices Douglas and Black thought no obscenity statute, state or federal, could be constitutional.

After the *Roth-Alberts* decision the lower Courts did the best they could with the test in the three cases which followed *Roth*, to wit, *One, Inc.* v. *Olesen*, 355 U. S. 371 (January 13, 1958); *Sunshine Book Co.* v. *Summerfield*, 355 U. S. 372 (January 13, 1958); and *Times Film Corp.* v. *Chicago*, 355 U. S. 35 (November 12, 1957). In each of these cases the material under consideration seems infinitely more obscene than the most daring of the magazines before the Court here. The material in *One, Inc.* was described by the Court of Appeals for the Ninth Circuit as follows:

> "It conveys information to the homosexual or any other reader as to where to get more of the material contained in 'One.'

"An examination of 'The Circle' clearly reveals that it contains obscene and filthy matter which is offensive to the moral senses, morally depraving and debasing, and that it is designed for persons having lecherous and salacious proclivities.

"The picture and the sketches are obscene and filthy by prevailing standards. The stories 'All This and Heaven Too' and 'Not Til the End', pages 32–36, are similar to the story 'Sappho Remembered', except that they relate to the activities of the homosexuals rather than lesbians. Such stories are obscene, lewd and lascivious. They are offensive to the moral senses, morally depraving and debasing." *One, Inc.* v. *Olesen*, 241 F. 2d 772, 778 (9th Cir., 1957).

The Court of Appeals condemned such materials as obscene.

The material in *Times Film Corp.* v. *Chicago* was described by the Court of Appeals for the Seventh Circuit in these terms:

"The film, as an exhibit in this case, was projected before and viewed by us. We found that, from beginning to end, the thread of the story is supercharged with a current of lewdness generated by a series of illicit sexual intimacies and acts. In the introductory scenes a flying start is made when a 16 year old boy is shown completely nude on a bathing beach in the presence of a group of younger girls. On that plane the narrative proceeds to reveal the seduction of this boy by a physically attractive woman old enough to be his mother. Under the influence of this experience and an arrangement to repeat it, the boy thereupon engages in sexual relations with a girl of his own age. The erotic thread of the story is carried, without deviation toward any wholesome idea, through scene after scene. The narrative is graphically pictured with nothing omitted except those sexual consummations which are plainly suggested but meaningfully omitted and thus, by the very fact of omission, emphasized. The words spoken in French are reproduced in printed English on the lower edge of the moving film. None of it palliates the effect of the scenes portrayed.

"We do not hesitate to say that the calculated purpose of the producer of this film, and its dominant effect, are substantially to arouse sexual desires." *Times Film Corp.* v. *City of Chicago*, 244 F. 2d 432, 436 (7th Cir., 1957).

Certainly this film is a far greater transgression of the laws of decency than the most ribald passages in the magazines involved in this case.

The third case to follow the *Roth* opinion was *Sunshine Book Company* v. *Summerfield*, 128 F. Supp. 564 (D. C. D. C. 1955), 249 F. 2d 114

(D. C. Cir., 1957). In the District Court Judge Kirkland followed meticulously the standards laid down by the majority opinion in the *Roth* case. He examined each nude in the magazine and tried to analyze which would cause prurient thoughts. He condemned some and passed others and finally held that the magazine as a whole was obscene. The Court of Appeals, three judges dissenting, affirmed Judge Kirkland's opinion. We think that on the lustful thoughts test Judge Kirkland and the Court of Appeals were unquestionably right.

Yet the Supreme Court in all three of these cases granted certiorari and, without permitting argument or the submission of briefs and without a written opinion, reversed all of them *on constitutional grounds* as appears from the cases cited to support the reversal. In *One, Inc.* v. *Olesen,* the Supreme Court opinion reads as follows:

> *"Per Curiam.* The petition for writ of certiorari is granted and the judgment of the United States Court of Appeals for the Ninth Circuit is reversed. Roth v. United States, 354 U. S. 476, 77 S. Ct. 1304, 1 L. Ed. 2d 1498" (355 U. S. 371).

In the *Sunshine Book* case the *per curiam* opinion is practically identical, as follows:

> "Jan. 13, 1958. *Per Curiam.* The petition for writ of certiorari is granted and the judgment of the United States Court of Appeals for the District of Columbia Circuit is reversed. Roth v. United States, 354 U. S. 476, 77 S. Ct. 1304, 1 L. Ed. 2d 1498" (355 U. S. 372).

The *per curiam* opinion in *Times Film* reads as follows:

> *"Per Curiam.* The petition for writ of certiorari is granted and the judgment of the United States Court of Appeals for the Seventh Circuit is reversed. Roth v. U. S. (Alberts v. California), 354 U. S. 476, 77 S. Ct. 1304, 1 L. Ed. 2d 1498. Mr. Justice Burton and Mr. Justice Clark are of the opinion that the petition for certiorari should not have been granted" (355 U. S. 35).

We do not see how it can be argued after these three *per curiam* opinions by the Supreme Court that any of the magazines in this case can be declared obscene. It is our own view that the Supreme Court has adopted the "hard core" pornography test suggested by the Government and approved by Justice Harlan in his dissent in *Roth*. Justice Harlan has apparently changed his mind about there being a different requirement in the application of state laws than there is in the application of federal law. Only two Justices—Burton and Clark—dissenting in *Times Film Cor-*

poration v. *Chicago* would preserve this distinction. Except on this one point the Supreme Court is unanimous.

Ordinarily when the Supreme Court grants certiorari and reverses *per curiam* without argument or submission of briefs it means that the law was clear without argument. But it cannot be said of these three cases that previous decisions compelled their results. There must be a different reason for the Court's silence. We think that reason becomes apparent from a reading of the hundreds of cases where the courts have tried to analyze the concepts of obscenity and which we have refrained from citing because no more unedifying section of judicial literature exists. Vermont has indeed been fortunate in escaping it. The spectacle of a judge poring over the picture of some nude, trying to ascertain the extent to which she arouses prurient interests, and then attempting to write an opinion which explains the difference between that nude and some other nude has elements of low comedy. Justice is supposed to be a blind Goddess. The task of explaining why the words "sexual relations" are decent and some other word with the same meaning is indecent is not one for which judicial techniques are adapted.

It is our belief, therefore, that the Supreme Court's refusal to write opinions in these three cases was exceedingly wise. No one can reason out why anything is or is not obscene. We cite as an instance the District Court's opinion in the *Sunshine* case. Here the judge, feeling compelled to apply the majority standards in the *Roth* case did analyze the magazine picture by picture. The language he had to use in describing the pictures is more repellent than the pictures themselves.[12] What the Supreme Court is saying to the lower court judges is that they don't have to write any more of that kind of stuff. If the material is bad enough they can leave the case to a jury. If it isn't the indictment should be dismissed or a verdict directed. This decision may be made at a glance. Studying the material for hours doesn't tell a judge any more about its obscene character than he knew when he first looked at it.

While it is apparent that the Supreme Court has adopted the "hard core" pornography as a Constitutional test its use of the *per curiam* opinion neatly avoided the trap of defining what "hard core" pornography is. Such an attempt would have started the futile and desperate game of definition all over again. As William James, the great psychologist, said: "Such discussions are tedious—not as hard subjects like physics or mathe-

---

[12] *Sunshine Book Co.* v. *Summerfield*, 128 F. Supp. 564 (D. C. D. C., 1955).

The only way to avoid such repellent descriptions is to hold that no nudes is good nudes.

matics are tedious, but as throwing feathers endlessly hour after hour is tedious".

The net result of these *per curiam* opinions taken in connection with the *Roth* case may be stated as follows: Obscenity laws are not unconstitutional on their face and legislatures are permitted to make this legislative bow to morality. But in applying an obscenity statute under the First and Fourteenth Amendments only the most extreme forms of erotica can be banned from distribution. Tendency to arouse lustful thoughts does not justify submitting a case to a jury even though, as in *One, Inc.* the author had no other purpose in mind. Courts are no longer required to undertake the undignified introspective task of putting themselves in the role of the general public and then deciding whether in that role the material has unduly aroused their sexual interest. Nor does the court any longer have to be a literary critic and decide whether the author is predominantly an artist or a pornographer. Judges have definitely been relieved of the responsibility of reducing the number of improper thoughts per capita.

However, where the material is so obscene as to constitute hard core pornography and the case *does* go to a jury the judge has to say something. In that case and in that case only does the lustful thoughts test have any relevance, perhaps because such an instruction is about the best anyone can do in this field of conflicting moral and social values. In this connection it should be carefully noted that in the *Roth* case the alleged obscene material was not in the record. The decision was limited to the abstract question whether *any* obscenity statute could be constitutional. Therefore, the majority in approving the instruction in the *Roth* case decided only that it was proper if the material was of the class which constitutionally could be submitted to a jury. But in the subsequent *per curiam* opinions the same majority held that material which would ordinarily be called depraved and vicious but which was not "hard core" pornography could not form the basis of a criminal conviction. In determining what constitutes "hard core" pornography the Court felt that further definition was useless and simply held that the material it saw in each case was not obscene, without attempting to explain in an opinion. The Court evidently concluded that its actions must speak for themselves in this field. This may be an unconventional way of making law, but in the field of pornography it is certainly sound judicial common sense.

We therefore suggest that this Court dismiss the indictment with a simple statement that while the Vermont statute is constitutional the particular material before the Court is not as a matter of law criminally obscene.

The argument before the Supreme Court of Vermont proved to be a *cause célèbre*. Pictures of myself and Judge Henry F. Black, of the Vermont bar, who was co-counsel for *Playboy*, were taken on the front steps of the courthouse. The Vermont Attorney General was indignant because of the flippant character of the presentation of our argument in the brief. He particularly took exception to the footnote in the brief that said, "No nudes is good nudes." The Supreme Court listened in silence. No questions were asked; not a word was said by any justice. When their decision came down, they dismissed the appeal without opinion on the highly technical ground that our motion to dismiss in the lower court, from which we had appealed, was "a speaking demurrer" (whatever that means) and not to be tolerated in Vermont jurisprudence.

The case was, therefore, remanded to the lower court in Vermont for trial. The day before the trial, when I was packing my brief case to appear in Vermont, I received a telephone call from Judge Black, who told me that the Attorney General of Vermont had dropped the indictment.

This was the end of a series of *Playboy* prosecutions. Today, the Supreme Court of the United States has clearly indicated, not by written opinions, but, rather, by a series of reversals of lower-court convictions for obscenity, that nothing less than so-called hard-core pornography can be made a crime by state legislation under the Constitution of the United States.

Today and for the future, unless the Supreme Court changes its mind, books formerly declared obscene can freely be published and distributed. In Washington today *Fanny Hill,* once considered the ultimate in pornography, is being sold at newsstands in paper covers for ninety-five cents a copy. No one seems the worse for it. In my view it is a step forward, because pornography exists only in the mind of the reader. He is stimulated by matters that he is not used to. If he reads *Fanny Hill* a couple of times, he will become used to it and fail to react. By the wisdom of the Supreme Court in reversing cases without explanation, the whole field of obscenity in American law, its delicate distinctions, its justifications that frankly erotic literature is not obscene if it has literary merit, and so on, has almost disappeared. And this has been done in spite of the Supreme Court's decision in the Roth case, holding that any book that appeals to prurient interests is obscene. Thus the elastic judicial process in the United States has adapted itself to changing times without in any way repudiating the great principle of the Roth case that obscenity is a crime.

CHAPTER NINETEEN

The Law Firm of Arnold, Fortas & Porter

In July, 1945, after I had resigned from the Court of Appeals, I formed a temporary partnership with one of my former associates in the Antitrust Division, Arne Wiprud. He was an expert in transportation and a necessary associate in handling my first case.

Robert Young, a colorful and controversial figure in railroad transportation, conceived the idea of forming an independent company to buy the equipment and service of the Pullman Company. He enlisted the financial support of Cyrus Eaton, of Cleveland, a financier who was noted for his independence of Wall Street financial interests and for his endorsement of the principles of the Sherman Act.

Young's opportunity to make this acquisition had arisen out of a prosecution I started when I was assistant attorney general. Sleeping-car service for all railroads in the United States was furnished by the Pullman Company, which had a complete monopoly over that service as well as over the manufacture of Pullman cars. No railroad could duplicate the nationwide organization of Pullman porters, conductors, and other personnel. It had no choice but to take Pullman service on Pullman's terms. Those terms were that the railroad should use only the cars manufactured by the Pullman Company. This excluded independent car-manufacturing companies, such as the Budd Company of Philadelphia, from the market. One of the incidental results of this restraint of trade is the fact that even today there are two conductors taking the tickets of each

Pullman passenger, an operation that could be carried on more efficiently by one conductor.

The government won the suit, and the Pullman Company was ordered to divest itself of either its manufacturing interests or its control over Pullman service. The company chose to sell its existing fleet of Pullman cars and its organization for servicing Pullman travel and to keep its car-manufacturing business. There were other bidders besides Robert Young, but Young and Eaton in my view offered the best plan for future competition in railroad service. A large part of the Pullman equipment was obsolete. In a day of roller bearings, Pullman passengers were traveling on friction axles. There was no way to get from New York to California without stopping a day in Chicago. Young dramatized this in a picturesque advertising campaign with the slogan, "A hog can cross the country without changing cars, but you can't."

Young had other plans for improving Pullman travel. He noted that one of the most inexpensive vacations that an American citizen could take was a pack trip in our wilderness areas. He figured that horses and tents were cheap; therefore, if a nationwide recreation company were organized, the Pullman Company could take the traveler to the edge of the mountains, get him up to the great forests in an automobile, put him on a horse in the morning, and bed him down in the tent at night, all as part of the same service and at a low cost. He argued also that, though the greater part of the Pullman equipment was owned by large Eastern railroads, an independent Pullman service company could transfer cars to the South in the wintertime, to the far western mountains in the summertime, and thus improve the competitive opportunity of the poorer railroads.

The entire Association of American Railroads opposed Young's bid. He had been a bitter critic of existing railroad management. He was even then trying to get control of the New York Central, a feat he subsequently accomplished. The existing railroad management wanted no part of him in its picture. The railroads, therefore, formed a combination to purchase the Pullman service themselves and offered the court a competing bid. We argued for Young that such a combination of railroads in itself was a violation of the

Sherman Act. In answer to this, the railroads got their program approved by the Interstate Commerce Commission.

At every session of the three-judge court in Philadelphia where the hearing took place, the general counsel of every American railroad appeared. They filled the courtroom. It was an impressive sight. It made Young and Eaton appear to be disputing the wise and expert recommendations of all the trained experts in railroading in the United States. We did not seem to be projecting the proper "image."

We lost the case, and the railroads' bid was accepted. This decision was later affirmed by the Supreme Court of the United States, by an equally divided Court, Justice Robert H. Jackson taking no part. Therefore no opinion could be written.

Thus two vital figures—Robert Young and Cyrus Eaton—were prevented from reforming railroad management, which has since that time had one principal objective, and that is the abandonment of passenger-car service. The luxurious trains in the East are becoming less and less luxurious. Passenger trains are being taken out of service. Commuter lines are going bankrupt. Japan, with the fastest commuter trains in the world, between Tokyo and Osaka, is far ahead of us. We are clogging our cities with automobiles. I have often wondered whether the suppression of the competitive ideas of Robert Young by the failure of the Supreme Court to get a majority on either side in the case is not in some way responsible for this.

At that point, since our firm's transportation business seemed to be at an end, Arne Wiprud, whose sole interest was in transportation law, dissolved our partnership to pursue his own speciality. My great hope then was to associate myself with Abe Fortas, a close friend and a former student of mine at Yale. I knew he was planning to resign his post as Under Secretary of the Interior and enter the practice of law. I asked him if he would form a partnership with me. This I consider the smartest decision I ever made. Abe accepted. And his decision was by all odds the luckiest thing that ever happened to me. And so the firm of Arnold and Fortas was launched in January, 1946.

In the meantime, Paul A. Porter had resigned as head of the Office of Price Administration to accept President Truman's appointment as roving ambassador to Greece. All he was asked to do was to end the disastrous civil war there, which was then being supported by the Soviets. This assignment lasted a year. As a close student of, and an authority on, international affairs, it is my considered opinion that the entire credit for the ending of that war should go to Paul Porter. Abe Fortas and I had the sagacity to invite Porter to become a member of the firm. The result was described by my cynical friend Edgar Goodrich, formerly a judge of the United States Court of Tax Appeals and now engaged in private practice, as follows: "Your firm used to be known as Arnold, Fortas & Integrity. Now that you have fired Integrity and taken on Paul Porter your future is very bright indeed." Some instinct told me that Goodrich was a born exaggerator.

Our firm had started out with two partners and four associates: Walton H. Hamilton, who had retired as a professor of law at Yale; Reed Miller and Norman Diamond, two young men who had been officers during the Second World War, and Milton Freeman, who resigned from the General Counsel's office of the Securities and Exchange Commission to come with us. Hamilton was a remarkable man. He was a brilliant and original economist, a writer of great distinction, and an inspiring teacher. He lost his eyesight when he was seventy, but he continued to handle difficult cases. He died, at the age of seventy-seven, in 1958. Freeman, Diamond, and Miller have been for many years partners in the firm, which now includes about forty lawyers. A country practitioner, I had inherited a dislike of large firms. Arnold, Fortas & Porter is not yet a big firm according to the standards of large American cities; nevertheless, I am still somewhat uncomfortable about its size, though nobody else seems to be.

The growth of a city law firm can be avoided only if the seniors turn down business. But the ambitious juniors, who start out carrying brief cases, get older, raise families, and want someone to carry brief cases for them. And so the firm expands. The only remedy to the inevitable growth of a city law firm is one that I proposed in a speech made at an annual banquet of the *University of Chicago Law Review*. I was asked what characteristics and talents a firm like ours was looking for in law graduates. I said we wanted bright young men of top standing with ability to grasp complicated legal problems and write persuasively and eloquently about them. We also wanted men who after three years of service and just about the time that their salaries were getting burdensome would come into the office, smile, and say good-by, and then gradually disappear like the Cheshire cat in *Alice in Wonderland*, leaving the smile behind them. If only such men could be obtained from our leading law schools, the problem of the unwieldy growth of a law firm would be solved. Unfortunately, my proposal came to nothing.

When I was at Harvard every law student knew the names of the leading lawyers in New York. The practice of law was far more personal and had less the appearance of the corporate practice of law that exists today. Increasingly, the law is being practiced anonymously. The names of senior partners of large city firms do not appear in the firm name. Highly successful lawyers are practicing under the names of dead men. The personal identities of lawyers are submerged. They are assuming the appearance of officers in large corporations. This has not happened in England, with its system of barristers and solicitors, nor has it happened in Germany, France, or Italy, where firms of one hundred or two hundred men are unknown.

The chief asset of a large firm in the United States is becoming the good-will value of its name rather than the personal reputation of any of its individual lawyers. In the days of John W. Davis, Rufus Choate, of Boston, and John S. Miller, of Chicago, this was not true. But my regret over this situation is purely nostalgic. I see no possibility of a change.

There is one great advantage in practicing under dead men's names. If you are depending upon clients who come to you on account of your own reputation, your first necessity is to persuade them that you are the indispensable man to handle their cases. Then as you get busy you must persuade them that some other member of your firm is just as much qualified—or even more qualified—than you are. In a firm where none, or only one, of the names of the partners appears in the firm name, legal talents are fungible. Any partner is presumed to be just as good as any other.

An anecdote may serve to show the skilled examination of witnesses that the members of Arnold, Fortas & Porter are able to produce on short notice.

The example is from the records of a case tried by Paul Porter before a hearing examiner of the Federal Communications Commission. The issue to be decided was whether the acquisition of the American Broadcasting Company by Paramount Theatres, a company that had emerged from a dissolution of the famous Paramount Pictures, would be approved by the FCC. The standards the FCC applies in such a case are necessarily vague. Among them, however, is the character and history of the applicant. On this occasion, counsel opposing our application appeared with a copy of my book *The Folklore of Capitalism*. Paul immediately became uneasy. I do not think he had ever read the book thoroughly, but he knew enough about it to be afraid that all sorts of assertions damaging to any reputable applicant before the Commission might be contained within its covers.

The witness on the stand was Paul Raibourn, the vice president of our client. At the end of opposing counsel's cross-examination of Mr. Raibourn, he produced the copy of my book. I repeat verbatim the examination and cross-examination that followed.

DIRECT EXAMINATION BY PAUL PORTER—CROSS EXAMINATION BY MR. ROBERTS. Pages 2354–2357.

Mr. Roberts: I think that concludes our examination, except for one question, Mr. Raibourn.

Mr. Raibourn, you were with Paramount throughout the reorganization days and, I believe, that you did work with the people in Paramount Publix, too, did you not?

A. Yes, sir.

Q. As to the value of the experience which would be contributed to a young and growing industry from Paramount Publix, I would like to read a reference from a standard and well-known work with regard to that company, and to ask you if it is a correct description.

Mr. Porter: Would you identify it, please?

Mr. Roberts: *The Folklore of Capitalism* by Thurman W. Arnold.

Mr. Porter: I submit, Mr. Examiner, that that is not proper cross-examination, to read to this witness excerpts from a publication that some people might characterize as the youthful effusions of an intellectual adolescent and a teacher at Yale Law School.

He can ask him what he thinks about the policies and the attitudes and the facts that happened during that period, but to check his opinions as to what somebody else said seems to me to be an improper field for cross-examination.

Mr. Roberts: Well, Your Honor—

The Presiding Officer: Objection is overruled.

Mr. Roberts: Your Honor, this is the twelfth printing in January, 1948 of this work, which really is a highly—

Mr. Salant: The objection has been overruled.

Mr. Roberts: I did not think Mr. Raibourn had known that it had gone past the twelfth printing.

By Mr. Roberts:

Q. Quite seriously, Mr. Raibourn—

A. I read one of the early editions.

Q. It is probably the same.

> On page 351 it says with respect to Paramount Publix: "Once the personality of an organization is fixed, it is as difficult to change as the habits of an individual. The same type of men succeed each other, moved by the same attitudes as their predecessors. Illustration: Paramount Publix grew to be a colossus in the amusement industry by virtue of the most wasteful and extravagant habits imaginable. It was a combination of the personalities of Lorenzo the Magnificent and Jean Jacques Casanova in the motley crowd of business enterprizes, many of which affected the dour attitudes of our Puritan Fathers. Came the reorganization. A distinguished businessman named Hertz was given power over the budget to effect economies. From a puritanical standpoint, this was an easy task. Waste was everywhere. Hertz cut down expenditures about $25 million in one year. He was promptly forced to resign. Every economy that he instituted was entirely defensible. Yet the institution, instead of improving, appeared to be going to pieces under the strain. The persons whom he discharged were, no doubt, parasites. Yet fear and anxiety spread to the most useful members of the organization. Mr. Swaine, the hard-boiled and able attorney for the bankers, had difficulty in explaining before the Securities and Exchange Commission why the activities of Hertz were stopped, because he was talking in the highly moral atmosphere of a public investigation, in which it is difficult to get a practical point across."

Now, assuming and granting a considerable author's liberty, a very able person, Judge Arnold, is it true that Mr. Hertz was placed in charge of the organization under conditions roughly as described, and was unable to reorganize the Paramount business so as to effect an efficient and orderly economy?

A. I was there; I assisted Mr. Hertz in his work. We tried to eliminate everything which by any possible conception would prevent the company from reaching its final destination, which was bankruptcy and reorganization.

The measures which were taken were not sufficient in the face of the rapid decline of American business to meet that situation.

I think Mr. Arnold's characterization of it looked at from a distance is interesting but highly inaccurate. . . .

REDIRECT EXAMINATION BY MR. PAUL PORTER. Pages 2378–2380.

Q. Mr. Raibourn, Mr. Roberts read to you from a distinguished author of some sixteen years ago.

I would like to ask your opinion on a more recent statement that was made some five or six years after the statement which Mr. Roberts has read. The same individual in an official capacity as Assistant Attorney General was appearing before a Senate committee in April of 1940, and stated, and I quote:

> "I want to pay my tribute to the American businessmen and the movie industry. They are as competent as any in the world. I want to applaud the tremendous advances they have made. Their technique is far in advance of anything in the world. As a matter of individual initiative they are outstanding."

I will ask you which of the two statements you think is the most accurate.

A. I think the second one is, by far, the most accurate.

Mr. Porter: I did not open this up, Mr. Examiner.

The Presiding Officer: Well, Mr. Arnold, the gentleman whom you described as being a youth sixteen years ago, developed rather rapidly.

Mr. Porter: He has reached an advanced stage of maturity.

Mr. Ford: I do not think that the Commission ought to decide this case on the declarations of Mr. Arnold, no matter how wise they may be, either at one period of his life or another.

Mr. Porter: If counsel had joined me in my objections to Colonel Roberts' previous statement I would not have felt it necessary to burden the record here with the several statements I read, and I will assure you that this is where I will stop, because there are numerous opinions of this same individual, and we could continue this indefinitely, but this is the last.

CHAPTER TWENTY

The Use of Legislative Hearings for the Purpose of Exposing Undesirable Characters

It is interesting to observe that the technique of Senatorial investigations for the purpose of exposure of undesirable elements in our society was not invented by Senator Joseph McCarthy. In 1951, before Senator McCarthy had attained the chairmanship of an investigating committee, Senator Estes Kefauver's Committee on Crime put on the greatest legislative exposure of the year over a nationwide television hook-up. Its purpose was to expose gambling and gamblers throughout the nation. It was a popular success. It increased the amount of public hypocrisy on gambling across the land. In Nevada, where gambling is an industry, the famous resorts of Reno and Las Vegas continued to flourish. It also contributed to the fame and prestige of the Senator. Liberals, including myself, admired the Senator. They were all opposed to public gambling. Therefore, there was no protest from the liberal side against this investigation even though one of its main purposes was to arouse the public.

The method was the same as that later adopted with so much success by Senator McCarthy. First the witness was examined at a private hearing to which the public was not admitted. Then such of his testimony as would elicit the greatest public interest was rehashed at a public hearing. The vehicle used was television.

Later still the same technique was adopted by Senator John McClellan, whose counsel was the liberal Robert Kennedy. At one of his committee hearings James Hoffa, famous head of the

Teamsters Union, had to repeat over and over again before a nationwide television audience his refusal to answer questions on the ground that it would incriminate him. This show also was a nationwide success.

Senator McCarthy himself became the principal victim of this process in a television show that led to the vote of censure against him. No one can dispute the utility of televised public hearings in arousing public indignation.

My own views on televised hearings I expressed in an article in the *Atlantic Monthly* for June 1951, entitled "Mob Justice and Television," in which I discussed the Kefauver Crime Committee's procedure. I republish the article here in the hope that it may interest the reader in a problem that is still alive. Recently Robert Baker's request not to have his appearance before a Senate committee televised was granted by the committee that investigated him, though there is no rule that required the committee to grant Baker's request.

The production put on by the Kefauver Committee on crime is unquestionably the best show of the year. My introduction to it was during the examination of Mr. Frank Costello. I missed an entire morning at the office, fascinated and at the same time appalled by the dramatic quality of this new form of public inquisition.

Mr. Costello was not visible. Instead the camera focused on his hands, which constantly moved and twitched in a decidedly guilty way. It was apparent that the committee did not regard Mr. Costello as a pillar of the church or as otherwise an object of hero worship. They were at the moment going back to his career during Prohibition. Counsel for the committee would read selected answers made by Costello at a previous examination and ask him if he didn't remember so answering. It was an effective dramatic device, particularly when the camera would switch from the stern and righteous faces of the committee and its counsel to the guilty twitching hands of the gambler. It soon appeared that Costello had started as a bootlegger. It became equally apparent that the questions were not for the purpose of finding out anything. The committee already had the information. And so Mr. Costello's attorney

thought he had a point. He objected on the ground that all the
committee was doing was castigating his client in public for mis-
deeds in the dim and distant past. He implied that an investigation into the violations of the Prohibition laws had become somewhat dated since the repeal of that great experiment. But the
presiding Senator had the answer. He observed that if Mr. Costello
had been engaged in a conspiracy to violate the Prohibition laws
at the time of his naturalization it might be a present ground for
revoking his citizenship as fraudulently obtained. Counsel agreed,
and Mr. Costello's hands twitched violently. The possibility was
considered sufficient to establish the relevancy of going back twenty
years. The camera then switched to Mr. Costello's attorney, whose
face registered complete frustration as effectively as I have ever seen
it done by any professional actor. In fact, the entire cast was good.
Everybody was having fun except Mr. Costello, and certainly no
one would suggest that gamblers deserve to be comfortable in a
land where gambling is quite often and under certain circumstances
illegal.

Nor, as is apparent from a later incident, are persons who associate with unsavory characters entitled to consideration. John P.
Crane testified that he gave Mayor William O'Dwyer $10,000 in
cash on a front porch in the dark. Ambassador O'Dwyer, fran-
tically flying up from Mexico, denied it. The publicly announced
verdict of the committee was that one of the two had perjured
himself. This verdict of guilt in the alternative against a public
figure is a new weapon in the arsenal of law enforcement for which
I predict a bright future. It gets two birds with one shot, and at
the same time is so simple to operate that even a child can handle
it without danger to himself.

Captious critics might, of course, argue that Mayor O'Dwyer's
official conduct in New York and Governor Thomas E. Dewey's
alleged indifference to Saratoga gambling were, under our federal
system, none of the business of Congress. But if so New York has
an easy answer. If Senators investigate state officials over television,
then let state legislators use the same medium to investigate the
Senators whenever they catch them in their state. Governor Dewey
requested the committee to come to Albany and learn about crime
from him. They declined. Immediately thereafter they should have

been hauled to Albany under subpoena for a compulsory course in the problem of crime. It makes a better game if the opposing side occasionally gets the ball.

Bishop James Cannon must be turning in his grave with disappointment because he lived before criminal inquisition by television. He had to contend with the grand jury system, a relic of the days when it was thought that investigations of crime had to be conducted in secret. The notion was that even suspicious and unsavory characters should not be publicly accused by a responsible tribunal unless there was enough evidence to support an indictment. And so the bootleggers who supplied liquor to respectable but wayward citizens escaped. If Senators who followed the inspiration of the good Bishop could have compelled the convivial elements of our various cities either to tell over television the names of their bootleggers or to decline on the ground of self-incrimination, they would have cleaned up every country club in the land.

Today the utility of this device in getting rid of subversive ideas on the screen, in the theater, on college campuses, is as yet unexplored. Anyone who has been on television knows the camera fright involved in a first appearance. College professors are shy and retiring folk. When their opinions are inquired into before twenty million listeners by an investigator experienced and skilled in television showmanship, millions of American housewives are going to enjoy the entrancing spectacle of seeing them go to pieces before their eyes with twitching hands, nervous voices, hesitating answers, and similar evidences of guilt which made the ancient trial by ordeal the effective instrument that it was.

Unfortunately Senator McCarthy has not yet attained the chairmanship of an investigating committee. He can now go on television himself but he cannot examine unwilling witnesses there. This is like trying to conduct a fox hunt without a live fox. But the process of time and seniority will soon remove that handicap, and when the Senator does put on his show I'll lay a substantial wager with my bookie (provided the Kefauver Committee has not deported him) that McCarthy will make the efforts of the present committee look like the work of inept amateurs.

Trials in our courts of justice are public but the audience is so limited that the ordinary housewife cannot see the show because, as we go to press, cameras are still banned. I suggest that if this rule cannot be changed, all the judge has to do is to hold a trial like that of Alger Hiss in Yankee Stadium. By this method, while the judge could not get television rights he would still have quite a crowd in any *cause célèbre*. And since judges do not have to run for office as often as Senators, this minor disadvantage creates no real injustice.

The beauty of criminal investigation by television is that it permits us to preserve intact our traditional principle against self-incrimination and at the same time prevents that privilege from getting in our way. No respectable public figure would dare invoke it over a coaxial cable, so that it is a rare case in which a verdict of guilty in the alternative between the accuser and the accused cannot be obtained against any prominent individual.

These are the outstanding virtues of this new technique for public hearings. Others might be added. This kind of presentation makes the problems of government simple enough to be understood by readers of comic strips. It eliminates the bores who are unable to discuss a public issue as a matter of black and white. When ex-Mayor O'Dwyer was testifying about the problem of crime from his vast experience as a prosecutor and a mayor, I am informed the stations were flooded with calls to get him off and put Virginia Hill back on. In my view these people had a point. How can anyone enjoy a good detective story when his train of thought is constantly interrupted by tiresome undramatic interpolation?

Yet in spite of these many and obvious advantages, I am prepared to argue that the entire show should be taken off the road and that hereafter no investigator should ever be permitted to use the long arm of a government subpoena to force any witness, however unsavory, to confess (or discuss) his sins before twenty million people. And I would maintain this view even if I were convinced that it meant the continuance of the horrid gambling at Saratoga that has shocked the conscience of the civilized world. And if the great television audience protested I would have Arthur Godfrey appear and read to them what Moses said to the children of Israel when they began the worship of the golden calf: "Ye have sinned a great sin" (Exodus 32:30). I would have him explain that justice is even more important than the enforcement of sumptuary laws.

The thing which I believe is overlooked by those who argue that television is a legitimate extension of our traditional public hearing is this. The reason that a criminal trial is public is not to obtain the maximum publicity for judges or prosecutors. It was not intended to make a *cause célèbre* out of criminal prosecutions. It is public for the protection of the accused against star-chamber methods, and for the protection of the public against secret deals and alliances. The notion that since a criminal trial is usually entertaining it should be so staged as to provide the greatest entertainment to the greatest number is not an American tradition. A criminal hearing should not be a star chamber. It is equally important that it should not be a circus.

I recognize that a legislative investigation of crime, such as the Kefauver Committee, is not strictly speaking a criminal proceeding. But anyone viewing the proceedings in New York will understand how easily it can be turned into one and how great the temptation is to do so. If the committee succeeds in arousing the American housewife, it is inevitable that there will be a counterreaction and the American housewife will arouse the committee. If this mutual excitement becomes a common incident to the legislative hearing, blind forces will be unleashed which I do not like to contemplate. When a Congressional hearing becomes through the osmosis of television more of a trial than an attempt to obtain information for legislative action, the punishment may be as severe as fine or imprisonment. For the screen actor it may be the loss of his career. For a college professor it may be the end of his job. The fact that these incidents can happen in a hearing even without television does not in my view justify magnifying them a thousand times in order to entertain housewives.

But apart from the injustice to witnesses, there is the effect on the legislative committee itself. It tends to degrade the subject matter of the hearings. The crucial nonmilitary problems before us concern inflation and the economics of mobilization. But these are dull subjects. Their Hooper rating would be nil. The sure-fire topics are sin, sex, and subversion, not presented abstractly but

pepped up with live witnesses. Sex presents its difficulties under
our present mores. But properly buttered up as an educational
show there is no reason why an investigation of vice in our high
schools would not be accepted. After all, are we trying to protect
the American home or aren't we?

My trouble here is not a moral one. It is only that the really important investigations cannot compete with these circuses. As a
result, at a time of national peril we see the time of our most
important Senators engaged in arousing the public on dangers
which the historian is going to regard as of the utmost triviality.
Indeed, if a sensible list of priorities for the expenditure of Congressional effort and for the education of the public were made
today and then turned upside down with the least important
thing put first, we would have the present situation. For this
distortion of government objectives, investigation by television
will bear an increasing responsibility.

And then there is the degrading effect of an audience of twenty
million on the manner in which the material is presented. It may
be that fox hunts began as an honest attempt to exterminate
these predatory animals. I do not think they are that today—at
least not the hunts I have seen. And I had an uneasy suspicion,
as I watched the Senate crime hearing, that the same metamor-
phosis was taking place there. I could be wrong, but it did not
seem to me that putting an unwilling witness under the strain of
a hot lamp and an audience of twenty million was any way of
obtaining objective information to be used in drafting legislation on a national problem. And why was Mr. Costello asked to repeat before this vast audience information about his activities of
twenty years ago which the committee already had?

I do not charge the Kefauver Committee with intolerance or
vindictiveness in the conduct of the hearings. Senators Kefauver
and Charles Tobey, who played the principal roles, have long been
distinguished for their fairness and generally liberal attitudes.
But the requirements of the television stage on which they have
been appearing make an objective investigation almost impossible.
It is too apt to become dull, and if it does it will go off the air.
And what will happen when intolerant men take over the management is not comfortable to contemplate.

The vice of this television proceeding is not in the way this particular committee conducted it, but in the proceeding itself. Any tribunal which takes on the trappings and aspects of a judicial hearing, particularly where there is compulsory examination of witnesses, must conform to our judicial traditions, or sooner or later it will develop into a monstrosity that demands reform. Those traditions are:

1. It must be public and at the same time not a device for publicity.

2. It must protect the innocent even at the cost of letting the guilty escape.

Television has no place in such a picture. For witnesses it is an ordeal not unlike the third degree. On those who sit as judges it imposes the demoralizing necessity of also being actors. For the accused it offers no protection whatever. Former Federal Judge Simon H. Rifkind recently said that our judicial procedure, "forged through the generations to the single end that issues shall be impartially determined on relevant evidence alone, works fairly well in all cases but one—the celebrated cause. As soon as the *cause célèbre* comes in, the judges and lawyers no longer enjoy a monopoly. They have a partner in the enterprise, and that partner is the press." I would add that when television is utilized in investigations or trials, *causes célèbres* will increase like guinea pigs and still another partner will be added—to wit, the mob.

CHAPTER TWENTY-ONE

The Un-American Activities of Government
Organizations to Suppress Un-American Activities

Our practice at Arnold, Fortas & Porter since the institution of the firm has been devoted largely to problems of corporate clients with the government, fascinating to those who are carrying it on but of little general interest. The cases that might interest the nonspecialist reader are those involving civil liberties during that hysterical era when Senator Joseph McCarthy had the power to call to heel anyone in the executive branch of government, any Cabinet officer, and indeed the President of the United States.

Our first case of this character was *Friedman* v. *Schwellenbach*, 159 F. 2d 22 (1946). Friedman, an official of the War Manpower Commission, had been discharged for alleged disloyalty. Had he been discharged for unsuitability, we would have felt that this was within the managerial discretion of the War Manpower Commission. Under civil service rules, he would have been entitled to a statement of the charges against him, which he could answer. After his answer, if the Commission had decided that he was still unsuitable for his job, he could have been discharged unless some personal bias or prejudice was shown that made the discharge an arbitrary act rather than an exercise of managerial discretion. No one has a right to a government job. Discharge on the grounds of unsuitability is unfortunate for the employee but implies no moral stigma.

But in 1947 the fear that culminated in the McCarthy hysteria was building up. It was not sufficient to discharge Communists and fellow travelers just to get rid of them. They had to be exposed in order to prove to the public that the government was not being soft on Communism. Hence, this official had to be branded with a badge of infamy in addition to the loss of his job owing to his left-wing opinions and associations. He had to be stigmatized as disloyal to his country. A lower court sustained the Commission's action in discharging him. We applied for a writ of certiorari to the Supreme Court of the United States. In his brief, in April, 1947, Abe Fortas wrote the following:

But this assault on freedom of opinion will not stop with Government employees. Assaults upon freedom have a habit of growing beyond a stated objective. They quickly attack not merely a manifestation, but freedom itself. So this crusade, once under way, will not stop with its victims in the federal service. It will spread and is now spreading over this country, blighting our democracy and bringing fear and distrust to American homes throughout the nation.

The granting of a writ of certiorari is not a decision on the merits of a case. It is simply an assertion by the Supreme Court that the decision of the lower court is of sufficient public importance to deserve review before the Supreme Court of the United States. This procedure has been adopted because the Court cannot possibly find the time to hear all the cases lawyers from all over the United States desire to bring before it.

In arguing for certiorari, we conceded that the government could fire anyone for unsuitability for his position after giving him charges setting out the reason he was unsuitable, as civil service rules required. But the government, we urged, could not fire an employee and then put upon his record a charge akin to treason, and thus not only get rid of him but also ruin his career in other fields. If an officer of a bank had become so connected with left-wing groups that depositors were leaving the bank, the president would call him in and say, "You may be a sincere idealist, but you are hurting the image of this bank. We can't afford to have you around. I suggest you find another job." But the president could not then follow this by taking additional action to prevent the discharged employee from ever getting another job. Although it was not put in these terms, this is exactly what the government was trying to do in this case.

Had the Supreme Court agreed with us, the power that McCarthy achieved later would have been impossible, or, at the least, impeded. But a majority of the Supreme Court, motivated, I suspect, by the principle that one of the functions of the Court is to keep out of trouble, denied certiorari. Justices Black and Douglas dissented. And Abe's prediction of the disastrous results that might follow the Court's refusal to protect an individual under these circumstances from penalties imposed after trials that had no semblance of due process of law proved all too true.

President Truman, sometime after this decision, realizing, no doubt, that a discharge for security reasons carries the penalty of disgrace and the loss of a career, set up a quasi-judicial system of loyalty boards with the appearance of impartiality to try persons accused of Communist leanings. These boards promptly adopted a device that robbed the proceedings of all semblance of a fair trial. They began to base their convictions for disloyalty in cases where all the evidence was favorable to the accused on secret information given to the board by unnamed informers, which the accused could not possibly rebut. And thus arose the case of *Bailey* v. *Richardson,* in which our firm defended Dorothy Bailey.

Dorothy Bailey was a highly intelligent young woman who occupied an important post in the Department of Labor. Seth W. Richardson was the head of the loyalty board that tried her. Dorothy Bailey's duties were not even remotely connected with national security. They consisted in drawing up training programs for use in educational work. She was charged with being a member of the Communist party and brought to trial before a loyalty board, set up according to President Truman's executive order.

At the trial she produced a host of affidavits from responsible people who had known her all her life attesting to her loyalty. She was examined at great length on the stand. There was not a line in the public record that in any way impeached her or threw any suspicion on her loyalty. In spite of this, she was convicted by the loyalty board. The evidence upon which this conviction was based consisted of either the testimony or the written statements of unknown accusers. We never knew. When asked whether this testimony or these statements were sworn to, the board informed her that they did not know, but that the FBI had certified that the unknown informers were reliable. The board was not only unwilling to disclose the names of the informers, but it would not even tell her the contents of or the time and place of her alleged disloyal acts, beliefs, or associations.

We appealed the case to the lower courts with high hopes of success. It seemed incredible that a citizen of the United States could have her entire career ruined and her livelihood taken away on a record such as this. We checked the record of the trial of the German judges conducted by an American court in Germany after the war. It appeared that these judges had sustained convictions on evidence given by faceless informers. The American tribunal sitting in Germany sentenced the judges to imprisonment because they had conducted their proceedings in this manner. In the Bailey case we were not asking for the imprisonment of the loyalty board that had convicted Dorothy Bailey; all we wanted was to have her conviction reversed and a fair trial given to her under American standards.

To our bitter disappointment, the United States District Court sustained her conviction. We appealed. For reasons I did not then and do not now understand, though I have read the opinion, the Court of Appeals sustained the trial court.

We then applied to the Supreme Court to review the decision. The brief that we filed before the Supreme Court to support our position in this case consisted of the great dissenting opinion filed in the United States Court of Appeals by Judge Henry White Edgerton in the Bailey case. He said in part (182 F. 2d 46, 74 (1950)):

The court (referring to the majority opinion) thinks Miss Bailey's interest and the public interest conflict. I think they coincide. Since Miss Bailey's dismissal from a nonsensitive job has nothing to do with protecting the security of the United States, the government's right to preserve itself in the world as it is has nothing to do with this case. The ominous theory that the right of fair trial ends where defense of security begins is irrelevant.

On this record we have no sufficient reason to doubt Miss Bailey's patriotism, or that her ability and experience were valuable to the government. We have no reason to suppose that an unpatriotic person in her job could do substantial harm of any kind. Whatever her actual thoughts may have been, to oust her as disloyal without trial is to pay too much for protection against any harm that could possibly be done in such a job. The cost is too great in morale and efficiency of government workers, in appeal of government employment to independent and inquiring minds, and in public confidence in democracy. But even if such dismissals strengthened the government instead of weakening it, they would still cost too much in constitutional rights. We cannot preserve our liberties by sacrificing them.

This time the Supreme Court of the United States thought the issue was of enough public importance to grant certiorari. The decision was a long time in coming down. One of the nine judges disqualified himself. Finally, in 1951, the Court announced that it had split four to four, and since the Court of Appeals had decided against her the dismissal of Dorothy Bailey was sustained (341 U. S. 918).

We were unable to believe that a full Court would sustain such a result and, therefore, when, in a later case, Dr. John P. Peters, of the Yale Medical faculty, was convicted of disloyalty by a loyalty board, we agreed to represent him in presenting the issue once more to the federal courts.

Dr. Peters was an expert in nutrition. He was not permanently employed in Washington. His position was that of a consultant. He had no specific duties and received no pay except when he was called on for advice by the Surgeon General. It was impossible that there could be any reasons involving national security that required the badge of infamy involved in a loyalty conviction to be pinned on him, except perhaps that he might breathe subversive theories of nutrition into the gullible ear of the Surgeon General of the United States. If the Surgeon General was suspicious of Dr. Peters, all he had to do was write him a polite letter saying that his services as a consultant were no longer required. Peters had no civil service status, as Dorothy Bailey had had.

But those were the days of the numbers game in loyalty cases. Everybody was afraid of McCarthy. Each department head prided himself on the number of scalps he could tie to his belt as a result of loyalty convictions. Each department had its own security officers, on whom millions of dollars were being spent. Victims had to be found in order to give these security officers something to do. And at the time Dr. Peters was tried, the departments had been combed and recombed in a search for subversives to such an extent that it was becoming difficult to find enough Communists to feed into this machine and keep its wheels of injustice grinding. Secretary of Health, Education, and Welfare Oveta Culp Hobby, under whose jurisdiction the Surgeon General operated, was particularly zealous in this respect.

So Dr. Peters, instead of quietly being told he was not needed any more, was brought before a loyalty board, charged with being either a Communist or a person with subversive notions and associations. He had no difficulty in getting long lists of distinguished people to testify in his favor. Men like Charles Seymour, of Yale, and Judge Charles E. Clark, of the United States Court of Appeals for the Second Circuit, testified that there could be no question as to his loyalty. He was tried before a loyalty board and promptly acquitted. But this did not satisfy Secretary Hobby, and so a second loyalty board convened to review the first board's decision. This review board ruled that Dr. Peters was disloyal and should be dismissed. The evidence on which this decision rested consisted, as in the case of Dorothy Bailey, of statements by unnamed informers the character of whose accusations the accused was never permitted to know.

We brought the case before the United States District Court for the District of Columbia for review. That court sustained Dr. Peters's conviction by the loyalty review board. The United States Court of Appeals then affirmed the trial court. Next, the Supreme Court of the United States granted certiorari. The basic question which all counsel felt was involved was whether, as a matter of due process of law, the government could stigmatize a person as disloyal on the basis of information from anonymous informants. When Paul Porter and I argued the case before that Court, Justice Felix Frankfurter raised the question of whether the loyalty review board, which had convicted Dr. Peters, was properly constituted. Both the government counsel and I were taken completely by surprise; neither of us had thought the point worth raising. I further protested to Justice Frankfurter that a decision on this ground would not take away the badge of infamy the second loyalty board had pinned on Dr. Peters, and which he must wear for the rest of his life. I stated that I did not want to win the case on that technical ground. But Justice Frankfurter informed me that it made no difference whatever what grounds I wanted the case decided on—a statement that later proved to be completely accurate.

At the close of the argument, the government and we were instructed to submit briefs on the question of whether the loyalty review board had power to consider the case in light of the favorable decision by the first board. Both sides took the position that there was no technical fault with either the organization or the jurisdiction of the loyalty review board, which had been properly set up under the regulations of the loyalty program. But when the decision came down, the Supreme Court ignored both the government and us with respect to our contention that the second board had jurisdiction, and reversed the decision on the ground that it did not. On this the Court was unanimous.

Thus the case was won on a technical ground that left the badge of infamy still hanging around the neck of Dr. Peters, and the basic issue before the Court—whether a government employee or consultant by accepting government pay puts himself into a position where he may be convicted for an offense akin to treason—was left hanging in the air. So in 1955, under this backhanded approval of the Supreme Court, which had dodged the issue, loyalty convictions on secret evidence continued in full fury.

Our firm had a third chance to present this issue to the federal courts and get a hearing in the case of the loyalty convictions of scientific personnel employed by the government at Fort Monmouth, New Jersey. During the early 1950's Senator McCarthy had made screaming headlines in every newspaper in the country by announcing that some thirty employees, most of them scientists, engaged in classified research at Fort Monmouth, were disloyal. They were discharged. As was customary in those hysterical days, anyone accused by McCarthy of anything was always discharged for security reasons in order to appease the Senator and prove to him that the particular department head was not soft on Communism. High government officials failed to understand that McCarthy never could be appeased. His whole career depended upon harassing the government, no matter what the department heads did.

My sister-in-law was employed by the Department of State at the time. One day when the firings were at their height, I expressed concern lest the State Department find out she was my relative and fire her. She replied, "There is no danger of that whatever. They are only firing the competent people."

The wheels of justice of the hierarchy of trial loyalty tribunals and appellate loyalty tribunals with jurisdiction over the crime of imagining the king's death were promptly thrown into gear and began to grind on the Fort Monmouth spy case. At the trial of ten of the accused before a loyalty board no evidence was produced to support the charges against them. The board relied on secret information given to it by unknown informers. The ten were nevertheless dismissed as disloyal.

Then began the long fight to rehabilitate the characters of the stigmatized employees, a fight that lasted about seven years from the time of their discharge. Their first recourse was an appeal to a review board, which, as usual, promptly sustained their convictions. But the process of appeal in the Fort Monmouth case was adorned with a new gimmick. The names of the members of the reviewing tribunal were kept secret from the accused and their counsel. The proceeding thus outdid the Dreyfus case. Not only was the evidence against the accused kept secret, but also it was reviewed and weighed by a secret tribunal. If there are any other spectacles like this in the history of American or English jurisprudence, I have been unable to find them.

We brought the case before the United States District Court for the District of Columbia, raising the same constitutional issues with respect to conviction on secret evidence as we had formerly presented in the Bailey and Peters cases. Further, we expressed doubt as to the constitutionality of sustaining a penalty involving the loss of the scientific careers of the accused imposed by a secret tribunal. We even went so far as to question the practical necessity in the interests of security of setting up a secret tribunal. But none of this trivia bothered the district court, which promptly sustained the decision of the secret loyalty board.

We finally won the Fort Monmouth case in the Court of Appeals. That court set aside the conviction of disloyalty, and the accused were subsequently awarded about eighty thousand dollars in back pay, which they were entitled to because their severance from the service had been illegal. We achieved this victory in a totally unexpected way.

As the law stood at that time, there was no constitutional requirement based on due process giving an accused the right to learn from findings furnished to him what the offense of which he had been convicted was. But a dismissal from government employment for an offense akin to treason based on secret evidence, reviewed by a secret tribunal, and imposing a severe social penalty seemed a little unreasonable even to the men who drafted the Army regulations governing procedure in loyalty cases. So the requirement was put in that a government employee convicted of disloyalty must be shown the findings of the board.

The Supreme Court of the United States in previous cases had held that though there was no necessity for a government department to adopt rules and regulations governing its loyalty procedures, if it did adopt them, the regulations had to be followed or the dismissal would be set aside. No findings in any of the Fort Monmouth cases had ever been shown to us. The only matter of record the accused had been permitted to see was a statement to the general effect that a doubt existed as to their loyalty. We felt confident that the court would compel the findings of the board to be delivered to us. We desperately needed them. Without them we could not know what offense we were defending our clients against. We therefore made a motion that the court order the Secretary of the Army to furnish us copies of the findings of the board. The government, to our complete amazement, informed the court that the Secretary of the Army would not furnish such findings. He rested that refusal on two grounds. The first was that if we were shown the findings, the names of secret informers would have to be disclosed and government security would thus be disastrously impaired. We met this argument by representing to the court that we had no interest in learning the names of the secret informers and would be satisfied if they were blocked out in the copies of the findings delivered to us. The second ground for refusing to comply with our motion was, according to government counsel, that if the findings were delivered to us, even with the names of the informers blocked out, they would disclose secret methods of investigation that, if the Russians ever got hold of them, would destroy the efficiency of the entire loyalty program, leaving the Army a helpless prey to Soviet spies, subversives, and what not.

I inquired what these mysterious findings could possibly contain of that character. Were rubber hoses concealed in the folds of these mysterious documents, or was it truth-telling serum? The District Court was not impressed. It denied our motion and subsequently sustained the dismissals. We filed our appeal in the United States Court of Appeals. The Court of Appeals had been recently reversed in sustaining a conviction by a loyalty tribunal that ignored the regulations adopted by its department. In our case, it therefore reversed the District Court and remanded the case for a trial to be held after the Secretary of the Army had provided the accused with copies of the findings against them.

At this point the government, to avoid showing us these findings, gave up and agreed to a judgment in favor of the accused for the back pay to which they were entitled because of their illegal separation from the service. The only condition imposed by the government on this settlement was that after reinstatement the accused would immediately resign from government service. Since nothing short of a draft could have induced the defendants in the Fort Monmouth trials ever to work for their government again, this was an easy condition to meet.

After seven years of humiliation, discouragement, and want, the discharged Fort Monmouth employees were finally vindicated. They were men of the highest ability in their field. I have no doubt that the research program at Fort Monmouth must have been seriously impaired by these idiotic carryings-on, indulged by a frightened and hysterical Department of the Army. And I still wake up at night wondering what those mysterious findings could possibly have contained. Certainly the Secretary of the Army must have believed that the security of the United States government would have been disastrously impaired had these findings been disclosed, or else he would not have so represented to the court. Protecting the security of the Army must indeed be a mysterious business filled with black magic. On mature consideration of this matter, I have finally come to the conclusion that the secret loyalty boards when they made their secret findings must have sat around a bubbling cauldron throwing in this and that like the witches in *Macbeth*.

Of all the cases in this area handled by our office, the most dramatic and at the same time the most productive of headaches was the prosecution of Owen Lattimore, a professor at Johns Hopkins University. For many years Lattimore had been a leading expert on the Orient. He knew practically all the Chinese dialects. He had spent years in China, Outer Mongolia, and other Asiatic countries. When he was in Afghanistan in March, 1950, McCarthy rose from his seat on the Senate floor and denounced Lattimore as a Soviet spy. Lattimore flew back immediately from Afghanistan and came to see Abe Fortas. Abe agreed to defend him.

The first hearings were before a subcommittee of the Senate Committee on the Judiciary, headed at that time by Millard Tydings, of Maryland. Senator Tydings was a man of unusual courage and integrity. He conducted hearings with fairness and impartiality. At the conclusion of these hearings, Tydings found that the charges against Lattimore were baseless.

Tydings was defeated in the next election because of his courageous stand in fairly appraising the evidence for and against Lattimore. He was an exception to the rule then current in public life that a man accused of Communism was not entitled to a fair hearing. Even John F. Kennedy, then a senator, faltered in those dark days under the tremendous pressure of McCarthy's power.

But Senator Tydings' findings in favor of Lattimore did not end the matter. Senator Pat McCarran, of the Senate Judiciary Committee, was determined to get Lattimore. A year and a half after Lattimore's exoneration by the Tydings committee, he was called before the McCarran subcommittee in executive session. He was asked hundreds of questions. His memory proved to be phenomenal. The committee then gathered together all the memorandums and letters it could find that could possibly cast suspicion on Lattimore from the files of the Institute of Pacific Relations, which was also under investigation for subversive activities.

Lattimore had long been associated with the Institute. It was an international organization founded at Honolulu in 1923 under the general auspices of members of the YMCA for the purpose of promoting mutual understanding and co-operation among the peoples of the Pacific area. It had autonomous local units in many countries, including Russia. They were engaged in a study of the whole

Pacific area, and the Institute published a quarterly magazine known as *Pacific Affairs*. This journal was edited by Lattimore from 1934 to 1941; during that period he was much on the move in China and elsewhere, not only as an expert in the problems of Mongolia, but also because it was necessary for him to maintain contacts with the various national units of the Institute in pursuit of the over-all objective of that organization. In the period of Lattimore's editorship, *Pacific Affairs* carried some two hundred and fifty leading articles and numerous shorter pieces.

As the records of the Institute accumulated over the years, they were moved for storage to a barn on the premises of the chief administrative officer of the Institute. In February, 1951, the McCarran committee investigators seized the records. In July, after a five-month study of this barnful of papers, the committee called Lattimore before it, and in executive session interrogated him in detail. It was at this hearing that five of the alleged episodes of perjury for which Lattimore was later prosecuted occurred.

The committee then went into open session, and from July 25, 1951, to February 21, 1952, took eight volumes of testimony, much of it attacking Lattimore in his absence, although he had asked to be heard. Finally, in February, 1952, the committee granted his request for an opportunity to answer the charges that for months had been given wide publicity from the committee forum. When at last Lattimore came to the stand for public hearings, the committee kept him under cross-examination for twelve days, the longest congressional interrogation of one man in congressional history. This cross-examination encompassed the story of his life; his associations; his conversations, even the most casual; his conferences, public and private; and in the utmost detail his activities during a period of from ten to fifteen years from the early 1930's until by his own voluntary action in 1950 he came to Washington from the center of Afghanistan to defend his loyalty and his good name before the Congress of this country.

During these open hearings he was never confronted by the witnesses against him, and in the course of the cross-examination to which he was subjected he was repeatedly denied the right to refresh his memory; he was ordered to answer without attempting to refresh his recollection—indeed, he was once ordered to answer but not to think—and several times his counsel was enjoined by the chairman of the committee not to speak unless spoken to. I recall one instance when the Professor's wife attempted to help him out in answering a question about matters of many years ago. McCarran pounded his gavel and thundered, "Mrs. Lattimore, you will either have to stop coaching your husband or you will be removed bodily from this room."

As an example of unfair and oppressive procedure, the open hearings were a masterpiece of hypocritical ingenuity. The countless questions were directed to Lattimore in no perceptible order, with no overt emphasis as to what was important and what was not important. Yet his interrogators were completely prepared with questions written out in advance, based often upon their own recent reading of correspondence many years old. The most striking fact about these questions and the manner in which they were propounded is that they were *not* asked in order to obtain information, but for the purpose of entrapment, for the committee, having seized the voluminous files of the Institute of Pacific Relations, was armed with documents dealing with the details the witness was commanded to dig up from the recesses of his memory of events of ten to fifteen years before.

McCarran had an excellent sense of timing with respect to headlines. I recall that one afternoon about four o'clock, a time when any startling piece of news could be carried in the morning headlines, he asked: "Mr. Lattimore, did you ever write articles which might convey to the Soviets secrets concerning our air bases?" The answer was "No." McCarran repeated the question three times, each time in a louder tone. Naturally, the next morning the papers carried headlines indicating that Lattimore must have been giving away Air Force secrets. But all the committee could produce with respect to this matter was a few sentences in an article which gave away no secrets whatever. And so it went day after day. I had heard of the third degree, but I had never before seen an investigation conducted with third-degree methods. It was hard to believe that we were in the United States of America, where our freedom of opinion and associations was supposed to be protected by the Supreme Court of the United States.

At the end of the hearings nothing except a few inconsistent statements on trivial matters appeared in the record to impeach the integrity or loyalty of Owen Lattimore. But McCarran was determined to convict this man. At the hearings on the confirmation of James P. McGranery, of Pennsylvania, who had been appointed attorney general of the United States by President Truman, McCarran exacted a promise from McGranery that Lattimore would be prosecuted for perjury. McGranery kept his word.

The indictment that followed at the end of 1952 was one of the most curious documents in the history of criminal law. Count I charged in part:

4. That at the time and place aforesaid, the defendant, OWEN LATTIMORE, duly appearing as a witness before the said Senate Subcommittee, and then and there being under oath as aforesaid, testified falsely before the said Senate Subcommittee with respect to the aforesaid material matter, to wit, said defendant testified that he had never been a sympathizer or any other kind of promoter of Communism or Communist interests.

5. That the aforesaid testimony of that defendant, as he then and there well knew and believed, was untrue, in that said defendant had been a sympathizer and promoter of Communism and Communist interests. [22 D.C. Code 2501]

There were six other counts of so frivolous a nature that they were later dismissed by the prosecution without going to trial. Lattimore got his first break since his exoneration by Senator Tydings when Luther Youngdahl was assigned to the case. Judge Youngdahl had been a Republican governor of Minnesota from 1947 to 1951, and had a long record of able and courageous political leadership before he was appointed to the bench by President Truman. The Lattimore case was a *cause célèbre*. The public and the press generally believed that there was something wrong with Lattimore, even if he was not a spy. The McCarthy hysteria was influencing the decisions of judges all over the country. But Judge Youngdahl happened to be a judge who could not be deterred by fear of public criticism.

Our first action was to move to dismiss the first count of the indictment on the ground that it was so vague that it would be impossible to prepare a defense. We argued that we did not see how any intelligent man, even a layman, could hold otherwise. When Lattimore made the statement for which he was being prosecuted in

Count I, it was a statement of his belief that he had never done or said anything in the interest of what he conceived to be Communism. The charge was that he lied about that belief. What were these Communist interests? Did the United States promote Communism when it aided Russia? Did President Roosevelt promote Communist interests when he furnished Lend-Lease to Russia? Did General George C. Marshall promote Communist interests when he criticized Chiang Kai-shek's government? Was Wendell Willkie a promoter of or a sympathizer with Communist interests because of passages in his book *One World?* Since Tito was a Communist and his interests were of necessity also Communist interests was the government of the United States a promoter of Communism and a sympathizer with Communist interests when by both legislative and executive action it came to the aid of Tito?

We were successful. The government appealed, but Judge Youngdahl was sustained. Count I was stricken out, as well as some of the minor counts, and the case was sent back for trial on the remaining counts. The government had no intention of going to trial on these trivial matters, and so, instead of seeking a review in the Supreme Court of the United States, it brought a new indictment in July, 1954, almost two years after the first indictment had been brought by the first grand jury.

This second indictment sought to cure the vice of vagueness that had caused the dismissal of the first. It is such a remarkable example of ingenious hypocrisy on the part of the prosecution that even the lay reader may be interested in following its corkscrew twists and turns. The former Count I, expanded into two counts, read in part as follows:

5. That at the time and place aforesaid, the defendant, OWEN LATTI-MORE, duly appearing as a witness before the said Senate Subcommittee, and then and there being under oath as aforesaid, testified unlawfully, wilfully and knowingly, and contrary to said oath, before the said Senate Subcommittee, with respect to the aforesaid material matter, to wit, said defendant testified that he had never been a follower of the Communist line, thereby meaning that he was one who had never knowingly and intentionally followed the Communist line in that in his expressed positions and policies as to political, diplomatic, military, economic and social

matters he had never knowingly and intentionally followed in time, conformed to, complied with and paralleled the positions taken, the policies expressed and the propaganda issued on the same matters by the Government of the Soviet Union, the Communist Party of the Soviet Union, the Comintern and its successors, the various Communist governments, parties and persons adhering to Communism and accepting the leadership of the Soviet Communist Party.

6. That the aforesaid testimony of the defendant as he then and there well knew and believed was untrue, in that said defendant during the period 1935 to 1950, both inclusive, knowingly and intentionally had been a "follower of the Communist line" as hereinbefore defined in Paragraph 5; that is to say he had knowingly and intentionally followed the Communist line in public and private statements, in his conversations, his correspondence, and in his widely disseminated writings, both in the United States and other parts of the world; that said statements, conversations, correspondence and writings contain several hundred instances denoting that the defendant was a "follower of the Communist line", as hereinbefore defined in Paragraph 5, which instances include but are not limited to the following topics and statements: . . .

The topics referred to were citations from Lattimore's writings without giving their context. We printed all these citations, giving the full text. The result was a hundred and forty-five pages of single-spaced, legal-size paper. The government had gone through every one of Lattimore's voluminous writings since the year 1935 to extract, out of context, any statement that might conceivably indicate that Lattimore agreed with any Communist country. There were four periods covered. The first was from 1935 to 1941, when a debate was going on about the active intervention of the United States against German, Italian, and Japanese aggression. Lattimore, along with Roosevelt, Chiang Kai-shek, and Churchill, was willing to accept Russian collaboration. His position was used to indicate that he had been a sympathizer and promoter of Communism. The second period was from 1941 to 1945, a period of cordiality among Allies. During that period the United States gave support to French, Italian, and Yugoslav Communist partisans and resistance groups. During the third period, 1945 to 1946, the United States was co-operating with Russia in trying to solve the problems of world peace. Late in 1945, General Eisenhower, after a trip to Moscow during which he had reviewed a Red Square parade from atop Lenin's tomb, told a House committee that "nothing guides Russian policy so much as a desire for friendship with the United States."

The fourth period, after 1946, covered Lattimore's views on the victory of Communists in China. He had pointed out the strength of the movement. One of the quotations used by the prosecution to show that he was a promoter of Communist interests was the following: "My own opinion is that now and for a long time to come the Chinese Communists will have great defensive strength if attacked, but little offensive strength beyond their own frontier." Later events showed the accuracy of this statement. Yet the government attempted to smear Lattimore by putting this citation under the heading "Chinese Communists are not a menace to China or the world" to make it appear that the statement promoted Communist interests. Thus the Department of Justice of the United States sought to convict Lattimore of perjury because of his opinions and writings since 1935, with nearly all of which most sensible men now agree. A more blatant invasion of the right of free speech has never occurred in our history.

The second count of the second indictment was even worse than the first. It read partially as follows:

5. That at the time and place aforesaid, the defendant, OWEN LATTI-MORE, duly appearing as a witness before the said Senate Subcommittee, then and there being under oath as aforesaid, testified unlawfully, knowingly and wilfully and contrary to said oath before the said Senate Subcommittee with respect to the aforesaid material matter, to wit, said defendant testified that he had never been a promoter of Communist interests, thereby meaning that he was one who had never knowingly and intentionally contributed to the growth, enlargement and prosperity of Communism by acting to further, encourage and advance those objectives of political, diplomatic, military, economic and social interest to the Government of the Soviet Union, the Communist party of the Soviet Union, the Comintern and its successors, the various Communist governments, parties and persons adhering to Communism and accepting the leadership of the Soviet Communist party.

6. That the aforesaid testimony of the defendant as he then and there well knew and believed was untrue, in that said defendant during the period 1935 to 1950, both inclusive, knowingly and intentionally had been a "promoter of Communist interests," as hereinbefore defined in Para-

graph 5, that is to say: He had knowingly and intentionally promoted Communist interests in his activities, including, but not limited to conversations, his correspondence and his widely disseminated writings, both in the United States and other parts of the world; and the defendant in furtherance of his promotion of Communist interests did and caused to be done, among other things, the following acts:

(a) During the period 1935 to 1950, both inclusive, the defendant as a writer, lecturer, editor of the Institute of Pacific Relations' publication "Pacific Affairs", employee of the National Government of China, and as a United States Government official, did make use of his position to engage directly and indirectly in the placing and disseminating within the United States and other countries throughout the world, oral and written statements containing the positions taken, the policies expressed and the propaganda issued on political, diplomatic, military, economic and social matters by the Government of the Soviet Union, the Communist Party of the Soviet Union, the Comintern and its successors, the various Communist governments, the parties and persons adhering to Communism and accepting the leadership of the Soviet Communist Party, by means of oral, written and pictorial information and matter, through books, periodicals, newspapers, lectures, broadcasts and otherwise; as to the statements of the defendant so promoting the objectives above-described, but not limited thereto, there are repeated and incorporated herein by reference the Communist positions taken and policies expressed by defendant which are more fully set forth in Paragraph 6 of Count I of this indictment, to wit, the twenty-five enumerated Topics and accompanying specifications as to defendant's statements;

(b) The defendant directly and indirectly, as editor of "Pacific Affairs", caused to be published therein writings by various individuals which followed the Communist line, which said line is described in Paragraph 5 of Count I of this indictment which description is repeated and incorporated herein by reference;

(c) The defendant directly and indirectly, as editor of "Pacific Affairs", prevented the publication of articles therein by persons when he learned such persons were considered by Soviet Communists to be anti-Soviet;

(d) The defendant directly and indirectly, when an editor of the publication "Amerasia", caused to be published therein writings by a Communist writer on China which followed the Communist line, which said line is described in Paragraph 5 of Count I of this indictment which description is repeated and incorporated herein by reference;

(e) The defendant directly and indirectly, as an official of the Institute of Pacific Relations, sought to have the said Institute in its "Inquiry Series" (an extensive research project inquiring into the factors underlying the hostilities in the Pacific Area in 1938) follow the official Chinese Communist positions;

(f) The defendant directly and indirectly, as an official of the Institute of Pacific Relations, sought to have the said Institute in its aforesaid "Inquiry Series" support the international policies of the Union of Soviet Socialist Republics;

(g) The defendant directly and indirectly in 1936 urged the United States Ambassador to the Soviet Union to endeavor officially to bring about United States recognition of Outer Mongolia as an independent state, although defendant knew said state was not in fact independent, but under the domination and control of the Soviet Union;

(h) The defendant directly and indirectly sought to influence the United States Department of State in 1949 as to the conduct of foreign relations with the National Government of China so as to advance the policies and positions of the Chinese Communists.

Since this indictment is complicated and lengthy, it may be helpful to translate it into plain English. In the first place, the reader should note that there are two separate kinds of subversive activity about which Lattimore is charged with perjuring himself. The first is set out in Count I as being a "follower of the Communist line." In Count II the subversive activity is being a "promoter of Communist interests." The difference between those two types of conduct was never clear to me as counsel for the defense.

The first step in each indictment is to tell the court, in paragraph five, what Lattimore actually meant when he said that he was not a promoter of Communist interests or follower of the Communist line. The prosecution claims that Lattimore meant to tell the McCarran committee that he had never done anything, written anything, or said anything to anyone that would encourage the objectives of "political, diplomatic, military, economic and social" interests of any Communist nation or party in the world. This is a somewhat large order. It would include helping Russia win the war against Germany. Indeed, no citizen of the United States could possibly testify that he had not promoted Communist interests or followed the Communist line under the definition of these activities contained in the indictment. Reduced to colloquial terms the case amounted to something like this: Lattimore: "I did not and never meant to say such a silly thing as you charge in the indictment." Department of Justice: "You did too, and you're lying when you deny it." The proof that Lattimore meant what the prosecutor said he did could be made by shouting at the jury in his closing speech.

As the next step in the prosecution, the prosecutor would have to prove that Lattimore did or said something to promote Communist interests or follow the Communist line under his definition. This would be easy. It covers every Communist country in the world, some of which, as in the case of Tito's Yugoslavia, the United States itself had aided and encouraged. The United States also collaborated with Russia during and for a period even after the Second World War, as, for example, in the Nuremberg trials. There is probably no soldier or citizen who, under this indictment, could testify that he was not a Communist follower without perjuring himself.

The government at the end of the second count set out what it considered eight glaring instances of Lattimore's promotion of Communist interests. It did not like his books or lectures. Though we printed Lattimore's writings listed in the indictment, we could not find anything we thought was subversive. Perhaps the prosecution did not like his statements that China might become a strong country. There was no way of finding out whether this was correct. Neither did the prosecution like the magazine *Pacific Affairs,* which Lattimore had edited. That magazine attempted to give an outline of both capitalistic and Communistic views and published some articles by Communist writers. Maybe this was wrong. (It is interesting to note that the U. S. Treasury in 1955 took away the educational exemption of the Institute of Pacific Relations. The Institute promptly sued to recover it, and the Treasury introduced the McCarran committee hearings as proof of subversion. The court restored the exemption, and the government did not appeal.)

Another step in the prosecution would be to show that Lattimore's writings actually did promote Communist interests. For example, the indictment charged that Lattimore in 1936 urged the recognition of Outer Mongolia as an independent state. We were not clear in what respect this promoted Communist interests. How would the prosecution prove that it did? Presumably, by calling experts in Chinese affairs to contradict Lattimore and the experts whom the defense called. The jury would then decide the international question as to which set of experts was right. The verdict on this issue might be of assistance to the State Department in determining Far Eastern policy.

Without going further, I think that I have sufficiently demonstrated the ghastly absurdity and injustice of this indictment. If the indictment were held valid, there was no possible way to prepare a defense, because it covered political and economic writings of thirty-five years and involved the proof before a jury selected by lot of the rightness or wrongness of international policy. Yet there were four out of the nine judges on the United States Court of Appeals for the District of Columbia who were willing to sustain this monstrosity.

Lattimore asked the District Court to dismiss the first two counts of the second indictment for substantially the same reason that the first count of the first indictment had been dismissed. At that point the Department of Justice, with the specific approval of Attorney General Herbert Brownell, filed an affidavit of bias and prejudice in an attempt to remove Judge Youngdahl from the case. In arguing that Judge Youngdahl was biased against the government, the United States Attorney was positively insulting to the Judge; indeed, his argument was not addressed to the Judge, but, rather, to a crowded courtroom with the press present. In order to illustrate the kind of argument this attorney made, I quote the following:

"Number six: Now, listen to this, in a memorandum that has to do only with the question as to whether perjury is properly charged.

'In our proper concern for the internal and external threat of Communism and in pursuing our efforts to strike down this threat, we should endeavor to be consistent and not attempt to require a conformity in thought and beliefs that has no relevancy to a present danger to our security.'

"Your Honor, that is astounding language. That is a gratuitous insult to the Government of the United States. It is a gratuitous insult to the grand jury. This indictment does not involve—nobody is attempting any conformity of thought and beliefs.

"Oh, it has the atmosphere of a great appeal to the liberal mind, that in exposing this threat of Communism, we must not put a man's mind in a strait jacket."

* * * * * *

"That language shows personal bias and prejudice on Your Honor's part, not the bent of mind that we should have in an impartial adjudication of this case."

To realize the enormity of the approval of the Attorney General to the filing of the affidavit of prejudice in this case requires a word of explanation. The law is that any defendant or his counsel may file an affidavit of bias and prejudice, stating some incident or course of conduct by a federal judge, *outside his rulings in the actual trial,* that indicates a bias. When such an affidavit is filed, the judge must excuse himself. He cannot try the issue as to whether the facts stated in the affidavit are true. He must immediately get off the bench, and the case will be assigned to another judge. The reason that the truth of the affidavit cannot be contested is that this would be putting a federal judge on trial as to his veracity; therefore, the law relies upon the good faith of counsel not to file such affidavits unless there are substantial grounds for them. Generally, this system works well enough.

But the affidavit filed in the Lattimore case based its charge of bias solely upon the judge's opinion and rulings from the bench. The theory of the Department of Justice was that any judge who did not rule in its favor was on that account presumed to be biased. Such a proposition is unthinkable in civilized jurisprudence. If it were the law, the Department of Justice would disqualify any judge it thought might rule against it, in order to get one it thought was favorable.

The Attorney General knew the law, as he must also have known that this public condemnation of Judge Youngdahl could not help but embarrass him. He must have relied on the fact that the press generally would not understand the law as to affidavits of prejudice, and that Judge Youngdahl would, therefore, stand prejudiced in the eyes of the public because of the public reprimand by the Attorney General. That being so, he took a chance that rather than face public misunderstanding, Judge Youngdahl would voluntarily disqualify himself.

It should be noted in this connection that the Attorney General of the United States approves the promotion of trial judges to the United States Court of Appeals. Without his approval such promotion is practically impossible. Therefore, the pressure the Department of Justice brought to bear on Judge Youngdahl was enormous.

But the Attorney General mistook his man. Judge Youngdahl indignantly struck the affidavit from the files. He declined to disqualify himself. Then later, on motion of Lattimore's counsel, he dismissed Counts I and II of the second indictment on the ground that they were impossibly vague. Again his dismissal of these counts was sustained. This time no opinion was written; the Court of Appeals was divided four to four, thereby sustaining the ruling of the trial court only because there was no majority to overrule him.

I have often wondered on what grounds half the judges of the Court of Appeals could have sustained the second indictment, which seems to me even worse than the first. Could it possibly be that the affidavit attacking Judge Youngdahl for ruling against the government made these four judges, whose names no one will ever know, hesitate? I do not know. I simply do not understand how these four judges could be willing to permit an American citizen to be tried criminally because of his opinions and beliefs.

In any event, the Attorney General did not feel enough confidence in his case at that point to seek a review by the Supreme Court of the United States, which we had hoped he would do. We could not appeal because the net effect of the split in the Court of Appeals was in our favor. So we began the laborious preparation necessary to try the trivial counts of the indictment that still remained.

We never had to try them. The Attorney General nol-prossed these counts on the ground that with the dismissal of general Counts I and II further prosecution of Lattimore was useless.

Thus from 1952 to 1955, Owen Lattimore went through the ordeal of being subjected to a relentless and unfair persecution. The Lattimore case is one of the dark pages in the history of the Department of Justice. The Attorney General did not succeed in convicting Lattimore; he did, however, succeed, at the expense of hundreds of thousands of dollars of the taxpayers' money, in getting him pilloried from coast to coast. The newspapers did not understand the case, and most of the comment was against Lattimore. It assumed that the Attorney General must be right and that Lattimore must be a dangerous character. Even the outrageous attempt to slander the District Court judge because his ruling was against the Department of Justice solicited no adverse comment. Indeed, some newspapers commented on it favorably. To their editors I wrote explaining the actual situation and what would happen if the prosecution were able, by attacking his judicial integrity, to remove from the bench any judge who ruled against it. I never received an answer from, nor was there a retraction by, any of these papers.

Why was the Attorney General so anxious to use any means, fair or foul, to prosecute Lattimore? Why were half the judges on the Court of Appeals so timid that in spite of their lifetime tenure they were unable to speak out in defense of justice? The answer is that it is always difficult and sometimes impossible to achieve impartial justice for a defendant in a *cause célèbre*. The prosecution loses its sense of balance. The judges get scared. In such situations Americans owe a debt of gratitude to men like Judge Luther Youngdahl.

CHAPTER TWENTY-TWO

The Criminal Trial as a Symbol of Public Morality

The significance of a criminal trial in civilized countries goes far beyond the question of public order and the enforcement of law. It embodies the notion that every man, however lowly and however guilty he may be, is entitled to a fair and impartial trial in which he must be presumed to be innocent. What is underneath the idea of a fair trial; what are its basic elements? First, the accused must be informed of the charges against him. Second, the judge must be impartial. Third, the accused must have the right to have counsel. Fourth, the judgment must be based on the evidence before the tribunal, and the accused must be entitled to confront and cross-examine the witnesses who testify against him.

These restrictions are unquestionably handicaps in the enforcement of the law. They prevent a trial from having the efficiency of an expert scientific investigation. No doubt some guilty men go free. Nevertheless, there is tremendous psychological need for the appearance of justice that a fair trial creates in the public mind.

The ideal of a fair trial is as old as Western civilization. Its significance in our culture is tremendous. It involves the humanitarian notion that the underdog is always entitled to a chance. It gives us a sense of security against what we are accustomed to call "mob rule." So persistent is it that once it has been violated, the matter is never at rest until the ideal is vindicated. An example of this can be found in the case of Tom Mooney, a labor leader convicted of responsibility for the deaths and injuries from a bomb explosion in San Francisco in 1916. The justice of the proceedings against him was subject to question in spite of the fact that the appellate courts of California affirmed the conviction and the Supreme Court of the United States refused to interfere. Condemned to death, he later had his sentence commuted to life imprisonment, but he was still a political issue in a campaign fifteen years after he had been sent to prison. The case was forgotten only after Mooney was finally pardoned in 1939. In much the same way, books pro and con are still, over forty years later, being written about the Sacco-Vanzetti case, which, like France's Dreyfus case, became for a time an issue argued all over the world.

During the mad days of Senator Joseph McCarthy it was not sufficient to get rid of government employees suspected of Communist tendencies by firing them. Though there was no law that compelled the government to give its employees a fair hearing, department heads wanted to show their zeal in pinning the stigma of disloyalty on suspected employees. They wanted a public ceremony to show that they realized the grave danger of the overthrow of the government by Communists and to proclaim their devotion to the cause of circumventing that threat. Firing an employee quietly did not do this. The appearance of a fair trial did. The emotions of the time demanded that the government set up an elaborate series of loyalty courts. These loyalty courts violated the very essence of a fair trial by relying on secret evidence given by undisclosed informers who were never cross-examined and who were not required to take an oath. Yet at least the trappings of justice were placed upon the proceedings. There had to be technical findings, often opinions were written, and there was a hierarchy of trial tribunals and appellate tribunals to give the appearance of justice.

Indeed, throughout history the appearance of justice and government morality have been symbolized by the use of the criminal trial. Jeanne d'Arc was unquestionably guilty of heresy as that offense was defined in 1431. She was setting herself up as a moral authority above the church. She followed the counsel of her voices instead of that of her bishop. In spite of the political need to get rid of her, hers was a fairer trial than other heresy trials of the time. The judges refused to employ the usual practice of getting a confession by torture. There was a preliminary hearing, an indictment that disclosed the nature of her offense in elaborate detail, a trial in which she was given the opportunity to meet all relevant issues, an appellate review on both the law and the evidence by the faculty of the University of Paris, who even reviewed the question whether she was not criminally responsible owing to insanity, and a permanent written transcript of the entire proceedings. So well was she permitted to conduct her defense that her canonization as a saint is in large part based upon this written record.

The most ruthless dictators are frequently compelled to utilize the trappings of a fair trial in at least a few representative cases in order to justify themselves in getting rid of their political enemies. Hitler sought justification through world-wide publicity of a sham trial of persons charged with burning the Reichstag. The Soviet purges, while largely conducted in the dark, were every now and then dignified by the ritual of an elaborate trial, in which all the defendants confessed. In an interesting book, *A Coffin for King Charles*, C. V. Wedgwood notes that Cromwell was careful to give the trial of Charles I an atmosphere of due process and legitimacy. She quotes King Charles, relying on the same symbol, speaking in his defense: "It is not my case alone, it is the freedom and liberty of the people of England; and do you pretend what you will, I stand more for their liberties. For if power without law may make laws, may alter the fundamental laws of the Kingdom, I do not know what subject he is in England, that can be sure of his life, or anything that he calls his own."

The trial resulting in the conviction of German government officials at Nuremberg for the offense of waging an aggressive war (as distinguished from the commission of specific atrocities) was a conspicuous use of the symbol of the criminal trial to establish a great moral principle, theretofore unknown in history, which would lead to peace. It was felt that no other ceremony, no signing of pacts, could have the same impact. It was not a fair trial; it lacked an impartial tribunal, and, furthermore, at the time that Germany started its aggressive war, it was not a criminal offense to do so. Its ex post facto character thus violated a principle of the United States Constitution. A trial for atrocities would not have done so.

But such a trial would have established no principle of international relations. The very fact that the Russians sat on the Nuremberg court dramatized the notion that Communist and capitalist nations alike would not in the happy future engage in aggression against other nations. The mood of the time demanded that comforting assurance, and only a conviction after what appeared to be a fair trial could give it.

Trials are like the miracle or morality plays of ancient times. They dramatically present the conflicting moral values of a community in a way that cannot be done by logical formalization. Civil trials perform this function as well as criminal, but the more important emotional impact upon a society results from a criminal trial.

One of the significant results of the growth of the ideal of a fair trial has been a change in attitude toward the insane or mentally ill criminal, which may well later extend toward the mentally retarded criminal. Insanity and criminal responsibility involve two conflicting ideas. One is that society should avenge itself against a criminal. If it does, there will be fewer criminals and we will all be safer. In teaching a lesson to a particular criminal we educate all other criminals not to commit crimes. The heavier the punishment, the better the lesson. As a practical matter there seems no support for this thesis. It has been noted frequently that when men were hanged for picking pockets in England, pickpockets were busy plying their trade among the crowd witnessing the hanging. Nevertheless, it is an emotional idea that nearly all of us share.

On the other side of the coin is the notion that you should not punish a man who is so abnormal that the punishment will not be a deterrent to him because he will not understand the reason for the punishment and it will not be a deterrent to others since they do not identify themselves with a madman. Punishing a wild bull for manslaughter seems wrong to most people. The average citizen cannot identify himself with the bull, but he can identify himself with a man who knows the difference between right and wrong. It is our duty to punish immorality, but a man who doesn't know the difference between right and wrong cannot be called immoral. Such a man should be put in a hospital instead of a penitentiary, whereas a man who knew he was doing wrong should be treated with the utmost severity, as a lesson to him and to other citizens.

Thus the knowledge-of-right-from-wrong test, representing as it does punishment for willful immorality, has survived in a majority of American jurisdictions since the M'Naghten case in London in 1843 led, in an examination of the judges by the House of Lords, to the formulation of rules that declared it to be the only legal test of insanity in criminal tests. This test, simply stated, is that an accused person is criminally responsible if he knows the difference between right and wrong. The M'Naghten Rules preach a simple moral lesson, but they are difficult to defend in the light of modern psychological knowledge. It sends a person who has one type of insanity to the penitentiary and sends another person, with a different type, to the hospital. Moreover, psychiatrists have demonstrated that most insane persons know the difference between right and wrong in an intellectual sense. However, because of an emotional disorder they are incapable of preventing themselves from committing certain deeds.

The M'Naghten Rules were vigorously denounced for years by psychiatrists, and even by some judges. Despite this criticism, the courts seemed unwilling to adopt a new rule. It was in this climate of opinion that the case of *Monte W. Durham* v. *United States* came to our office, in 1953. Durham had been convicted of housebreaking and grand larceny. Prior to his trial in 1951 a hearing had been held before a judge to determine after a psychiatric examination whether Durham was "presently insane or *otherwise so mentally incompetent* as to be unable to understand the proceedings against him or properly to assist in his own defense." It will be noted that this is an entirely different test from the right-and-wrong standard. Under it a criminal who knew the difference between right and wrong nevertheless could not be tried if his mental illness prevented him from co-operating with his counsel. It was thought unfair to try such a person even though he was morally deserving of punishment. A person who was insane from a psychiatric point of view could not be tried even though he was sane according to prevailing legal views.

Durham was found incompetent to be tried, and was hospitalized. After several years the hospital concluded that he was fit to be tried. At Durham's trial, where the right-and-wrong test of the M'Naghten Rules was applicable, a psychiatrist called by the defense testified that Durham was *medically* of unsound mind at the time of the offense. But when he was asked whether Durham knew the difference between right and wrong at the time of the crime, he said he did not know and could not tell.

In a criminal trial the defendant is presumed to be sane in the absence of evidence to the contrary. Therefore, because the defense psychiatrist could not tell whether Durham knew right from wrong, the trial judge (the case was tried without a jury) ruled as follows:

"I don't think it has been established that the defendant was of unsound mind as of July 13, 1951, in the sense that he didn't know the difference between right and wrong or that even if he did, he was subject to an irresistible impulse by reason of the derangement of mind." He accordingly ruled that Durham was criminally responsible, and sentenced him to a long term in prison.

An appeal was taken to the United States Court of Appeals for the District of Columbia, and because Durham was indigent the court appointed my partner Abe Fortas to argue whether or not the above ruling of the trial judge was proper.

Abe argued that the right-and-wrong test was obsolete in the light of modern psychological knowledge. The test was based on the old notion of reason versus impulse. If reason told the criminal that it was wrong to give in to impulse and he disregarded that advice, he should be sent to the penitentiary because he did not deserve the expensive care he would get in a hospital. To the psychiatrist who regarded thought as part of human behavior, this was nonsense. No well-trained psychiatrist would testify whether or not a criminal knew the difference between right and wrong.

The court was faced with the dilemma that if it persisted in applying the right-and-wrong test, no psychologist, skilled in the basic premises of his art, could testify at all. It decided that the M'Naghten formula was obsolete and that it was the duty of the court to keep abreast of scientific knowledge in the psychological field (214 F. 2d 862 (1954)). The decision was made easier by the fact that in the District of Columbia a defendant acquitted on the ground of insanity would not be released, but would be sent to a hospital until he was cured and the court was satisfied that he would not be dangerous if released. A new test was therefore laid down in the Durham case, broader than the right-and-wrong test. The jury from then on would be instructed that if they believed from the psychiatric testimony that the criminal act was the result of mental disease, they should acquit the defendant on the ground of insanity. Thus the criminal law was brought abreast of modern science, and in this case without incurring the danger to society of turning habitual criminals like Durham loose to continue their life of crime.

The decision did Durham no good whatever. At his second trial he was convicted as promptly under the new rule as he was under the old. But because of the peculiar importance of the criminal trial as a symbol of public morality, the Durham case created a storm of controversy all over the United States. It was argued that the law should represent moral principles, and there were none under the Durham Rule. Editorials were written expressing alarm about the consequences of coddling habitual criminals by sending them to hospitals. The criminal law was no longer a deterrent to criminals who heard the voice of reason and did not follow it. There was a movement in Congress to repeal the Durham Rule.

The psychiatrists, on the other hand, were jubilant. At last their science had been recognized by the courts. Articles were written claiming the triumph of scientific knowledge over superstition. What the psychiatrists failed to discuss, however, was how they could tell that a crime was the result of mental disease. Recent statistics have shown that a mentally retarded person has three times as much chance of becoming a criminal as one not so handicapped. On this theory, why shouldn't every mentally retarded criminal be sent to a hospital?

There is no logical or scientific answer to this question. The inescapable fact is that a decision on whether a criminal should be acquitted on the ground of insanity is entirely a moral problem, on which the psychiatrist can no more testify than on the question whether he knew right from wrong. It is like asking a psychiatrist "How crazy must a crazy man be before he is insane?" But the union of science and religion or morality is something that all of us would like to see accomplished, and the Durham Rule satisfied that feeling. A criminal law was at last in accord with scientific theory. We also like to feel that mental illness is a fact within the knowledge of experts and that it can be proved or disproved by expert testimony. That need was also met by the Durham Rule.

And while it is probably true that in a doubtful case no psychiatrist can possibly tell whether the crime was the result of mental disease or the exercise of free will, there are many psychiatrists who think they can. Those who do not think so can always describe the symptoms and leave the issue to the jury. In other words, after the Durham Rule the psychiatrist could talk about concepts with which he was familiar. Before the Durham Rule he could not.

The value of the Durham Rule is that it gives a trial on the issue of insanity the appearance of justice achieved by scientific methods. So far as getting a conviction in a particular case is concerned, the new test will probably make little difference. The great importance of the Durham Rule is, rather, that it includes a more compassionate attitude toward crime, and from that attitude will flow a greater understanding by the public of the causes of crime, and may even induce a feeling that our entire penal system needs reform. The Durham Rule is an advance in human understanding that may well be of tremendous consequence.

After the Durham decision mentally disturbed criminals began to realize that if they pleaded insanity and were committed to a hospital, they might be confined for a longer time than they would be if they were convicted. For that reason, many refused to allow insanity to be pleaded in their defense.

This raised another difficult philosophical problem. Should a court consider insanity as a defense over the objection of the "insane" criminal? On the one hand, if the criminal was insane, he should have treatment for his disease whether he liked it or not. It was society's duty to cure him rather than to give him a few years in the penitentiary and then turn him out to repeat his insane offenses. On the other hand, every defendant in a criminal case is entitled to decide how his defense should be conducted. Indeed, he may represent himself, without counsel, if he chooses to do so. The Supreme Court of the United States settled this philosophical difficulty by holding that an insane person can go to the penitentiary as a penalty for his crime if he wants to, even though that decision itself may be the product of mental disease (*Lynch* v. *Overholser*, 369 U. S. 705).

Some of the judges in the courts of the District of Columbia were morally opposed to the Durham Rule. Some of them tried to whittle it down. There have been over a hundred decisions in the District of Columbia alone interpreting the rule and the procedure to be followed in cases involving the insanity issue. As in the case of the old effort to reconcile science with religion, the theology of criminal insanity has become complicated indeed.

Another interesting case involving public attitudes toward the defense of insanity was the strange case of the noted poet Ezra Pound. When the United States entered the Second World War, Ezra Pound was living in Italy with his wife. He became obsessed with the grandiose idea that the entry of the United States into the war was a conspiracy between President Roosevelt and the Jews in violation of the United States Constitution, and that it was his duty to defend the Constitution. In this frame of mind he made a number of broadcasts during the war for the Italian government which were hostile to the United States in tone but generally unintelligible. Indeed, so unintelligible were they that the Italians took him off the air because they were afraid that he was giving signals to the American troops in some sort of poetic code. He was arrested when the Americans occupied Italy, and for a while, according to his story, he was put in an iron cage with a light shining on him day and night.

He was returned to this country and indicted for treason on November 26, 1945. In December a board of psychiatrists appointed by the court gave their unanimous opinion that the defendant was mentally unfit to advise properly with counsel or to participate intelligibly in his own defense. On the basis of this testimony the trial court held that Pound was mentally unfit, as of the date of the trial. No one could testify with any certainty as to what his mental condition was at the date of his alleged treason some years before. Pound was committed to the criminal ward of St. Elizabeths Hospital in Washington, D. C., to receive treatment until he might become mentally competent to stand trial.

It soon became apparent to the staff of St. Elizabeths that from a point of view of ability to co-operate with his counsel Pound was incurably insane. Had he been tried, he would have insisted on testifying that America's entry into the war was a conspiracy between Roosevelt and the Jews and that in opposing such a war over the Italian broadcasting system he was saving our Constitution. From the point of view of the philosophical morality of our judicial system, it would have been an injustice to Pound to try him until psychological therapy had cured him of these delusions so that he would not have insisted on testifying against himself.

Yet the philosophical morality that saved Pound from a criminal trial was of little advantage to him so far as confinement was concerned. Had he been tried, his testimony, together with the unintelligible nature of his broadcasts, might have convinced the jury that—insane or not—he did not have the requisite intent to commit treason. Or, if the jury did convict him under these peculiar circumstances, he certainly would not have been given the sentence that he actually served.

To the increasing horror of the literary world here and abroad, Pound was detained in the criminal ward of St. Elizabeths for thirteen years. I seriously doubt if anyone in the Department of Justice wanted to keep him there. But there seemed no way of getting him out. The fact that he was too mentally ill to be tried was not a reason for releasing him, because this had nothing to do with whether he was insane at the time of the offense. He could not be pardoned, because he was not convicted of any offense and there was nothing to pardon him for. He could not be tried and acquitted on the ground of insanity, because he refused to make that defense and, insane or not, the Supreme Court had held that he could not be forced to. It is my own opinion that had Mrs. Pound, acting as Pound's guardian, asked for habeas corpus on the ground that it was absurd to confine Pound for life because he could not be tried, she might have succeeded, though this had been tried once, and failed, in the lower court. So there was no way in conformity with the philosophical legal logic of the situation to release Pound except for the prosecution to dismiss the indictment.

But such voluntary action on the part of the Department of Justice involved the risk of damage to the image of the department. It might have been considered by the public as an attempt to release a traitor just because he happened to be a great poet. It would have been inconsistent with the policy of former attorneys general who had insisted on keeping Pound in confinement.

Pound's continued incarceration cast a stigma on the American system of justice in the eyes of the world. During his incarceration he won a distinguished prize, conferred on him by the Library of Congress, for a new volume of poetry. Many distinguished writers were of the opinion that he was one of the best American poets. Petitions were submitted by scores of well-known writers and poets, among them Ernest Hemingway, Archibald MacLeish, and Carl Sandburg. Dag Hammarskjöld, the late Secretary-General of the United Nations, petitioned for his release. Richard Rovere wrote: "The main thing about Ezra Pound is that he is a poet of tower-ing gifts and attainments. . . ."

The staff at St. Elizabeths was becoming increasingly sensitive to the situation. Pound had reached the age of seventy-two, and they thought with dismay of the world-wide protest that would occur if he died in confinement. In such a case a great poet accused of a serious crime would have served a life sentence simply because he was too insane to be tried. In addition, Pound was becoming an intolerable nuisance at St. Elizabeths, though this was hardly his fault. Since he was perfectly harmless, no security measures needed to be taken. He was permitted to hold court for his admirers from all over the world. At such sessions people with a reputation for hating Jews were particularly welcome. The situation had become ridiculous during the last six or seven years of his confinement.

Then Robert Frost stepped in. He was probably the only Amer-ican poet who could have accomplished what he did. He was uni-versally admired. He was a rock-ribbed conservative. He had come to be a great literary figure of the United States. His espousal of Pound's cause gave it a dignity sufficient to protect the government if it permitted him to be freed. Such protection could be afforded by few other distinguished authors or poets. In the eyes of a great many of the American public, authors and poets are queer ducks apt to be tainted with radicalism and not to be trusted with serious decisions involving the punishment for treason. Hammarskjöld did not make it any easier for the Department of Justice by his inter-vention. What right had a foreigner to interfere with our domestic affairs? But with Robert Frost it was different.

Frost instinctively knew the right political action to take. Instead of circulating another petition, he went directly to Sherman Adams, who had been his close friend for many years and who was at the time the most powerful figure in government next to the President of the United States. He convinced Adams that something had to be done about Pound. Adams was a man of courage and integrity, and I assert this in spite of the fact that he later became a victim of his own injudicious conduct. He conveyed Frost's views about Pound to the Attorney General.

When Frost was assured that something could and would be done, he asked Will Shafroth, then Deputy Director of the Administrative Office of the United States Courts, to get him an attorney. Shafroth chose me, and I agreed. But there was a procedural difficulty that had not been cleared away. Mrs. Pound was Ezra Pound's guardian. I did not know whether she had an attorney, or whether she would desire my services. The agreement with Frost had been made on a weekend, and, before I could see her, Frost had, in good faith, told reporters, and the Sunday newspapers had carried the story, that I was representing Pound in the matter of his release from St. Elizabeths. I was worried that Mrs. Pound might consider it a deprivation of her constitutional right to be permitted to select her own attorney. But Mrs. Pound came to my office on Monday and expressed herself pleased with the arrangement for counsel Frost had made, though she did admit she was a bit startled when she learned for the first time through the press that I was representing her.

As I have indicated, the only way to liberate Pound without offending the logic of the law was to dismiss the indictment. This the Attorney General declined to do, for understandable reasons. To take affirmative action liberating a man who had broadcast against the United States in time of war, and who in addition was a notorious anti-Semite, would have put the Department of Justice under sharp attack. But I had gathered from Frost that while the Attorney General would not affirmatively dismiss the indictment, he would not oppose a motion to dismiss it if I made it.

The difficulty was that Mrs. Pound, as the guardian of her husband, had no standing to move to dismiss the indictment on any other ground than that the document itself was defective, which, of course, it was not. In fact, defendant Pound's motion to dismiss his own indictment was not based on any legal ground, but only on the general principle that the situation had become ridiculous. The court had no jurisdiction over such a motion. Therefore, I asked the Department of Justice what position it would take if I filed a motion to dismiss. The department said it was not in a position to give me any information. Though I was not given its reason for refusing to state what would be done with respect to my motion, it was easy to figure it out. The case was too well known for the department to put itself in the position of making advance deals or doing anything that looked like an advance deal. Yet it would be most embarrassing to me if I filed a motion to dismiss and the department objected. The court would instantly deny the motion on the ground of lack of jurisdiction, and I would appear before the public as ignorant of ordinary criminal procedure. Still, I had to take the chance and file my motion.

I supported the motion with an affidavit from Dr. Winfred Overholser, Superintendent of St. Elizabeths, saying that Pound was insane and could never be in a position to stand trial, and that he would not be dangerous if released. I also prepared a statement for Robert Frost. Frost read it and said he wanted to do his own. He then quickly wrote out the following, which I consider a gem:

I am here to register my admiration for a government that can rouse in conscience to a case like this. Relief seems in sight for many of us besides the Ezra Pound in question and his faithful wife. He has countless admirers the world over who will rejoice in the news that he has hopes of freedom. I append a page or so of what they have been saying lately about him and his predicament. I myself speak as much in the general interest as in his. And I feel authorized to speak very specially for my friends, Archibald MacLeish, Ernest Hemingway and T. S. Eliot. None of us can bear the disgrace of our letting Ezra Pound come to his end where he is. It would leave too woeful a story in American literature. He went very wrongheaded in his egotism, but he insists it was from patriotism—love of America. He has never admitted that he went over to the enemy any more than the writers at home who have despaired of the Republic. I hate such nonsense and can only listen to it as an evidence of mental disorder. But mental disorder is what we are considering. I rest the case on Dr. Overholser's pronouncement that

Ezra Pound is not too dangerous to go free in his wife's care, and too insane ever to be tried—a very nice discrimination.

Mr. Thurman Arnold admirably put this problem of a sick man being held too long in prison to see if he won't get well enough to be tried for a prison offense. There is probably legal precedent to help toward a solution of the problem. But I should think it would have to be reached more by magnanimity than by logic and it is chiefly on magnanimity I am counting. I can see how the Department of Justice would hesitate in the matter from fear of looking more just to a great poet than it would be to a mere nobody. The bigger the Department the longer it might have to take thinking things through.

In addition to these, I filed statements from a large number of men of literary prominence to the effect that Pound was a great poet and it would be a national disgrace if he were to die in confinement. Technically, none of these laudatory remarks or appeals to the sympathy of the court could properly be put in evidence. Had counsel for the Department of Justice objected, they could not have been read.

Judge Bolitha Laws heard the motion. Since it was a criminal proceeding, it was necessary for Pound to be in the courtroom. I was afraid that he might rise and object to an order releasing him on the ground that he was incurably insane. But he was so pleased by the complimentary statements of the leading literary figures at home and abroad that I do not believe he paid any attention to anything else that went on. When I had completed my statement, the attorney for the Department of Justice rose and announced that he did not oppose the motion. Judge Laws was troubled about his jurisdiction in the absence of an affirmative motion on the part of the Attorney General. He said, "Failure to oppose is not enough. Do you consent?" Counsel for the department thereupon consented. Thus my motion to dismiss became in a backhanded way a motion to dismiss by the prosecution, and the court granted it.

Pound and his wife left the courtroom with his confidence in his own sanity undiminished and happy in the belief that he was being released on the sole ground that he was a great poet.

By this curious procedure the conflicting political, moral, and logical values that the case represented were resolved by a public ceremony. The Department of Justice escaped the charge that it had taken affirmative action to release a traitor on the ground that he was a great poet. The proceeding had the blessing of that admired literary figure Robert Frost. At the same time, it had the judicial sanction of a decision by a judge on the evidence. A simple motion to dismiss on the part of the Department of Justice would not have embodied these values. And as for Pound himself, the tribute of internationally known artists and writers and the editorials acclaiming his release were perhaps worth waiting for, although he declined to admit it at the time.

The case illustrates how many important moral values are symbolized by the miracle play of a criminal trial. There is the idea that if crime is the result of mental illness the defendant should be sent to a hospital to be cured rather than to a penitentiary to be punished. There is the notion that even if a man is insane, he cannot be forced into hospital confinement if he refuses to plead insanity, even if his refusal is a result of mental disease. There is the idea that psychiatrists can study mental symptoms and determine whether a crime is the result of insanity or the result of the exercise of free will on the part of a mentally disturbed person.

From a realistic point of view a trial cannot be a product of exact logical analysis, but the dignity of the law requires that it appear to be.

The enforcement of criminal law represents the moral values of society in other ways. Recently, in the case of *Gideon* v. *Wainwright,* 372 U. S. 335 (1963), my partner Abe Fortas was appointed by the Supreme Court to represent a fifty-year-old white man who had been in and out of prison most of his life. He had been convicted of four previous felonies. He was serving a five-year term for breaking into a poolroom. At the trial for the last offense he had asked for legal counsel and had been refused it. The Supreme Court had held in 1942, in *Betts* v. *Brady* 316 U. S. 455, that for minor offenses prosecuted in the state courts it was not necessary that the accused have an attorney. This decision was based on a realistic appraisal: many offenders in such minor cases were guilty, and the burden on the courts and the difficulty of finding enough counsel to represent the thousands of habitual criminals justified the rule. Yet Abe succeeded in convincing the Supreme Court that every man, including seemingly worthless, habitual criminals, must have the same rights before a court.

The case had been brought before the Supreme Court in a peculiar way. Gideon had written a letter from prison in Florida which he called a petition for certiorari. It was not technically correct. Nevertheless, the Court, using its discretionary powers, agreed to review the case, appointed Abe as counsel, and concluded by reversing its decision in *Betts* v. *Brady*.

There are no doubt thousands of people in penitentiaries in the United States who could be released under the Gideon decision. As a practical matter, I doubt if many of them get out, because few of them will ever have learned about the Gideon case, and the mentally retarded persons, who make up forty per cent of our prison population, have probably never heard of the Supreme Court of the United States. Nevertheless, the moral impact of this dramatic case was terrific. The idea that the busy judges of our highest tribunal would reach down into a prison and review the case of a habitual criminal was so moving that a book about it by Anthony Lewis, called *Gideon's Trumpet,* became a best seller. In addition, a nationwide television network devoted a full hour of its prime time to a dramatic portrayal of the case in which all of the principal actors were interviewed. I doubt if any of the millions of people who saw this presentation of a great moral issue were not deeply moved.

Some of the moral values that the criminal law represents make little sense. For example, vast sums are spent in prosecuting narcotics peddlers. This raises the price of narcotics so high that an opportunity for tremendous profits is given to highly intelligent but extremely evil masters of organized crime. Under our laws the treatment of addicts by physicians has become so hazardous that few doctors will undertake it. Organized criminal rings engage in a nationwide effort to create addicts, because once created they are sources of revenue for the indefinite future. O. W. Wilson, Superintendent of Police of Chicago, reported in an article in *Harper's Magazine* in April, 1964, that the major part of the police job is to suppress gambling, vice, and trafficking in narcotics. He is able to bring in only the minor participants in these illegal activities. He reported that, for the most part, the men higher up, who control the vast gambling and other vice operations, cannot be convicted, although he knows who they are. He placed the blame on our principles of criminal justice, which give too much protection to the accused. This is a common police complaint.

Policemen, understandably enough, feel themselves handicapped by the tendency of judges to adhere to our notion of a fair trial. They resent the fact that under recent decisions of the Supreme Court it has become very difficult for a policeman to extort a confession which can be used in evidence against a criminal. The answer, however, is not to destroy the value of a fair trial. In the case of the narcotics evil, the answer is to treat it not as a moral problem, but as a disease. This is the way it is treated in England, and in that country narcotics is apparently not a serious criminal problem.

One of the persistent obsessions that stand in the way of a realistic and compassionate treatment of the problem of crime is the notion that we cannot afford the cost. People are continually compiling statistics about the cost of crime. They add up all the expenses of our penitentiaries, our psychiatric care of insane criminals, the budgets of the various police forces, the time criminal lawyers spend defending cases, and the time spent by judges in convicting criminals, and reach a fantastic figure, which represents a serious financial burden on the taxpayer. They argue in Congress that we cannot afford to provide adequate defense counsel to a criminal defendant; we cannot afford to rehabilitate him through expensive psychiatric treatment.

Yet if by some miracle criminals were removed from our society, all penitentiaries were closed, all psychiatric treatment of insane criminals were no longer necessary, and attorneys who represented criminals ceased to earn an income, and the wealthy free-spending masters of organized crime were reduced to poverty, the decrease in national income might have a serious impact upon every citizen. How many people would be thrown out of employment I do not know, but it would certainly be a substantial number.

But once the idea is accepted that there is a moral obligation on the part of society to spend whatever is necessary for the rehabilitation of the criminal and the removal of the environmental causes that breed crime, the complicated mythology that leads to the conclusion that we cannot afford such measures because of their cost will disappear. In time of war all notions of cost are removed from the public mind by the necessity of achieving victory. Though during the Great Depression it was psychologically impossible for us to make the public expenditures we needed, once we were in the war, we forgot all notions of cost, and became rich in spite of tremendous waste. The war increased our real wealth, our capacity to produce goods. Without it we might still have been in the midst of depression. In the same way, the increased economic activity required to eliminate the conditions that are the principal cause of crime will make us richer instead of poorer.

This is not an argument in favor of crime as a means to acquire a stable economy. It is simply an attempt to expose the utter irrelevance of the idea of social cost to the problem. In a society where the goods and services the industrial plant is capable of producing are fully utilized, any money spent on goods and services devoted to rehabilitating criminals would mean that law-abiding citizens would have to go without something. But in an economy that is utilizing only seventy-five per cent of its actual productive capacity, even the most foolish distribution of the unused twenty-five per cent would cost no one anything in terms of goods and services he is now receiving.

To bring this about, the important thing needed is the recognition of a national obligation to remove the misery and economic destitution into which criminals are born. Once that obligation is accepted, the goods and services to meet it can easily be forthcoming from the constantly increasing productive capacity of the twentieth-century industrial revolution. The necessity to produce these goods will make us not poorer but more prosperous than we were before. The tremendously important result of the exposure of the moral values implicit in the Durham case and in the Gideon case is that these moving dramas on the courtroom stage tend to create a compassionate society. Only a compassionate society can take the measures that will solve the problems of crime and violence in our great cities.

———◆———

CHAPTER TWENTY-THREE

A Lady from Colorado

No book about life in Washington from the beginning of the Depression to the Second World War would be complete without a reference to one of the most extraordinary women of our time, Evalyn Walsh McLean.

The daughter of Thomas Walsh, who had made a great fortune in Western mining ventures, she had married John R. McLean, a man of large fortune. She wrote a lively and interesting autobiography entitled *Father Struck It Rich.* She was a part of that fabulous era when rich men gathered from all points of the compass to build elaborate rococo palaces in the capital city, to entertain foreign diplomats and visiting noblemen and perhaps marry their daughters to someone with a title. That kind of society disappeared with the Depression and will never be revived so long as the progressive income tax continues to deprive American businessmen of their incentive.

Though Evalyn loved to entertain on a lavish scale, she had little regard for the Social Register. She was always in revolt against people whom she regarded as smug or conventional. When I knew her, only a few of her intimate friends were wealthy. She had little interest in organized charity; her generosity was toward individuals whom she knew and thought she could help.

In 1932, as a result of the Depression, a great army of poverty-stricken veterans of the First World War gathered from all sections of the nation and marched on Washington. They were known as the "Bonus Army." They established themselves in a miserable camp on the Anacostia River and asserted they were going to stay there until Congress granted them a bonus. It was a dramatic and desperate gesture. It carried with it the radical notion that it was the moral obligation of the government not to let its former soldiers starve. No idea could have been more shocking to the respectable members of the community than this. If the government under organized pressure handed out money to anyone, that would be the end of the capitalist system. You could prove this by going back to Roman history, when the emperors furnished free bread and circuses to the people of Rome. It was this, combined with the lack of proper moral standards, that was the cause of the decline and fall of the Roman Empire, as every educated man knew.

Evalyn did not claim to know anything about economics, nor was she at all sure just why the Roman Empire fell. But here on her doorstep was camped a group of starving soldiers, so she bought food for them. She never got over her burning indignation when, under the orders of the President, the Bonus Army was driven out by tanks and tear gas.

Equally characteristic of Evalyn was her contribution of one hundred thousand dollars to find the kidnapped Lindbergh baby. Gaston Means, a plausible rogue, persuaded her that for this sum he could do it. Without consulting anyone, she pawned the famous Hope diamond to raise the cash. Gestures like this were characteristic of her.

When I came to Washington Evalyn's weekly dinners at her home, "Friendship," were an established institution. Sometimes they would be for as few as one hundred people. Other times there might be three hundred. She developed a great liking for the New Dealers. This was somewhat of an amorphous group. At the top were the Brain Trusters. Following them there was a larger group known as "eggheads." Then at the bottom there was a vast army, known as the bureaucrats, devoted to the senseless harassment of American business. By and large they were the most interesting group of people that had ever come to Washington, and Evalyn loved to meet and talk with them.

She was equally fond of conservatives and industrialists and prominent politicians. At one of her large dinners you could find

General William S. Knudsen, who had left his position as president of General Motors to work for the government; Leon Henderson, Clare Boothe Luce, Walter Lippmann, and Walter Winchell; members of the Supreme Court; Martin Dies, head of the Un-American Activities Committee of the House of Representatives; Lord and Lady Halifax, Joseph Hergesheimer and other authors, and a goodly scattering of motion-picture actors. She managed to have on her list the most colorful cross section, all shades of opinion from reactionary to radical. If some government official had been attacked by a Senator, she took particular pleasure in seating them at the same table at her next dinner.

It was at one of Evalyn's dinners that I first met Governor Alf Landon, who had been such a notoriously unsuccessful candidate against President Roosevelt in 1936. Evalyn had a motion picture to entertain such guests as wanted to see it. Those who did not could play bridge. The picture to be shown did not interest me, so I was sitting sipping a drink when Charlie Michelson—one of Roosevelt's principal assistants—asked me to make up a fourth at bridge. I told him I knew little about the game, but he said they could not find anybody else, so I joined him. At the table was Governor Landon. My first partner was Michelson. I did not make many mistakes, and this caused Landon a not insubstantial loss—I think we were playing for two cents a point. In the next rubber I was Landon's partner. I picked up an extraordinary hand. I thought we could not lose and that boldness was indicated. I kept raising Landon's bids until we were playing for a little slam. It was doubled; I redoubled. Then I laid down my hand and discovered to my horror that what I thought was the ace of spades was the ace of clubs. It was a financial catastrophe for both Landon and myself. I apologized profusely, of course. Landon smiled and said, "Don't give it a thought. It serves me right for having anything to do with a New Dealer."

After that incident I got to know Landon and came to admire him greatly. He was an old Bull Mooser. He believed in the enforcement of the antitrust laws. The campaign he had conducted against Roosevelt under the pressure of the conservative financial interests who were supporting him did not represent his true character. My friend Raymond Clapper, the late columnist, admired him, too, and with complete justification.

Landon had a great sense of humor. A few years ago, when I was invited to lecture at the University of Kansas, he asked me to stay at his beautiful home in Topeka. My wife had brought enough clothes to outfit a musical-comedy chorus, and her suitcase was very heavy. Landon insisted on carrying it when we arrived, but I said, "Governor, if it ever gets out that a Republican candidate for President ended up by carrying the suitcase of an old New Dealer, it would ruin the Republican party." "You're so right," he answered, and dropped the suitcase.

To return to Evalyn Walsh McLean, I remember an incident that occurred at the end of the first of her dinners that I attended. Every sort of conveyance, from chauffeur-driven Cadillacs to battered tin jalopies, could be found at her front door. Needing a second car when I came to Washington, I had purchased a vehicle known as a Stearns-Knight Falcon. It was about ten years old and cost me fifty dollars. It had hard narrow tires, and a sunshade at each of its two windows. But it ran, and that was the important thing. When my wife and I left that evening, the footman asked, "Shall I call your car, sir?" I replied, "You can call it, all right, but I doubt very much if it will come."

Evalyn was famous for her jewels, which included a pear-shaped diamond called "The Star of the East" and the Hope diamond. She loved to load her arms with priceless bracelets, but there was something irresistible and original about the way she did it. At every move she sparkled like the Milky Way. One evening when she was entertaining my wife and me in her suite at the Waldorf Towers in New York, two gentlemen from Cartier's, very solemn and dignified persons indeed, wearing striped pants, came in to fit some diamond earrings Cartier's was making for her. She asked, "Can't you get more diamonds on these things?" There was a shocked pause, after which the head man said, "My dear madam, no lady could possibly wear earrings with stones bigger than these." She replied, "Dammit, I'm not a lady—I want to know if you can put more stones on and keep them from falling off my ears." Everybody in the room laughed, and Evalyn joined in.

She was extraordinarily careless in leaving her jewelry around, and none of it was insured. She told my wife that if you cared for jewelry so much that you insured it, you shouldn't buy any.

When the United States entered the war, Evalyn began to entertain each week wounded or disabled servicemen who were resident at military hospitals in the community. There would be a hundred to a hundred and fifty of them with their wives or girl friends on a Saturday evening at her house. After dinner she would slip off her jewelry and let the girls wear it. My wife and I assisted at those parties, and the scattering of all that uninsured jewelry worried us. When the party broke up, it was our duty to retrieve the jewelry. Nothing was ever lost.

I remember the afternoon she died. Father Edmund A. Walsh, her favorite priest, who was vice president of Georgetown University, was there. Also present were Frank Murphy, Associate Justice of the Supreme Court of the United States, Cissy Patterson, owner of the Washington *Times-Herald,* Frank Waldrop, managing editor of that paper, Mrs. Arnold, and myself. Her death was sudden, and none of her family could get there in time.

After Father Walsh had given her the last rites, Waldrop and I gathered up her jewelry, which was scattered around the room, and put it into a shoe box. We knew it was worth between one and two million dollars and felt that it was dangerous to leave it where it was, so we decided to put it in a safe-deposit box. Domenic, Evalyn's butler, drove us to her bank. But it was late on a Saturday afternoon, and we learned that the time locks all over town were on and no one could get into a safe-deposit box until Monday morning. We then tried the jewelry stores. None of them would take our shoe box; they were afraid it might create questions with respect to the insurance they carried.

Finally Waldrop had a bright idea. We went up to J. Edgar Hoover's office at the Federal Bureau of Investigation. His chief assistant, now Judge Edward A. Tamm of the United States District Court for the District of Columbia, was there. After Tamm got Hoover's approval by phone, we sealed the shoe box and got a receipt from him saying that the FBI was holding a shoe box with an unknown quantity of diamonds in it which would not be released until called for by the duly qualified executor of Mrs. McLean's estate.

Under Evalyn's will, Justice Frank Murphy and I were the executors. After the will was probated, we retrieved the shoe box from the FBI. The jewelry was finally sold to Harry Winston of New York, for about a million dollars. He gave the Hope diamond to the Smithsonian Institution, in Washington, where it is now on display.

No one could know Evalyn Walsh McLean without feeling the deepest respect and affection for her. She brought to Washington the atmosphere of a Western mining camp. She had the gift of originality, sympathy for people in distress, the love of jovial companionship, and the desire to bring people of all sorts of positions and ideas together. Since her death there has been no one like her and no institution like her parties, and there probably never will be again.

CHAPTER TWENTY-FOUR

The Practice of the Law Is a Profession of Great Dignity the Pursuit of Which Requires Great Learning

Clarence Darrow, whom I knew and admired, once told me of an occasion when he was asked to state for a magazine article the principal cause of his success. He asked the interviewer what the other successful people whose names were to appear in the article had thought was the cause of their success. The interviewer informed Darrow that most of them had said that their success was due to hard work.

"Put me down for that too," said Darrow. He continued, "I was brought up on a farm. When I was a young man, on a very hot day I was engaged in distributing and packing down the hay which a horse-propelled stacker was constantly dumping on top of me. By noon I was completely exhausted. That afternoon I left the farm, never to return, and I haven't done a day of hard work since."

Darrow's concept was accurate. I would advise any young man who has an allergy toward hard work to train himself for the law, where he can achieve reasonable affluence by writing, talking, and thinking. Thus he will give the appearance of working hard, for the hours are long and the law appears to the layman to be abstruse and difficult. But, as I have observed before, legal learning is the art of making simple things complicated, which should be an easy task for anyone. Paradoxically, the great lawyer is frequently one who can make simple and intelligible matters which lawyers and judges regard as complex.

In addition, as I hope I have proved, the law is more abreast of the times and more flexible in adapting itself to changing conditions than any other learned pursuit. It offers to its high priests an entrancing variety of avenues to pursue. In my view, next to teaching, the practice of the law offers to its disciples more excitement than any other profession.

It may be interesting to contrast the legal profession in the United States with that of England, from which the American legal system springs. England clothes its lawyers, both barristers and solicitors, with more dignity than they can have in the United States. This is particularly true of barristers. Their right to plead in open court is a privilege that can only be acquired through an invitation to become a member of one of the celebrated Inns of Court and obtaining chambers there. The chief requirements a student must fulfill to be called to the bar of an Inn are to pass the law examinations given by the Council of Legal Education (an organization jointly sponsored by the four Inns of Court), to dine in the hall of the Inn six times (in some cases only three) during each dining term, of which there are four a year, and to spend a year as pupil of a junior member of the bar. This takes four years. After that time he becomes a full-fledged barrister and, if room for him is available, a tenant of the chambers.

In form, at least, the privilege of practicing before the London courts is more like membership in a private club than a right. The fortunate members eat together and go to church together. I once attended services at the Middle Temple, where the choir was the most beautiful I have ever heard. After the services the judges and lawyers had cocktails and lunch.

One wonders, noting the small capacity of the Inns as compared with the space taken up by the great law offices of New York, how the London system could accommodate a rapidly expanding bar such as we have had in the United States. There is no evidence, however, of any arbitrary exclusion of qualified persons, in spite of the fact that an invitation, from what appears on its face to be a private club, is a requisite to admission. Sometimes the failure to obtain chambers leads to fortuitous exclusion from practice. But since the number of barristers in all England is only about two thousand, this limitation does not seem of serious concern to anyone to whom I have talked.

In contrast, in the United States, where there never has been any distinction between solicitors and barristers, the right to practice law is a right protected by the due process clause of the United States Constitution. The Supreme Court of the United States has in a number of cases reversed state courts in their disbarment of attorneys or in their refusal to admit them without a hearing on the facts, which conforms to the due process standard. The result is that an American lawyer on the way up will refer to his need for more "law business," a term seldom used by an English barrister.

The profession of law in England, though its admission requirements are offensive to the democratic tradition of the United States, has acquired a dignity that United States practice can never achieve. There are certain practical advantages to this dignity. As a result of the close association and camaraderie of London barristers through the Inns of Court, English judges and members of the bar trust each other. The British judge has neither a law clerk nor a full-time stenographer. He must work with a pen or pencil and investigate and analyze the authorities for himself, aided only by the arguments of the barristers who appear before him in any given case. As a result, it is a practical necessity for a British judge to rely on the fairness and objectivity of the barristers. A barrister is under the corresponding practical necessity to see to it that he does not lose the confidence of the bench by advancing preposterous legal theories or by making misleading analyses of the authorities he cites in support of his position.

In the United States a lawyer is expected to take advantage of every technicality to advance every conceivable legal theory, however preposterous, and to use his ingenuity in delaying proceedings where such delay would be of advantage to his client.

As an illustration of the inability of the judge in the United States to rely on counsel as the English judge does, I cite a rule of the Supreme Court of the United States that a petition for rehearing must be accompanied by an affidavit of counsel that it is not brought for purposes of delay. Implicit in this rule is the assumption that members of the bar of our highest tribunal, duly admitted with an appropriate ceremony, are apt to mislead the Court if they are not put under oath. But a casual sampling of the huge number of rehearing petitions filed in the Supreme Court in-

dicates that the required oaths are not an effective deterrent to
frivolous petitions. It is hard to believe that many of such petitions could be filed for anything else but delay. Yet I know of no
case where a lawyer has been penalized or even seriously questioned
because he filed such an affidavit.

In the United States a principal part of the proceeding is a written argument citing every case that conceivably bears on any issue
of the case at hand. If the work is thoroughly done, the brief will
be long. In an important case the judge will be confronted with a
brief containing all the cases that by any stretch of the imagination
could be called relevant, running sometimes into the hundreds,
and an opposing brief asserting that these cases are all irrelevant
and citing another long list. The judge will feel he has to read
these cases. To facilitate this task he has a clerk and a stenographer.
He will tend to postpone his decision until all this work has been
done. By that time he will have forgotten what was said in oral
argument. Therefore, one of the results of the voluminous brief is
the decline of oral argument in the United States.

In England the long written arguments we call briefs are unknown. A "brief" there is a summary of the case. The argument on
which the court relies is oral. Each opposing barrister submits a
list of cases. Books containing them are brought to the courtroom,
with copies for the judge and counsel. Obviously counsel in England are not going to pile a hundred books on the judge's desk;
there would not be time to discuss them.

There is no limit put on the time for oral argument in England.
It proceeds like a class in an American law school. The opposing
barristers are the instructors; the judges are the students. When
the judges think they have learned enough, the opinion is delivered
orally from the bench. It may be polished up later if publication is
desired. But it is unusual for a case to be taken under advisement
for further study.

In the United States all appellate cases are taken under advisement for months and months while the clerks read and read, and
write memorandums, and the judges think and think and confer
and confer. This is in line with our tradition of thorough legal
scholarship. This notion makes oral argument seem superficial, and
hence it is growing of less and less importance. Gone is the time

when a Daniel Webster could argue before the Supreme Court for days. In that Court one hour is the maximum time counsel can take, and he often has to sit down before he has presented all his points, leaving most of his arguments to his brief. In most of our federal courts of appeal the time is limited to half an hour. Persuasive oral advocacy is becoming a lost art in the United States.

It is obvious that the English practice is faster. Cases cannot accumulate and decisions be delayed until long after the judge has forgotten what was said in oral argument. It is also a more impressive spectacle because of the ceremonial costumes of the participants, which give a background of tradition that enhances reverence for the ideal of impartial law. I would imagine, though I do not know from experience, that it might be more difficult to advance a phony argument dressed in a ceremonial robe. It is psychologically true that costumes do affect men's attitudes. Even an American thinks and talks differently when he puts on a high silk hat (which, unfortunately, is seldom today) than when he is in his shirt sleeves with a glass in his hand.

But the English system offends one of our most cherished legal traditions: that legal principles are difficult and cannot be applied, even by a well-trained lawyer, without exhaustive and profound research. How can the law become a seamless web of consistent principles, growing more and more certain with each decision, if judges are permitted to decide a case without long conferences and deep study?

At Harvard the faculty are seeking impartial principles of abstract justice that will remove whim and prejudice from the judicial scene. According to Professor Henry Hart, this can be done only by what he calls "the maturing of collective thought" on the part of judges. Recently he sharply criticized the Supreme Court of the United States for not doing more of this kind of thing. He suggested that if they had done so in one particular case, which he used as a horrible example of the failure of the justices to comprehend the applicable legal principles, they would have reached the same conclusions he had, instead of erring and straying like lost sheep.

I happened to agree with the decision of the Court on the case Hart used as an example of judicial delinquency. I disagreed with the idea of encouraging judges to spend more time making up their minds. In an article in the *Harvard Law Review* I replied to Hart by saying that I did not believe that judicial opinion would be improved by the maturing of collective thought. The process would only be slowed down. Indeed, I asserted that the law would not be clarified; it would only become more confused.

As a result of my article legal scholars swung into action with other articles. Some defended my point of view. Others asserted that more thought and research would produce the impartial legal principles so badly needed for the guidance of our judiciary. These articles appeared in law reviews from coast to coast. They were supported by hundreds of footnotes. Gradually, it seems to me, the winds died down, but since I am not a devoted reader of law reviews, the controversy may still be going on.

The British believe just as firmly as we do that the law must be applied to a given case with the guidance of abstract, impartial principles. But they seem to discover these principles faster and with less labor than we do in the United States. They believe their judges are capable of applying legal principles after hearing a brief discussion by a barrister trained in the art of explaining them. In the United States we are filled with doubt and conduct philosophical debates in an outpouring of learned articles as to the proper theology we should use for the guidance of our courts. The English, therefore, have no publications similar to our fifty or sixty university law reviews.

In the United States, the belief in the efficacy of exhaustive research and long reflection as a means of making the law clearer and more certain for those to come is reflected in the length and complexity of the brief. This has become a real problem. Most appellate courts attempt to solve it by limiting the length of the brief, usually to not more than fifty pages. But this is an exceedingly difficult rule to enforce. Lawyers who want to file longer briefs can always explain that the case is so complicated that fifty pages are utterly inadequate to enable the judges to understand the finer points on which their decision should depend. And since the motion to expand a brief is accompanied by the brief itself, the case is made to appear even more complicated than the lawyer claims it to be. If the court denies the motion, the result is that it has no brief before it. And the lawyer must be given time to rewrite it, which delays the case. So motions to expand briefs are usually granted.

Owing to this complex process practically all our courts are far behind on their dockets. The law's delay has become a subject of voluminous writings and study. Statistics are kept in many courts as an incident of this study, and committees are constantly being formed to prepare reports in which these statistics are analyzed. The conclusion is always the same: we need more judges. In England they seem always to have enough.

I confess an admiration for the superior dignity, the faster pace, and the economy of clerks, lawyers, and judges that the English legal system has achieved. There are only about two thousand barristers and thirty thousand solicitors to serve an English population of nearly fifty-three million. It requires 286,000 lawyers and 8,000 judges and others in the judicial service in courts of general jurisdiction and appeal to carry on the law business of this country. It may be that the British are less litigious than Americans. It is my belief that England has traditionally followed a policy of reducing the amount of litigation by making it expensive and hazardous. For example, contingent fees, paid to a lawyer only if he wins the case, are not permitted in England. How can an indigent victim of negligence get his case tried under these circumstances? The British lawyer will tell you that he can go to Legal Aid. Certainly the legal-aid idea is far more advanced in Great Britain than in the United States, but I doubt that it could possibly provide adequate representation for the vast mass of negligence cases that the contingent-fee system brings to our courts.

Another major deterrent to bringing suit in England is the practice of compelling the unsuccessful party to pay the fees of even the most expensive counsel on the other side. My friend Harold Laski was financially ruined by a libel suit he lost. If suit is brought, this practice might be a factor in compelling a small settlement.

This is not in the American tradition. We want the freest possible access to the courts; we are willing to see them used by a plaintiff whose attorney is on a contingent fee to determine whether or not he actually has the case he thinks he has. Indeed, in the antitrust field, and in many others, we encourage private litigation. If plaintiff in an antitrust suit wins, he gets three times the award of damages and, if he loses, the defendant may be required to pay a reasonable fee to the plaintiff's lawyers. This enables the plaintiff to hire able counsel on a contingent fee. It is the American belief that the enforcement of the antitrust laws is aided and supplemented by encouraging private litigants to supplement government prosecutions. This throws an enormous burden on our courts in antitrust litigation, but the consensus is that this cost is worthwhile.

Furthermore, counsel are encouraged to bring litigation against directors of a corporation who are abusing their power. A single stockholder can bring such an action. If successful, his attorney will be remunerated by compelling the corporation to pay a large contingent fee based on the benefit the stockholder's suit has given the corporation.

Our pretrial discovery proceedings in civil cases, unknown in England, further add to the amount of litigation, because a plaintiff may start a suit without being sure he has a cause of action and obtain the necessary evidence after the suit is started. He does this by requiring the opposite party to answer questions or produce documents in his possession. Thus our legal system actively encourages citizens to bring their troubles to court. The English does not. Certainly this must have some effect on the comparatively small number of members of the British bar and judges.

Restricting access to the courts by making litigation hazardous and by refusing to give it positive encouragement other than by legal aid permits a neater and tidier image of the judicial process in England. Yet, in my view the American tradition is more in accord with justice.

The British practice would be psychologically unsuited to this country. The ideal of an impartial judiciary applying impartial principles of law can be supported here only by the ceremony of learning and research. Our great law schools, which are much more significant in symbolizing the rule of law above men than anything similar in England, are devoted to the idea that it is only through theological learning that justice can be done. Books piled on books give us a vision of the impartiality of legal learning, and the possibility of its constant improvement toward the end of abstract justice.

This ideal can never be achieved. An objective psychologist would probably say that it has no scientific basis, that no amount of research and conferences can eliminate the instinctive reactions that the environment and the training of a judge have created and that condition his reasoning. But such a psychologist would be forgetting that a more important purpose of the judicial process, exceeding in social value what happens in an individual case, is the belief it induces in the public that there is and can be impartial justice. This ideal is celebrated by our law schools and by our tradition of legal scholarship. It is offended by oral decisions made immediately after oral argument. We can never attain to Britain's speedy administration of justice.

There are other differences. The opportunity to make a large income through the practice of law is far greater here than in England. In England, unless there are exceptional circumstances, no more than two counsel take part in a proceeding. While their remuneration is not on an hourly basis, it is inevitable that it have some relationship to the number of hours spent. On the other hand, it is customary in the United States in a case where large corporate interests are involved to put all the men in a law office who are not otherwise engaged to work on the case. Under the system of exhausting all possible theories and reading all cases that remotely bear on these theories, there is no limit on the number of lawyers who can be engaged or the time that they spend in research. Memorandum after memorandum issues in rapid succession from the lower echelons. The files grow bulkier and bulkier. This mass of material is analyzed and rewritten by the higher echelons. The lights burn brightly long after midnight as many of our larger law offices have felt compelled to run night shifts.

The result of this on the income of a law firm can easily be imagined. If a lawyer is able not only to charge for his own time, but also to engage a number of men whose salaries run from ten to twenty thousand dollars a year and charge from twenty-five to thirty-five dollars an hour for their time, the amount of money in the kitty increases by leaps and bounds. For example, my own office was recently engaged in complicated and protracted litigation. A large New York firm representing another corporate interest was working with us on the same side of a case. Both offices were in constant consultation and were in effect duplicating each other's work. Yet the New York office was able to charge much more than we were. This was not owing to better work performed, but because it was much larger and was able to put more associates to work on the case than we were.

The simplicity of English legal argument is greatly aided by the fact that it is difficult for anyone, even with the utmost diligence, to find all of the relevant British cases. In the first place, there are far fewer courts in England than in this country, where we have fifty state Supreme Courts. They have there no such institution as the West Publishing Company, which publishes cases and cross references, key numbers, and citations, by means of which the American lawyer can find out every instance in which a case has been mentioned in any court. This makes research more thorough in the United States, but it creates another problem that does not exist in England. Here the law reports keep pouring off the presses in staggering numbers. Law libraries expand in size in arithmetical progression. If a lawyer bought a complete set of law reports he would not have enough room to house them. Hence he must go to bar-association libraries. This results in his own profit but increases the expense of his client, for if he had his own library he could not charge for portal-to-portal time.

A complete law library is a fearsome thing. Harvard possesses the largest collection in this country. Professor Thomas Reed Powell, when asked whether Harvard was the largest law library in the world, replied, "I am sure it must be, because it is the only library where three hundred thousand books can be lost at the same time." Harvard is now acquiring complete sets of all the world's legal literature. A large separate building to house this foreign collection has been built. The problem of what use these books could be put to was a difficult one, but Dean Erwin N. Griswold solved it in a most ingenious way. He issued a report conceding that in the past the United States had muddled through without such a collection. But, he observed, times had changed. Isolationism had gone forever, and we had become responsible, or might become responsible, for problems in every nation in the world. How could we, he argued, understand and solve the problems of our relations with other nations without the assistance of some experts in the law of all other nations? Thus legal research and scholarship could aid us in foreign policy.

Having acquired this collection of foreign law in order to aid our foreign policy, the next step was to get someone to read it. To that end students are given scholarships and set to work. Since the real reward is a degree, the labor cost is low. And the Harvard faculty received an incidental benefit, because it was necessary to expand its personnel so that someone could read what the students had written.

England, having dropped the white man's burden shortly before the United States assumed it, is able to face the future without so many books.

Legal education is a far less serious undertaking in England than it is in the United States. In England, law is given as an undergraduate course, and there does not appear to be the intense pressure on the students that there is in our schools. Law students there are not required to go through intense research of cases, and they do not write for law reviews. In addition, no law degree is required for membership in the bar. Any individual is permitted to "read" for the bar and prepare himself for examination, and private quiz courses are given unconnected with any educational institution to prepare applicants for their bar examinations. A bright student can prepare for admission to the bar in about fifteen months.

In the United States, if an applicant were permitted to take the bar examinations without going to law school, I have no doubt that he could pass them with fifteen months' preparation. But the applicant must have a degree from an accredited law school, and nearly all such schools require an undergraduate degree for admission. It is interesting to note that even after an applicant has passed the three-year law-school course, he stands a good chance of failing the state bar examinations in many states. This is because the philosophical approach to the law in a great law school is entirely different from the technical approach of the bar examinations of many states. The law student is therefore well advised to take a private quiz course before his bar examinations.

It would seem to follow that as a result of his more thorough legal training the American lawyer should be superior to the British lawyer. But when one meets the British bar that difference is

not discernible. I have heard Americans who have engaged in litigation in Great Britain complain that the British lawyer is not a
fighter, like the American lawyer, that he will not advance arguments his client wishes him to make. I suspect this means only that
the British lawyer feels more responsibility to the judge than the
American lawyer does. There are also those who think that the
British barrister is superior in the general run. This leads to the
suspicion that the long and intensive training in an American law
school is unnecessary because the so-called science of the law is not
nearly as complicated and requires much less training than the faculty of our law schools thinks it does.

Another difference in law education in the two countries is that
English law faculties have resolutely refused to adopt the case system of studying law, which was imposed on our law schools by
Dean Christopher C. Langdell, of Harvard, more than half a century ago. No more time-wasting system of studying law has ever
been devised. The English law professor imparts his learning to his
students through lectures and textbooks. He can thus cover in an
hour what would take a week in an American law school. The
theory behind the case system is that the student, by confining himself to cases and avoiding textbooks, can develop mental muscles in
the same way that physical muscles are developed by daily set-
ting-up exercises. But any competent psychologist will tell you that
mental agility cannot be achieved in this way. Yet a blind faith in
the case-by-case system still persists in the great majority of American law schools.

There is a sharp variation in English and American practice in
the division of labor and responsibility. In an American law office
the preparation of the witnesses in a complicated case involving
large financial interests, the preparation of pleadings and motions,
and the trial itself are done by a closely organized firm of partners
and their legal employees. In England such a case is prepared and
tried by at least three independent lawyers, each with a separate responsibility and without the employer-employee relationship. There
is the solicitor, who sees the witnesses and prepares the factual case.
There is the junior barrister, who prepares the pleadings and argues intermediate motions. And there is the senior barrister, who presents the case in court. While we may assume that all these inde-

pendent counsel co-operate, none of them is in a position to deal with the others as a senior partner deals with his associates and law clerks here.

The division of responsibility in the trial of an English case may be less efficient than the organized work in law offices here, but certainly it seems more dignified. The leading barrister is set apart from the rest of the hive like a queen bee. The junior barrister has a more dignified appearance than the solicitor. In the United States anyone who has been a member of the bar for three years may be admitted to practice before the Supreme Court of the United States. Recently one of my partners moved the admission of a prominent newspaper columnist to the Supreme Court of the United States. He had a law degree and thereby had attained membership in the bar of the state of New York. This was all that was required for admission to the highest tribunal in the United States. An English barrister would probably have shuddered at the thought that such a thing could happen in a high court of law.

The division of functions between barristers and solicitors in England results in an important difference in the preparation of a case for trial. The English barrister is not permitted to interview witnesses, whom he will have to examine at the trial, except expert witnesses. His first sight of a witness is usually when he appears in the witness box. He must rely on written "proofs" of the witness's testimony prepared by the solicitor. This is to prevent the coaching of the witness by counsel, which is such a large part of American trial preparation.

In the United States, where "coaching" is freely permitted, many trial attorneys will have the questions and answers of the witness in written form if the case involves a complicated set of facts and the witness is unable to tell a good connected story without being prompted by leading questions. The witness will often be given the transcript of the questions and answers to study so that he will not get mixed up on the stand.

A conscientious American lawyer will prepare his witness only so that he will be at ease and tell a connected story. The witness will know what questions are coming and what answers will further the orderly expedition of the case. Yet there is no doubt that the lawyer's access to witnesses offers grave temptation, even though it is fair to assume that there are few who would induce a witness to perjure himself. By training the witness to put his best foot forward, and by causing him to emphasize some facts and minimize others, the story he tells on the witness stand may give a far different impression from the story told by the witness to the lawyer. An anecdote is told about a lawyer who won a substantial verdict for his client. He gave his client twenty-five per cent of the amount won. The client protested, saying: "After all, it's my case that won; you only argued it." The lawyer replied: "The case you brought me wouldn't have won you a cent. The case that got the verdict was my case, not yours."

Nevertheless, I prefer the American system of coaching witnesses. An inarticulate witness, subject to stage fright, who jumps from point to point and is unable to walk a straight path through a set of complicated facts, needs to know in advance precisely what questions are going to be asked him by the examining attorney in the order in which they are going to come. Once such a witness gets confused, there is no way on direct examination to straighten him out and get him back on the track except by asking leading questions, questions that can be answered yes or no. Such questions are permitted on cross-examination, but not on direct examination. And so counsel examining a witness who is mixed up on his dates asks in desperation: "Now, it was the fourteenth of June that you saw X, wasn't it?" Before the witness can answer, there is an objection, which is sustained. The attorney then asks: "When did you see X?" The witness, having been coached by the leading question, answers: "On the fourteenth." The opposing counsel then objects to the coaching of the witness. Since rulings on leading questions are largely discretionary, attempts to coach the witness by this method will get by if the judge is tolerant. But, even so, it adds a note of confusion. All this can be avoided if the witness is properly prepared in advance.

In my view one of the defects in English procedure is the failure to permit adequate pretrial discovery in civil cases. There is no legal process more important in the administration of justice than the right of litigants before the trial to discover evidence on their own behalf and the evidence that will be used against them. There was no effective discovery process in the United States, either, prior to the Federal Rules of Civil Procedure adopted by the Supreme Court in 1938. Since that date, similar rules have been adopted in nearly all the states.

At first this reform met with intense opposition. Dean Charles E. Clark, of Yale, was its leading proponent. Most successful lawyers were bitterly opposed. It interfered with what was satirically called "the sporting theory of justice." A skilled trial lawyer liked to spring surprises during the trial on his unwary opponents. Any procedure that took away that element of surprise was condemned as a "fishing expedition"—a deadly legal sin. Hence, what discovery procedure existed was hemmed in by a host of technical limitations.

The discovery procedure contemplated by Clark went farther than anything any God-fearing lawyer ever dreamed of. It gave a plaintiff suing a great corporation the right to obtain copies of its confidential records and, worst of all, it was felt, it required the corporation to produce in advance of the trial not only documents that could be admitted in evidence, but also documents that would be excluded at the actual trial, provided there was any chance that by reading these documents the plaintiff could get a key to what the relevant evidence was. In the same way, corporate executives and other witnesses could be examined in advance of trial in a way not permitted by rules of evidence. In other words, discovery was to be a free-for-all inquiry, uninhibited by the legal principles established after centuries of careful thought and profound study by eminent legal scholars. Anarchy and disaster were predicted if these rules passed.

Today they permit a litigant who suspects he has a good case as either plaintiff or defendant to file a complaint or an answer without knowing whether the allegations are true or not, and then use the process of discovery to find out if he is right.

In spite of their defiance of formerly accepted legal theology, these rules have tremendously advanced the cause of justice in the United States. For an attorney who diligently invokes them there can be no surprises. He may tell his client that he does not know whether or not he has a good cause of action or defense, but he will be able to find out after the case is started. Thus the rules of discovery have increased the possiblity of a litigant obtaining a summary judgment, a judgment without a formal trial of the issues of fact, based on the depositions and documents the discovery proceeding has disclosed. This kind of discovery is unknown in England or on the Continent. The British bench and bar still recoil with horror at the thought of permitting such a fishing expedition. In my view this is a grave defect in British procedure.

On the other hand, the failure to adopt any adequate discovery proceedings to aid the defendant in a criminal case is one of the gravest defects in our practice. In the federal courts indictments are usually obtained through secret hearings before a grand jury. Only extraordinary circumstances give a criminal defendant the right to find out either the names of the witnesses or their testimony through examination of the grand jury minutes. Thus, an over-zealous prosecutor may conceal from the defendant the witnesses and the documents that would aid him in his defense.

I am now representing a client who I am convinced is entirely innocent. Indeed, he is unable to tell me why he is being prosecuted. His crime is being guilty of a conspiracy to defraud purchasers of securities in a company he represented only as an attorney. The indictment is seventy-six pages long. It is impossible to tell from reading it what acts my client is accused of doing, because the theory of the indictment is that he is equally responsible for the acts of the ten other defendants who are charged with conspiring with him. My client is convinced that if there is any evidence against him, it is either perjured or distorted. But he cannot find out what that evidence is before the trial.

All I could do under current practice was file a motion for a bill of particulars, asking not for the evidence against my client, but only for a more precise statement of the acts the United States attorney claims he committed. The attorney protested giving even this limited information on the ground that disclosing the precise acts the prosecution would rely on for conviction would be equivalent to disclosing evidence to the defendant. The court granted our motion, but there is a thin line between asking for information about a particular act and asking for evidence. Had the court declined to grant the motion, since it is discretionary, there would have been nothing we could do before trial. But we profited very little from the Court's ruling. After more than a month's time we received a bill of particulars explaining the seventy-six-page indictment in 226 pages of elaborate obfuscation. We still do not have the faintest idea of the particular acts with which our client is charged in this trial. All we know is that he is responsible for everything all the other defendants did, and they are responsible for what he did, and what anybody did is lost in the fog of obscurity.

In England a preliminary hearing would have been held, in which the government would have had to produce enough evidence to show the probability that the defendant had committed some particular act or acts. The government could withhold some surprise witnesses but at least the defendant would be able to prepare his case. This is not true with respect to criminal indictments in the United States. The evidence showing the probability that the defendant committed the crime is in the secret files of the grand jury and only under extraordinary circumstances is it disclosed to the defendant.

One wonders why American courts, which allow the broadest possible discovery in a civil case, deny it to a criminal defendant. The theory is that doing so would hamper the enforcement of the law. In these days of increasing crime we must see that those who are guilty do not escape by using false testimony that they can make up the moment they know what the evidence is against them. The reason for the rise in crime is that we are coddling criminals. England has no such fear. The idea of giving a man with a criminal record an even chance with the prosecution is far stronger there than it is in the United States. Here criminal practice is shunned by our best lawyers, and it is felt that the criminal bar is not quite respectable. In England a barrister is not permitted to turn down a defendant, however notorious a criminal he may be, unless he has a much better reason than the mere fact that he does not want to represent that type of character. England's most distinguished barristers appear in criminal cases.

By way of parenthesis, I would like to say that I am not attempting here to review the various proceedings in the fifty state jurisdictions that might lead to adequate discovery in a criminal case. For example, anyone who reads the trials of Perry Mason, the famous criminal lawyer invented by Erle Stanley Gardner, knows that he finds out all about the evidence for the prosecution, and, indeed, wins most of his cases at a preliminary hearing where all the prosecution's evidence is disclosed. But our federal system permits no such practice.

One of the most interesting ceremonials in British legal practice is the custom commonly called "taking silk." After a period of successful practice, a junior barrister is privileged to apply to the Lord Chancellor for consideration for an appointment to be a king's, or, now, queen's, counsel. This is an honor, but it entails a risk. As long as a barrister remains a junior he may take the lead in one case and have the assistance of another junior to do the paper work. In another case he may do the paper work with some other barrister in the lead. But once he has taken silk and become a queen's counsel, he may no longer do the paper work (apart from writing opinions). Since the paper work he does as a junior may be an important source of his income, when he is restricted as a queen's counsel from doing any paper work at all this source of his income is cut off. However, if he remains a junior he loses considerable prestige. Traditionally, members of the high courts are selected from those who have taken silk. Those who remain juniors may be appointed as county judges only.

In the United States there are no absolute qualifications for appointment to the federal bench except admission to the bar. Anyone may be appointed, regardless of his professional standing. In addition, senators have a practical veto power over appointments to the federal bench in their own states, and the recommendations of the state bar associations are often disregarded by them. Also, in the majority of states the judges are elected.

Does the English system ensure better judges? Certainly it would seem to prevent the selection of judges who have not acquired some distinction at the bar and who are not qualified by actual experience in trial work. It would also seem to eliminate political appointments.

In any event, both the English and the American judicial systems embody, I think, better than do those of any other country the ideal of the rule of law above men. To make that ideal real there must be a priesthood dedicated to the service of justice. To give sanctity to that priesthood, England relies much more on robes and ceremony than does the United States, which regards them as superficial trappings. Here law is a science, which can be improved by constantly increasing scholarship and research. Books, rather than robes, are the heart of American law. One can only say that to us scholarship and learning and an infinite number of books seem to fit in with our Protestant tradition. Which is the better method of enshrining the ideal of the law in the hearts of people, I do not know.

In spite of its imperfections and its aspects of high comedy, there is no career in the world more interesting than the law in the United States. You have an orchestra seat from which you observe the most fascinating spectacles.

On the educational level Harvard is busy collecting books, giving scholarships to persons who are willing to read them, and employing professors to read what the scholarship students have written. The Yale Law School is busily engaged in renting computing machines, and in hiring sociologists and psychiatrists to make a science out of the law. I am informed by my spies and underpaid agents in New Haven that Yale now contemplates the employment of two astronomers and one bright Swede in order to obtain a well-rounded law faculty. Lesser law schools are trying to project images like Harvard's and Yale's.

On the professional side, great law offices composed of hundreds of lawyers are keeping open night and day to find cases to put in briefs and thus confuse the courts.

On the judicial side the judges, with the aid of their law clerks and secretaries, with knowledge that they cannot trust the briefs of counsel are engaged in looking up the law for their own benefit.

Counsel for parties in litigation before the courts are engaged in exhausting the authorities they cite in their briefs. Judges are valiantly attempting to cut down the size and complexity of these briefs, in which task they are constantly frustrated by the ingenuity of counsel.

While all this is going on, the high priests of our economic faith are thundering denunciations of the unsound thinkers who are leading the American public astray. The public-relations men, occupying positions of high prestige and power, are teaching our political leaders how to project proper images. The public, fully aware of the image-projecting techniques, is making its decision with respect to political candidates by using standards similar to those used to choose Miss America at Atlantic City. And at the same time scientists, who are the only knowledgeable hard workers of the lot, are devising means by which the human race can exterminate itself.

It is like watching a gorgeous ballet with a whole variety of dancers moving back and forth across the stage to create a scene of beauty and rhythm. The hard practical tasks of science and business management are less attractive to a man who would rather talk than work. And the Soviets have demonstrated by their cautionary example that reverence for the ideals of the law is more important in a civilized country than advances in either science or industry.

As a small-town lawyer, as a professor of law, as a government official, as an appellate judge, and as a practitioner in a big city, I have been privileged to watch this scene from every angle.

CHAPTER TWENTY-FIVE

The Education of the Educated Voter

To turn from justice and the law, where everything seems orderly and rational (except to a rabid minority who would impeach the Chief Justice of the Supreme Court), to the principles that should govern the distribution of the new productive wealth of the twentieth century has meant, since the days of the New Deal, to enter the land of hobgoblins and imaginary horribles. Its principal demon has been government planning. Lesser devils include inflation, invasion of states' rights, the intolerable burden of a national debt that cannot be paid, and loss of individual freedom if the fiscal budget is not balanced.

One of the few useful things to come out of the Bolshevik revolution and the Second World War was the growing realization that production is wealth and that money is a form of national bookkeeping necessary for the distribution of that wealth. That was the basic idea behind the Full Employment Act of 1946, which has since been ignored. But it is an idea that has had a slower acceptance in the United States than in any other civilized nation. In Russia, if more schools are needed, the planners ascertain whether there are enough bricks and lumber and steel to build them without interference with the military budget. That, at least, is the Soviet theory; and it has got Russia, at enormous social cost, as far as it is today.

In the United States any activity that cannot be envisaged as income-producing in monetary terms for the future has been held to be a burden on the taxpayer and a step toward inflation. It is for that reason that we cannot balance or expand our productive capacity to meet our needs except in time of war.

Ever since the Depression it has been apparent to any objective observer not looking at our economy through the lenses of economic theory that there has not been enough effective purchasing power to run our industrial plant at capacity. Yet the only legitimate means of increasing that purchasing power has been through private financial operations. These have been successful beyond the dreams of anyone living prior to the First World War. The automobile companies through their financing affiliates "print" all the money that is necessary to sell more cars per capita than are sold in any other country in the world. Prior to the First World War, if a young man on a modest salary had gone to his banker and asked for an unlimited letter of credit to finance a trip to Europe, he would have risked being sent to some institution for the treatment of the insane. Today for a small sum he may obtain an unlimited letter of credit for travel from the Diners' Club, the American Express Company, or another similar credit institution. The Federal Housing Act has created a system whereby we can move into houses now and gradually pay for them over periods lasting as long as thirty years. The houses themselves are built by bank loans guaranteed by the government, the builder having to advance only ten per cent of the estimated cost. A client of mine engaged in building apartments under the Federal Housing Authority received a profit of five million dollars on an actual cash investment of only a few hundred thousand. Naturally he went on to build more apartments. Department stores "print" the money for which they sell their goods under so-called revolving credit plans. The private debt, which was one hundred and four billion dollars after the First World War, has risen to the astronomical sum of five hundred and eighty-five billion dollars, and still we are unable to provide enough money to distribute the vast productive capacity of the twentieth-century industrial revolution.

This is not because we are unwilling to allow the government to be a major financial agent in our economy. It is, rather, as already indicated, because under our conservative economic ideas neither the government nor private financial institutions can print the money to finance any activity the future benefits of which cannot be translated in terms of dollar income.

There are exceptions to this, but they are minor ones. The theories of John Maynard Keynes are no longer considered unsound or radical. We are reconciled to the idea, unheard of before the Depression, that public works can be built in a depressed area as a stimulus to the local economy. What we cannot do is build public works because they are needed. If there were some way of treating the conservation of our water supply, for example, as a national asset, or of thinking about a trained physician as an asset, and then translating the benefits these investments would confer on society in terms of the dollar, private financing would give us all the money we needed. But at present we are stopped from developing such resources by rigid economic theory. It is inevitable that in the long run such ideas must change to fit the real world in which we live.

Our educated voters have been the prisoners of an obsolete bookkeeping system. The idea behind that system is that the production of goods should be cut down to fit the supply of money and credit instead of increasing the amount of money and credit to fit the expanding industrial capacity of our productive plants. Under this bookkeeping system, money is considered to be the real wealth of the country. It follows from that notion that the principal duty of the government is to save its money and pay off the national debt. For a government to expand its money supply would make money worth less than it was before. This process is called inflation. In addition, the national debt is said to be a mortgage on our grandchildren's future. The living generation has no right to treat coming generations so shabbily.

The result of this system of bookkeeping has been to prevent the government from effectively using the productive resources of the country in the fields of education, public health, and the preservation of our water supply and our recreational areas, all the way down to a series of desperately needed public programs. It is admitted by the educated voter that these programs are desirable, but he feels that we cannot afford them. To undertake them on any large scale might cause a deficit and increase the national debt. Increasing the national debt would increase the supply of money and lower its value. Once such an unsound course was adopted by

the government, the citizens who benefited by it would demand
more and more. Such citizens are thought to be the least deserving
of our population because most of them are poor. They would not
be poor except for some defect of character. They do not have the
intelligence to understand sound economic principles, but their
numbers give them vast political power, as was shown in the election of Franklin Roosevelt for four terms in spite of all the efforts
of our educated voters to defeat him. And so, even small amounts
of government spending were like the initial taking of small
amounts of drugs. Once that habit had been started, there was no
stopping, short of the inflationary destruction of the purchasing
power of the dollar.

There have been other impelling objections asserted against action by the government to eliminate the squalor that defaces our
cities and steps to improve health and education. It has been an
article of faith for more than a century that anything that the
government does, it does inefficiently. As the editor of the *Wall
Street Journal* noted on February 19, 1965:

> More broadly as applied to the newly expansionist policies of the U.S.
> Government, bureaucracies which have so ineptly operated so many pro-
> grams should not be allowed to assume still larger responsibilities with-
> out a full accounting of their past errors. *For it is by now well established,
> almost as a political law, that a government's propensity to mismanage
> increases with the increase of its undertakings.*
>
> Given honest money and minimum of supervision, people can handle
> their affairs better than a central authority can do it for them. And when
> overbearing governments multiply their burdens and restrictions, it is
> always the people who pay the price of control. [Emphasis supplied.]

It is certainly true, as I have previously pointed out, that the
failure of the government to offer a dignified professional career
to the persons who remain with it does drain its agencies of their
best personnel. In other words, conservatives do everything they
can to make the government bureaucratic. But even so, no proof
has ever been adduced that the evils of bureaucracy do not apply
as well to large corporate management as they do to government.
For example, our railroad management seems incapable of providing adequate passenger service or commuter service. The Washington *Post* of Saturday, February 20, 1965, satirically noted:

The natives here were impressed by a movie shown by the Japanese National Railways this week which showed what a developed country can do to make rail travel a pleasure. True enough, the American economy is still too backward to contemplate immediate emulation of Japan's advanced methods. But perhaps the World Bank can send us a mission staffed with Japanese experts to explain how to build something like the New Tokaido Line.

Furthermore, speaking of efficiency, even assuming that some political law makes private organizations more efficient than the government and that the Department of Defense under Robert S. McNamara is less efficient than it would be if it were in private hands, the fact remains that the government is never permitted to take over any segment of the economy until after private management has made a failure of it, or to initiate any project that can possibly be done by private industry.

And in any event, it is clear that since the Great Depression private industry cannot generate the purchasing power to absorb the product of the tremendously increasing production of the scientific revolution. Commenting upon the loss during the past decade of $550 billion in goods and services arising from idle productive capacity, Leon Keyserling stated in a recent pamphlet, *Progress or Poverty:*

If these revenues had not been lost, half of this gigantic sum could have provided more than 5 billion dollars a year, during the 11½ year period, to make war upon poverty. And the other half could have been used for reducing public deficits and for tax reductions beyond those which actually occurred.

The problem facing the American economy is a psychological one. We have unused productive capacity to a greater extent than any nation in the world's history. In creating consumer demand to distribute the products that our industrial plant is capable of producing, we have expanded our private credit and government-guaranteed credit to an extent that would have been thought to lead to disastrous inflation prior to the Second World War. But even this tremendous increase in the private "printing" of money has been falling increasingly short of absorbing the productive capacity of the twentieth-century scientific revolution.

These were the ideas behind the Full Employment Act of 1946, which was put on the shelf for so many years because our educated voters could not understand it.

Man is a slave to his vocabulary. Adjustment to the industrial revolution of the twentieth century will be accomplished only when we invent new words to describe the problems that face us. Today we need a set of words that will convey the idea that the wealth of a nation consists of its capacity to produce goods, that programs for the public welfare that cannot be translated into monetary terms are nevertheless assets of incalculable value.

How does the educated voter acquire a new vocabulary that will enable him to see the problems of our national economy as they actually exist? Certainly it is not through a process of sudden conversion to new ideas. Nor can it be accomplished by persuasive rhetoric. But in the close election of President Kennedy there were signs that the sacredness of old principles was eroding. In a book published in 1935, *The Symbols of Government,* I predicted what I think has actually occurred. I said:

There are signs of a new popular orientation about the theories and symbols of government which is arising from a new conception of the function of reason and ideals in the personality of the individual. A new creed called psychiatry is dimly understood by millions of people. Popular magazines are appearing, discussing from an objective point of view problems which used to be considered the exclusive property of the moralist. A conception of an adult personality is bringing a new sense of tolerance and common sense to replace the notion of the great man who lived and died for moral and rational purposes. Under these new attitudes men are becoming free to observe the effects of changing beliefs, without the discomfort of an older generation which swung from complete certainty to utter disillusionment.

Such a conception, once accepted, will in the long run spread to government and social institutions. Governments can act in no other way than in accordance with the popular ideals of what great abstract personalities should do. In medieval times nations were holy and kings led crusades to dramatize that ideal. In modern times governments act in the image of great businessmen. The codes to which national conduct attempts to conform are only enlargements of popular ideals of individual codes. When individuals must be logical, consistent, courageous, thrifty, generous, forgiving, implacable, and morally upright, governments dramatize all these values. National policies can only be a confused representation of popular ideals. As the notion of a tolerant adult personality grows in popular comprehension, the opportunity for a scientific attitude toward government will necessarily broaden. Once that conception becomes an unquestioned assumption, the day of the high-class psychopath and fanatic in social control will be over. (Pp. 269–270.)

It seems to me that the prediction I made in 1935 has come true. The extent to which this new attitude toward economic principles has penetrated into our political thinking was first made apparent during the 1960 presidential campaign. The two presidential candidates did not go around advocating political or economic principles; instead, they admittedly devoted all their efforts to projecting images. The debates between them were not debates at all in the old-fashioned sense. They were contests in image projection, which John F. Kennedy won, though it was a close call. The issues in these debates were not selected by the candidates; they were chosen by the reporters who asked the questions. Everybody knew these things, and no one thought it either hypocritical or sinful.

The old Brain Trusters of the Roosevelt era were still with us, but they had been pushed out of their place in the sun by public-relations men skilled in the magic art of image projection. Nothing like them has appeared on the American political scene before.

This has an exceedingly comic aspect, and though it certainly does relieve us of a sense of guilt and gives us freedom of political action, it is not nearly as funny as monetary theory. Everybody knows that President Johnson is not going to balance the budget by turning off lights in the White House. The public regards this gesture with approval although it knows that it is only a gesture of respect to a great American tradition. That gesture having been made, the President is left free to advocate deficit financing.

Speaking of the 1960 presidential campaign, when all the voters adopted cynical attitudes toward principle and emphasized image projection, Karl E. Meyer, in a brilliant book entitled *The New America: Politics and Society in the Age of the Smooth Deal* (Basic Books, 1961), commented as follows:

The term [image] has become so widely accepted that it seemed wholly in order during the 1960 campaign for an Associated Press profile of Richard M. Nixon to be subheaded "Man and Image"—with the undeniable implication that there was a difference between the two. Inevitably, Rabbi Max Nussbaum of Los Angeles opened the third session of the Democratic Convention by beseeching divine assistance for an "America with a new image." At the Republican Convention, images flew like hailstones—most memorably, perhaps, when the Governor of West Virginia retroactively endowed Lincoln with the "image of freedom."

During the campaign, the combatants hurled loaded images at each other. This came to a crescendo at the end of October, when President Eisenhower accused Candidate Kennedy of having "cruelly distorted the image of America." On the same day, the Washington *Post* quoted Mr. Kennedy's rejoinder: "Our prestige is not so high. No longer do we give the image of being on the rise. No longer do we give an image of vitality."

Political reporters vied with each other to find new and daring uses of the term. Chalmers M. Roberts of the Washington *Post* wrote that in agreeing to run together, Senators Kennedy and Johnson "broke the standardized image so many have of them." But what can be broken can be mended, and the same week columnist William S. White explained that Kennedy approached Johnson "and asked him to provide the cement so sorely needed—the image of a Protestant Southwesterner— so that the total image would not be solely that of a Catholic Easterner."

Cemented or broken, images come in a variety of shapes and sizes, are negative, bright or blurred, and even come in the big family-size package. The most basic of all images is the father image—the fellow who used to be in the White House. But coming up fast is the image of the sixties which was heralded in August of 1960 by a front-page headline in the Washington *Star:* "The Son You Vote For May Become President." So testified Dr. Martin Grotjahn, a psychiatrist at the University of Southern California, who found that Mr. Kennedy and Mr. Nixon "have remarkably similar images."

"Both appear as victorious sons," quoth the good doctor, "but they are also brothers, *alter egos* in a sense, to many middle-aged persons who feel 'I realize I cannot be President but my brother can.' "

Thus, among other distinctions, the 1960 election afforded the first instance of sibling image rivalry. But, with a bow to the growth issue, Dr. Grotjahn also held out this bipartisan consolation: "Of course, the son may grow later—in the voter's conception—into a benevolent father image the way Franklin Delano Roosevelt did." (Pp. 76–77.)

Mr. Meyer deplored the atmosphere of a campaign in which public relations and the projection of images were considered more important by the voter than debates on principles. It is my own belief that the cynical psychiatric attitude of the voters toward the issues represented a growing distrust of the fundamental economic faiths that had been so powerful a source of frustration during the Great Depression.

The presidential campaign of 1960, in which by public assent in an open secret the power to project images was considered more important than the sincere advocacy of fundamental principles, marked a revolutionary change in the attitude of the American voter toward the old-time economic religion. As a result a sincere and devoted segment of the Republican party became convinced that the time had come to get rid of the cynicism and hypocrisy of the 1960 campaign and return in 1964 to fundamental truths, without the recognition of which America could no longer be free.

The Goldwater campaign was a last crusade to free the holy city of Washington from the domination of hypocritical infidels and image projectors. The crusaders hoped that they could drive the "me-tooers" out of the Republican party and in the campaign, based on the immutable principles of the past, win the election. Even if they couldn't win it, they could reform the Republican party and make it a standard to which the wise and honest could repair, and which would eventually conquer when truth, crushed to earth, would rise again. This simple and devout faith on which the Goldwater campaign was based has nowhere been better expressed than in a column by John Chamberlain in the Washington *Post,* October 30, 1964. He said:

I am for Barry Goldwater for one big reason: I think he would slow down the drift to the omnipresent, do-it-all state. I wouldn't expect him to repeal the 30 years of New Deal legislation; I wouldn't even expect him to sell the fertilizer accessories of the TVA, though I wish he could. After all, Barry Goldwater is no Congressional arm-twister, and he would respect the wishes of the legislative majority in regard to laws already on the books.

But he would, I think, be the greatest vetoer of bad bills since Grover Cleveland, and that is the best reason in the world for putting him in the White House. We haven't had a Grover Cleveland in a long time, and it is time for a repeat performance of what that massive character did to restore integrity to the processes of government after the "great barbecue" that followed the Civil War. He thought the people should support the Government, not vice versa.

My reason for voting for Barry Goldwater has nothing whatsoever to do with the character of Lyndon Johnson. It is simply a matter of supporting my philosophical convictions. . . .

This was to have been a year of confrontation. Confrontation of the individual and the do-it-all state idea. Confrontation of the freedom philosophy and communism on the world stage, which would make foreign policy a legitimate part of the campaign. Well, it's still not too late for the confrontation. Next Tuesday will tell the story.

Such burning zeal, such devotion to a sacred cause, was characteristic of the Goldwater campaign for the nomination. It gave an impetus and drive to Goldwater supporters that was completely lacking in the vacillating and indecisive "moderate" Republican group. The Republicans arrayed in disorder against Goldwater for the nomination were not men of conviction. They knew they didn't like Goldwater. They knew they didn't like Johnson. But they were incapable of expressing in intelligible terms what they did like. The 1964 campaign for the Republican presidential nomination was, therefore, an attempt to beat somebody with nobody.

In the meantime, during the four preceding years under President Kennedy and, later, President Johnson, there had been an increasing feeling that it was the moral obligation of the United States government to use its productive resources to the utmost to achieve what President Johnson happily describes as the "Great Society." The slogans "Fair Deal" and "New Frontier" hark back to Franklin Roosevelt. Roosevelt's ideas had been accepted, but reluctantly accepted, by the educated voters who voted against him. The words "Great Society" indicate a positive step forward toward a goal that most of the business community and the educated voter are beginning dimly to understand. It was the first departure from the Roosevelt atmosphere and tradition since his death.

The 1964 campaign, unlike that of 1960, was not a campaign in which the public was thinking of the projection of images. In the simple style of a devout country preacher, Johnson told the people that they owed a moral obligation to the future of America. Goldwater told them that they owed a moral obligation to the past. The cynical attitude of the voters in the 1960 campaign disappeared. The business community and the educated voter became alarmed when presented for the first time with the consequences that might follow a return to the principles of the past.

The overwhelming defeat of the Goldwater principles and the acceptance of the most challenging idea ever put forth to the American public by an American President—the war on poverty and the opportunity to build a Great Society—will be a turning point in our history. The old gods are dead and new gods have taken their place. The ideological warfare between the business community and the administration is ended. In the future, what conflicts may arise will be conflicts about practical matters and not about philosophical differences.

Following his election, President Johnson promptly proceeded to prove that his idea of the moral obligation of American citizens was not a philosophical abstraction but a practical program. In his Inaugural Address, President Kennedy had stressed the dangers of the period we were in and the duty of citizens not to ask what their country could do for them, but what they could do for their country. Kennedy's program lacked definite objectives. I do not criticize him for that; it is my conviction that if Kennedy had declared a war on poverty in 1960, he would have been defeated. And if, in 1961, he had advocated anything approaching President Johnson's 1965 message to Congress on the State of the Union it would have been productive of alarm and dissension rather than of a unified purpose.

But as the defeat of the Goldwater principles showed, something had happened to American economic philosophy during the four years preceding 1964. American businessmen had begun to realize the tremendous industrial potential of the scientific revolution. They had learned that the private credits that had so fantastically increased were still not enough to utilize that potential. And so, when President Johnson in his State of the Union message, implemented by bills sent to Congress in rapid succession, told the industrialists and the educated voters of the country that they had a moral obligation to utilize American resources to the fullest and make America into the greatest society the world had ever known, they were not alarmed.

The appropriations the President asked for are pitifully inadequate to carry out the moral obligation that he has proposed.

The crucial thing, however, is that they envisage for the future expenditures for the rebuilding of American society that are incalculably greater than any expenditures in the past except in time of war. Only the chiefs of the last of the Mohicans located in places like the Chicago *Tribune* and the *Wall Street Journal* are alarmed. The business community has at last begun to recognize that the productive capacity of this nation is equal to the task of achieving the President's ideal of a Great Society. And, more important still, the educated voter and the business community have begun to understand that American private enterprise will become richer rather than poorer in carrying out the moral obligations imposed by President Johnson, just as America came out of the Second World War richer than it was when the war began.

Unlike President Kennedy, President Johnson has not emphasized sacrifice on the part of anyone. Instead, he has imposed a great moral obligation on the nation and assured its citizens that they have abundant capacity to perform that obligation if they have the will to do so. Thus, the economic principles of the immediate future have been released from the prison of philosophical abstractions which for so long have hampered the growth of our economy and have been brought into the daylight of practical reality.

And so, in answer to the question arising from the title of this chapter, "The Education of the Educated Voter" in times when old principles become obsolete in the light of rapid industrial change, I would say that the progress of his education since the Great Depression has been this: His first reaction was to restrict and limit the production of new wealth because there seemed no way to distribute it. When that remedy failed, as it always does, and the Roosevelt administration was forced into new and unprecedented government activity, there was a period of intense bitterness and philosophical conflict which lasted through the Truman administration. Then there was a last desperate attempt by the Eisenhower administration to apply the old philosophy. This effort ended in a lagging economy, increasing pollution of our rivers and streams and air, a larger number of unemployed, and an increased number of American citizens living in poverty, a number that now amounts to one-fifth of the nation.

In the Kennedy campaign, the educated voter had lost his traditional capacity to believe in the economic principle that only a do-nothing government could save us from the twin evils of inflation and socialism. The educated voter expressed that disillusionment by knowingly approving of a campaign in which both candidates were trying to project images rather than follow principles. This cynical attitude was, I think, a very necessary phase in the education of the educated voter. But it proved to be a temporary thing because government by public relations cannot be a dignified and inspiring form of government.

And finally, in 1964, the time was ripe for the rededication of America to a new principle in the form of a moral obligation that few could refuse to accept because by that time everyone knew that our industrial potential was enough to carry it out and that it was not going to be a burden on our economy.

I am not one who believes that the enunciation of a great moral principle will be followed by the business community just because it thinks the principle is right.

Samuel Butler observed of the New Testament that men "would be equally horified to hear [it] . . . doubted or to see it practiced." Men will fight, kill each other and lay waste the land for ideals and symbols. But in the conduct of a nation's peacetime business something more is needed than mere agreement on moral principle. That something is the fact that the business community can get rich by following the moral principle. A dynamic economy must be based on the kind of moral principle that will make it prosperous. So Great Britain built the greatest industrial empire in previous history on the moral principle that it was its duty to take up the white man's burden and bring British civilization to the unenlightened areas of the world.

President Johnson, in his 1965 State of the Union message to Congress, has given us a moral principle which, if followed, will make us rich. It consists in the assertion that it is the duty of a government to follow an economic policy that requires the full use of the productive capacity of the nation. Economic sacrifice is something that cannot be expected in an economy based on private enterprise in time of peace. But the policy announced by the President requires no economic sacrifice. It will add to the profits of private enterprise instead of taking them away. It rests on the common-sense notion that the wealth of a nation is not its supply of money and credit, but its capacity to produce goods and services, and that the function of money and credit is to distribute.

The initial appropriations that the President asks are inadequate, as the liberals are already beginning to point out. But they are probably all that the various organizations committed to the various tasks can presently use without waste and confusion. The importance of the President's program is the idea it expresses, an idea that enables the educated voter to look at the economy of the scientific revolution without the preconceptions of the past that have prevented him from seeing what is there.

The human brain is like a computing machine. When new ideas or new data are fed into it, it flashes electrical impulses into a compartment ordinarily called "memory." When the new data hit the memory of either the machine or the mind, the results come forth instantaneously. But what those results are depends upon what has been previously stored in the memory of the machine. The advantage of the computer is that by merely mechanical processes the memory of the machine can be changed to fit realities. To remove the rag bag of phobias, prejudices, principles, and ideas that condition the reactions of the human computer to new data is a long and painful process. It involves fighting revolutionary wars and means endless suffering and slaughter. But gradually the change comes about, principally through the substitution of new words, words that have a different emotional content from those previously used.

Index

Abrams v. *United States,* 162
Absentee ownership, 33–34
Adams, Sherman, 239
Agricultural Adjustment Administration, 131, 132–33
Agricultural depression of 1925, 34
Aldrich, Nelson W., 124
Alliance for Progress, 154
Almond, J. Lindsay, Jr., 157
American Law Institute, 58
American Medical Association, antitrust suit, 114
American Mercury case, 168–70
American Telephone and Telegraph, 46–47
Amsler-Morton Company, 141
Anheuser-Busch, 116
Antitrust laws: American, *see* Sherman Antitrust Law; European, 146
Arnold, Carl Franklin (grandfather), 3–4, 5, 13
Arnold, Constantine Peter (father), 4, 6, 11–12, 14, 15
Arnold, Thurman: with Agricultural Adjustment Administration, 131; ancestry, 3–6; with Antitrust Division, Department of Justice, 113–19; Arnold, Fortas & Porter, 190–95; Assistant Attorney General of United States, 147; birth, 3; childhood, 5–6, 8–9; Dean, West Virginia University College of Law, 35; faculty, Yale Law School, 35, 61–63, 135–36; and Harvard Law School, 20–22; judge, United States Court of Appeals, 156; love of the West, 6, 11; Mayor of Laramie, 32; and National Guard, 24–26; and Nuremberg Trials, 85–86; practice in Chicago, 23, 26; practice in Laramie, 30–35, 65–66; at Princeton, 16–18; with Tax Division, De-

partment of Justice, 135; views on crime and economics, 244–45; on economics, 273–74, 276–77, 283–85; on legal practice, 191–92, 252–53, 256–59, 265, 267, 268, 269–71; on legislative hearings, 196–203; on Presidential election of 1960, 277, 278, 279–80; of 1964, 280, 282; trials, 228–32; in Wyoming House of Representatives, 32–33
Arnold's Corollary, 155
Aspirin Age, 1919–1941, The, quoted, 38–53
Associated Press, antitrust suit, 114
Association of American Railroads, 189–90

Bailey v. *Richardson,* 206–08
Baker, Robert, 197
Bank of the United States, 98–99
Banks and Politics in America, 99–101, 105–06
Bell, E. J., 6, 7–8, 19–20
Bergson, Herbert, 149
Betts v. *Brady,* 242
Bicks, Robert A., 147–48
Biddle, Anthony, 101
Black, Henry F., 186
Black, Hugo, 180, 181, 206
"Blue Eagle," *see* National Industrial Recovery Act
Bonus Army, 26–47
Borah, William, 137
Borkin, Joseph, 114, 140, 145
Bottlenecks of Business, The, 120
Brandeis, Louis, 162, 163
Brewer, David, 127
Brownell, Herbert, 224–26
Burnham, James, 111
Butler v. *Michigan,* 175–76
Butler, Nicholas Murray, 46

Butler, Samuel, 284
Byrd, Harry, 157
Byrnes, James E., 117

Cardozo, Benjamin, 111
Carnegie, Andrew, 43, 121
Cartel systems, in America, 109–12; in Europe, 108
Caudle, Lamar, 148–49
Chamberlain, John, 280–81
Civil liberties: *Bailey* v. *Richardson*, 206–08; Fort Monmouth case, 210–13; *Friedman* v. *Schwellenbach*, 204–05; Lattimore case, 214–27; Peters case, 208–10
Clapper, Raymond, 249
Clark, Charles E.: federal judge, 209; Dean, Yale Law School, 35–36; legal reform movement, 63–67, 266
Cohen, Benjamin, 137
Conflict of interest rules: Bergson case, 149; Caudle case, 148–49; impairment to government efficiency, 150–51
Conservatives in Power, 93–94
Coolidge, Calvin, 82, 91
Corning Glass Company, 140–41
Corporate reorganization, New Deal legislation, 135
Costello, Frank, 197–98, 202
Cox, Hugh B., 114, 140
Crash of 1929, *see* Depression of 1929
Crane, John P., 198

Dale, Edwin L., Jr., 93–94
Darrow, Clarence, 252
de Gaulle, Charles, 95
Democratic Roosevelt, The, 138, 144
Depression of 1929, 38–53; changing jurisprudence, 54–70; the corporate bureaucracy, 44, fails to stop the slump, 47; government intervention, 47–53, under Hoover, 47, under Roosevelt, 47–49; the National Industrial Recovery Act, 50; the stock market, 39–42
Dewey, Thomas E., 198
Diamond, Norman, 191

Dies, Martin, 248
Dillon, C. Douglas, 150
Douglas, William O.: quoted, 172–73, 180–81; with Securities and Exchange Commission, 135; on Supreme Court, 206; on Yale faculty, 63, 68
Durham Rule, 234–35
Durham v. *United States*, 232–34

Eaton, Cyrus, 188, 190
Economic planning: before World War I, 91; Full Employment Act, 1946, 93; National Industrial Recovery Act, 1933, 92; National Resources Planning Board (World War I), 91
Economic programs: of Eisenhower administration, 88–91, 283; of Johnson administration, 282–83, 284–85; of Kennedy administration, 282; of Soviet Russia, 91
Economic theory: credit, 273, 276; free market and market control, 120–21; government efficiency, 275–76; government planning and competition, 138–39; public works, 274–75; wealth, 272–73, 284–85
Edgerton, Henry White, 207–08
Eisenhower, Dwight David, 88, 219–20, 279, 283
Election of 1960, 277, 278–81; of 1964, 280–82
Esquire case, 160–70

Farben, I. G., 115
Father Struck It Rich, 246
Federal Antitrust Policy, The, 124–25
Federal Housing Authority, 273
Federal judgeships: financial security of, 156; and political patronage, 157
Federal Reserve Board, 79–80, 101
Federal Rules of Civil Procedure, 67, 266–67
Fisher, Irving, 33
Folklore of Capitalism, The, 68, 135; quoted, 136, 137; Paramount Theatres case, 193–95
Ford, Henry, 121

Fort Monmouth case, 210–13
Fortas, Abe, 190; with Agricultural Adjustment Administration, 133; and Durham case, 233; and *Friedman* v. *Schwellenbach*, 205; and *Gideon* v. *Wainwright*, 242–43; and Lattimore case, 214; with Arnold, Fortas & Porter, 190–95
Fortune, 51–52
Frank, Jerome, 131
Frankfurter, Felix, 75, 209–10; quoted, 175–76
Freeman, Milton, 191
Friedman v. *Schwellenbach*, 204–05
Frost, Robert, 238–42
Full Employment Act, 1946, 76–81, 272, 277

Garrett, Garet, 102–03
General Electric, antitrust suit, 114–15
Gideon v. *Wainwright*, 242–43
Ginzburg, Ralph, 174–75
Goodrich, Edgar, 191
Goldwater campaign, 280–81
Government service, impediments: civil service system, 151–52; conflict of interest rules, 148–51; lack of dignity and respect, 153; public distrust, 148; salary scale, 153
Grapes of Wrath, The, 102
Griswold, Erwin N., 261–62
Grotjahn, Martin, 279
Guss v. *Utah Labor Relations Board*, 117

Hamilton, Alexander, 98, 106–07
Hamilton, Fowler, 114, 140
Hamilton, Walton, 68, 191
Harding, Warren G., 37, 91
Harlan, John Marshall, 125–26, 179–80, 181, 183
Harrison, Benjamin, 124
Hart, Henry, 61, 256–57
Hartford Empire Company, investigated by Temporary National Economic Committee, 140–41
Harvard Law Library, 261–62

Harvard Law School, 20–22, 270
Henderson, Leon, 248
Hergesheimer, Joseph, 248
Hitler, Adolf, 83
Hobby, Oveta Culp, 209
Hoffa, James, 118, 196–97
Holding companies, 123; Northern Securities Company case, 126; *see also* Sherman Anti-Trust Act
Holmes, Oliver Wendell, 127–28, 162, 163
Hoover, Herbert, 40, 46, 92
Hoover, J. Edgar, 88–89, 250
Horn, Tom, 13–14
Hutchins, Robert, 16; and "legal realism," 57–70; and Yale Law School, 35
Hutcheson, William L., 115

Income Levels in American Life (1938), 142
Institute of Human Relations, at Yale, 59
Institute of Pacific Relations, 214–15, 223
International Hod Carriers Union, 117

Jackson, Andrew, 99, 101, 107
Jackson, Robert H., 137, 190
James, William, 184–85
Jeanne d'Arc, 229–30
Jefferson, Thomas, 99
Johnson, Hugh, 50, 110
Johnson, Lyndon, 278; economic program of, 96–97, 282–83, 284–85; State of the Union message of 1965, 284

Kahn, Eugene, 62
Karpman, Benjamin, 173
Kefauver, Estes, Committee on Crime, 196, 197–98, 201, 202
Kennedy, John F.: appointment of Almond, 157; and campaign of 1960, 279; and economic policy, 96; inaugural address of, 282; and McCarthy era, 214; and steel price rises, 130
Kennedy, Robert, 196
Keynes, John Maynard, 274

Keyserling, Leon, 96, 276
Knox, Philander C., 127
Knudson, William S., 248
Krock, Arthur, 114

Labor unions: rights under the National Industrial Recovery Act, 110, 112; prosecution under Sherman law and antiracketeering law, 116–19
Landon, Alfred M., 248–49
Langdell, Christopher C., 263
Lattimore, Owen, 214–27; before McCarran Committee, 214–16; charges against, 217, 218–19, 220–22; perjury trials of, 217–26; views on China, 220; views on Russian collaboration, 219–20
Laws, Bolitha, 241
Laws quoted: Full Employment Act, 1946, 78; National Industrial Recovery Act, Section 7(a), 112; Postal Law, 161 *passim;* Sherman Antitrust Act, 121
Legal practices, American and British: admission to bar, 253–54; appointment to bench, 269; briefs, 255, 257–58; costs, 258–59, 260; criminal practice, 267–68; education, 262–63; and foreign law, 261–62; law libraries, 261–62; litigation, 258–59; number of practitioners, 258; oral argument, 255–56; pretrial discovery proceedings, 259, 265–68; research, 255–58, 259–62; rules of civil procedure, 266–67; "taking silk," 269; theories, 256–57, 259–60, 269–70; witnesses, 263–65
"Legal realism," 57, 59–70
Legislative hearings: Kefauver Committee, 196, 197–98, 201, 202; McCarran Committee, 214–16; Temporary National Economic Committee, 139–43
Levi, Edward, 114, 145
Lippmann, Walter, 248
Loyalty boards, 206, 229
Luce, Clare Boothe, 248
Luckman, Charles, 41–42
Lynch v. *Overholser,* 235–36

McCarran Committee, 214–16
McCarran, Pat, 214, 216, 217
McCarthy, Joseph, 86–87, 196, 197, 199, 211
McClellan, John, 196
McCloy, John, 85–86
McGranery, James, 217
McLean, Evalyn Walsh, 246–51; and Bonus Army, 246–47; and Lindbergh kidnapping, 247; dinners, 247–48; jewelry, 249–51
McNamara, Robert S., 276
McReynolds, James C., 59
Madison, James, 104
Managerial Revolution, The, 111
Marbury v. *Madison,* 75
Marx, Karl, 91
Masters of Deceit, 88–89
Means, Gaston, 247
Mellon, Andrew, 45
Mencken, Henry L., 168–70
Meyer, Karl E., 278–79
Michelson, Charles, 248
Miller, Reed, 191
Money, privately printed: "wildcat banks," 100; private corporations, 101
Monopolies: in World War II, 52–53; Roosevelt's message of 1935 on, 51; *see also* Trusts, Holding companies, Absentee ownership
Mooney, Tom, 228–29
Morgan, J. P., 43–44, 121, 124, 126–27
Morganthau, Henry, 85
M'Naghten Rules, 232–33
Murphy, Frank, 134, 250–51

Narcotics offenses, 243–44
National Committee on Law Observance, 62–63
National Industrial Recovery Act, 49–50, 92, 109–12, 128–29
National Labor Relations Board, 112, 116, 117–18
National Resources Planning Board, 91
New America: Politics and Society in

the Age of the Smooth Deal, The, 278–79
New Dealers, 92, 247
New York Times, 39, 114
Nixon, Richard, 279
Norris–La Guardia Act, 115–16
Northern Securities Company, 126
Northrup, F. S. C., 18–19
Nuremberg Trials, 84, 230–31
Nussbaum, Max, 279
Nye, Bill, 9–10

O'Brien, John Lord, 144–45
Obscenity cases, 160–87; Esquire case, 160–70; Playboy case, 170–86; One, Inc. v. Olesen, 181–82, 183; Times Film Corp. v. Chicago, 181, 182, 183; Sunshine Book Co. v. Summerfield, 181, 182–83
O'Dwyer, William, 198
O'Mahoney, Joseph, 139–140
One, Inc. v. Olesen, 181–182, 183
Overholser, Winfred, 240
Owens-Illinois Glass Company, 141

Paramount Theatres case, 193–95
Parkinson's Law, 154–55; see Arnold's Corollary
Patterson, Cissy, 250
Pepper, George Wharton, 158
Peters, John P., 208–10
Pike v. Walker, 163
Playboy case, 170–86
Police problems, 243–45
Porter, Paul A.: ambassador to Greece, 190–91; and Playboy case, 171–72; and Paramount Theatres case, 193–95; and Peters case, 209; quoted, 143
Postal Law, 161 passim
Pound, Ezra, 236–42
Powell, Thomas Reed, 20–21, 261
President's Council of Economic Advisers, 79
Princeton University: in 1907, the Club system, 16–17, the curriculum, 17–18; in 1964, student political views, 57, curriculum, 19

Progress or Poverty, 276
Pullman case, 188–90
Pullman strike, 125

Raibourn, Paul, 193–95
Railroad problems, 188–90
Reconstruction Finance Corporation, 47, 92
Richardson, Seth W., 206
Rifkind, Simon H., 203
Roberts, Chalmers, 279
Robinson, Edwin, 68
Rockefeller, John D., 3
Roosevelt, Franklin D.: appoints Arnold to federal bench, 156, 157–58; and court-packing fight, 69; economics platform in first campaign, 92; gift of leadership, 146; influence of in 1960's, 281; as monopoly fighter, 113, 135; monopoly message of 1935, 137, 139, quoted, 51; and National Recovery Act, 112
Roosevelt, Theodore, 120, 126; fight for federal supremacy, 126–28; and economic freedom, 128; and trusts, 139
Root, Elihu, 127
Roth v. United States, 172–73, 178, 179–80
Rovere, Richard, 238

Sanity, legal, 231–41
Schechter, A. L. A., Poultry Corporation v. United States, 110–11
Securities and Exchange Commission, 135
Seymour, Charles, 209
Shafroth, Will, 239
Shays' Rebellion, 100
Sherman, John, 120, 122, 123–24
Sherman Anti-Trust Act, 50; in effect, 1890, 124; used in Pullman strike, 125; defined, 125; virtual repeal of by Supreme Court, 125; shelved, 125; revived by Theodore Roosevelt, 126; under Franklin D. Roosevelt, 113–130
Standard Oil Company, 115, 123, 145

Sullivan, Harry Stack, 61–62
Sunshine Book Co. v. *Summerfield,* 181, 182–83
Supreme Court, United States: and Agricultural Adjustment Act, 133; and judicial decision and "judicial legislation," 58–59, 71–75; in McCarthy era, 86–87; and National Recovery Act, 92; recent civil liberties and civil rights decisions of, 72–75
Symbols of Government, The, 68, 277–78
Sturges, Wesley, 67–68

Taft-Hartley Act, 112, 159
Tamm, Edward A., 250
Teamsters Union, 117, 118
Temporary National Economic Committee, 139–43
Tennessee Valley Authority, 48
Thompson, William Hale, 23
Thorelli, Hans B., 124–25
Tierney, Leo F., 114
Times Film Corp. v. *Chicago,* 181, 182, 183
Tobey, Charles, 202
Trial, definition of, 228–32
Trials: Charles I, 230; Jeanne d'Arc, 229–30; Nuremberg, 230–31; Lattimore, 217–26; Durham, 233–34
Truman, Harry, 86; and Loyalty boards, 206; and Special Committee Investigating the National Defense Programs, 145
Trusts: history of, 122; Standard Oil, 123; prosecutions of by states, 123; Sherman Anti-Trust Act, 123–24; prosecution of under F. D. Roosevelt, 113–30
Tugwell, Rexford, 145; quoted, 138, 144
Tydings, Millard, 214

Un-American Activities Committee, 87
United Automobile Workers, 118

United Nations, 84
United States v. *Butler,* 134
United States v. *Hutchison,* 115
United States v. *E. C. Knight Co.,* 125
United States v. *Local 807, Teamsters,* 117
United States ex. rel. Milwaukee S. D. Pub. Co. v. *Burleson,* 163–64
United Steelworkers of America, 118

Waldrop, Frank, 250
Walker, Frank C., 162–67
Wall Street Journal, 60, 103, 155, 275, 283
Wallace, Henry, 131–32
Walsh, Edmund A., 250
War on Poverty, 154, 282–83
War Production Board, 144–45
Warren, Earl, 181
Washington *Post,* 275–76, 279, 280–81
Washington *Star,* 279
Weimar Republic, 82–83
Weizsaecker, Baron Freiherr von, 85–86
White, William S., 279
Whitney, Richard, 41
Wickersham Commission on Prohibition, *see* National Committee on Law Observance
"Wildcat banks," 99–101
Wilson, Charles E., 150
Wilson, O. W., 243–44
Wilson, Woodrow: at Princeton, 17; economic policy, 37, 91
Winchell, Walter, 248
Wiprud, Arne, 188, 190
Wisconsin Alumni Research Foundation, antitrust suit, 113
Works Progress Administration, 48
Wright, Skelly, 157

Yale Law School, 270; in 1930, 35; and "legal realism," 57, 59–70
Young, Robert, 188–90
Youngdahl, Luther W., 171, 217, 224–26

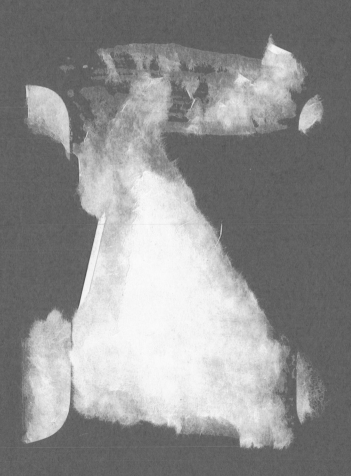